AF538463

Digital Literature for Children

Texts, Readers and Educational Practices

P.I.E. Peter Lang

Bruxelles · Bern · Berlin · Frankfurt am Main · New York · Oxford · Wien

Mireia Manresa & Neus Real (eds.)

Digital Literature for Children

Texts, Readers and Educational Practices

“Recherches comparatives sur les livres
et le multimédia d’enfance”
Vol. 9

Financial support for publication: Proyecto I+D del Ministerio de Economía y Competitividad (MINECO), ref. EDU2011-26141/EDU (2012-2015). Dir.: Dra. Teresa Colomer (Universitat Autònoma de Barcelona).

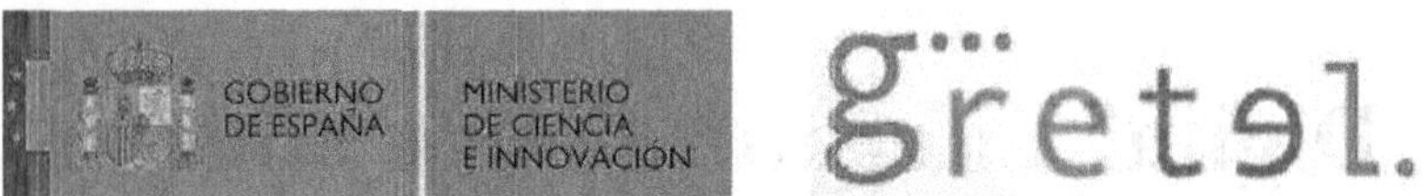

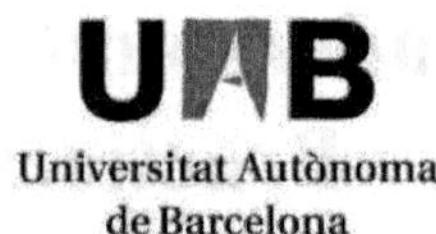

This book has been peer-reviewed.

Éditions scientifiques internationales
Brussels, 2015
1 avenue Maurice, B-1050 Brussels, Belgium
info@peterlang.com; www.peterlang.com

ISSN 1379-5473
ISBN 978-2-87574-272-8
e-ISBN 978-3-0352-6577-4
D/2015/5678/61

Printed in Germany

CIP available from the British Library and from the Library of Congress, USA.

Bibliographic information published by "Die Deutsche Nationalbibliothek".

"Die Deutsche Nationalbibliothek" lists this publication in the "Deutsche National-bibliografie"; detailed bibliographic data is available on the Internet at <http://dnb.de>.

Table of Contents

Introduction

Mireia MANRESA and Neus REAL

Universitat Autònoma de Barcelona

Literacy is currently facing new demands that have arisen from the expansion of the languages and codes in cultural products. This means that integration into 21st century society requires the ability to interpret a reality that is no longer represented and expressed merely through the written word. In the virtual context, literature and reading socialisation circuits are spaces where the digitality and different codes that configure the messages clearly demand an increase in the reader's interpretive skills within the framework of the digital literacy of the population. Although the new forms of electronic fiction present a notable specificity with regard to other digital products, they are completely located in this new cultural and communication paradigm which allows access to knowledge, interaction with others, the communication of one's own ideas, access to information in a virtual and virtualised world and the interpretation of different semiotic systems in coexistence with the products on the analogue circuit.

Teachers are therefore required to investigate the most suitable strategies in order to provide support to the receiver with this type of reading and with a focus on educating citizens in the interpretation of the different codes that contribute to forming the construction of meaning in the texts. It is therefore necessary for schools to take into account the expansion of these fictional and artistic designs and to introduce effective ways of facilitating the access keys to the multimedia, interactive and hypertextual messages and products that exist in today's different fictional products.

In light of these changes, we in the GRETEL research group at the Universitat Autònoma de Barcelona (UAB, Autonomous University of Barcelona, Spain), which specialises in children's literature and literary education, proposed to mark out a line of continuity based on our previous research to distinguish and analyse this new fictional product from the perspective of literary reader training. As this is the focal point of our research and training activities, our main objective was to explore the effects that digital literature can have on literary learning. More specifically we aimed to study the changes that digital literature has introduced in the production of fiction addressed to children and adolescents, in the reading reception of this population group and in the reading habits that usually take place in family and school situations. *Digital Literature for Children: Texts, Readers and Educational Practices*, as its title suggests, aims to provide a contribution to these three specific fields of knowledge using as a backdrop the potentials and limitations of digital literary reading and the associated practices thereof in relation to the reading of printed works.

In this research we focus specifically on app- or web-based literature that builds its meaning in a digital way by using the resources inherent to the electronic medium such as multimodality, interactivity and hypertextuality. This literature is referred to differently depending on the academic discipline, tradition and context. The most common terms are *electronic literature* (e-lit), *digital literature*, *digital fiction* and *digital picturebooks*. In order to be as unrestrictive and distinctive as possible regarding our object of study, in this work we use indistinctively the terms *e-lit* and *digital literature*. *E-lit* was formalised by the Electronic Literature Organization (ELO, the institution of reference for this new literature, albeit for an adult public) and is of constantly wider usage in children's literature research. *Digital literature*, in turn, has been and still is of much generalised use in children's literature studies. Hence its choice in the title of the book. *Digital fiction* would have been excessively general because it includes all types of digital fictional products (videogames among others) and does not necessarily have the specifically literary character required for our focus of study. On the contrary, *digital picturebooks* refers to the electronic transfer of a single type of analogue works (print picturebooks), and therefore it would have only included some of the products under analysis.

Emergent fields of study

In current societies the transformations in the uses and requirements of literacy brought about by reading in digital media have led to new lines of research in children's digital literature and in its sociocultural scope in different fields (transformation of texts, reading and writing uses and practices, editorial market, etcetera). All of these contribute to the creation of a map to (re)situate the modifications and educational practices aimed at the digital training of the population and more specifically at the literary education of children and adolescents today.

With regard to literacy, *The New Literacy Studies* and literacy practices in context have defined the factors involved in the citizens' processes of access to written culture within the framework of virtuality, as well as the skills of reading and text production that are activated through participation in a context configured by new technologies (Lankshear, and Nobel 2006; New London Group 1996; Pahl, and Rowsell 2005; Street 2003). As described by Alvermann (2004) or Cassany and Hernández (2012), the new *native digital* (Prensky 2001) generations are developing abilities that correspond to these forms of reading. The current immersion of children and adolescents in a technological environment leads to constant interaction on the net (through social networks, videogaming, personal blogging, etc.) and to fragmented reading with hyperlinks or to other emergent phenomena such as the collaborative writing of fiction stories. It may be considered, therefore, that these activities bring the reader closer to the narrative forms of children's digital fiction that have begun to emerge and that there is an urgent requirement for educational reflection on the literary reading that is promoted within the school context.

Also, from the sociology of reading, mainly from the qualitative research paradigm point of view, results have been provided on the socialisation exchanges of literary reading on the Internet (Leveratto, and Leontsini 2008; Lluch 2012, 2014) and on the transformations introduced by virtuality in social reading practices. In this way, the profile of the new digital reader in society has been described as having more of a tendency to share the reading experience which is focused towards interactions that transfer the reader from having an amateur role to an expert role with regard to literary reading (Manresa, and Margallo 2013). In short, this framework describes the habitual reading routines and practices of current readers and shows the emergence of new ways of relating to the literary.

Literary theory and the studies on the characterisation of contemporary children's literature also provide an essential basis for approaching literary education in the classroom. The evolution and typology of children's fiction in the last decades, configured through the integration of text and image and described by international research (Arizpe, and Styles 2003; Colomer 1995, 2002, 2005, 2010; Kress 2005; Nikolajeva 2001; Silva-Díaz 2005), prefigured the composition of fiction through multimodal and digital resources. The variations introduced by e-lit in the current production panorama place us before the studies of literary theory, comparative literature and the advances of digital resources in literary fiction which are mostly focused on adult production (Borràs 2005; Hayles 2008; Koskimaa 2000); the most relevant of these are the approaches on the effects of hypertextuality (Ensslin 2007; Landow 2006), on interaction (Juul 2001; Moreno 2002; Ryan 2001, 2004) and on multimodality (Bolter, and Grusin 2000; Ryan 2004).

Despite all these contributions, only recently has there begun to appear some reflections and research on children's digital literature that describe its current typology and characteristics and analyse in depth the variety of the existing corpus on the market in a clear effort to delimit the field of study and specify concepts (Al-Yaqout 2011; Al-Yaqout, and Nikolajeva 2015; Borràs 2012; Stichnothe 2014; Turrión 2013, 2014; Turrión, and Ramada 2014; Unsworth 2006; Yokota 2013). In summary, it has been stated that this is a type of literature that is still defining its creative limits – especially in the areas more foreign to the literary field such as the sequential and interactive potentiality of the digital environment –, and whose greatest achievements, especially regarding multimodality (with priority given to sound and movement), are still very dependent on the adjacent artistic disciplines. In parallel, this is a type of literature that situates the reader in a different place which requires a new type of interpretation and new keys of access to the literary product. To begin with the consideration of the transformations in interactive, hypertextual and multimodal products in relation to printed literature would seem to offer an efficient action framework for the precision of literary planning in the classroom.

These studies are complemented with explorations on reader strategies of comprehension, interpretation, reception and perception of digital and digitised texts. This field, explored from different research paradigms, is still very incipient with regard to literature. Most studies have investigated informative texts and have shown the differences between the reading of digital texts and the reading of printed texts, not merely in terms of comprehension skills and strategies but also in terms of reading habits and routines in general (Clark *et al.* 2008; Coiro 2007; Liu 2005). Specific research on the reception of digital literature has been mainly limited to works of textual fiction, that is to say e-books; it has been based on comparative studies on comprehension of printed and digital works, on case studies on the reading of stories using e-readers such as Amazon's Kindle, or on the focalisation of distinctive specific aspects of digital works such as, for example, hypertextuality.

Therefore we have studies based on diverse aspects that, from different methodological perspectives, offer important results on what happens when reading non-printed literature. For example, studies that show the comprehension differences between subjects who read the same narrative texts in both printed and digitised formats and show lower levels of understanding among the readers who read in digital format (Mangen, Walgermo, and Brønnick 2013). Or studies on the effects of the physical participation of the reader in digital reading such as the importance of the use of the fingers and hands for *immersion* in the fiction (Mangen 2008); on the impact of hypertextual reading in the reflexive mode which is characteristic of traditional literary reading (Miall, and Dobson 2001); on the ways of locating oneself in the temporality of fiction when it is not read in print (Mangen, Walgermo, and Brønnick 2013) or on the involvement possibilities when reading narrative works on electronic devices (Clark *et al.* 2008; Larson 2010). Nonetheless, we still know little of the reader's experience regarding the specificity of e-lit.

Equally interesting are the studies situated within the framework of the mobilisation and integration of electronic fiction in school and family situations with adult facilitation. Noteworthy among these are the studies that have examined the impact of technologies on learning processes (Coll, Mauri, and Onrubia 2008; Krashen 1993) and more specifically those that have focused on the incorporation of digital devices in the classroom. For example, the observations of Hutchison, Beschorner and Schmidt-Crawford (2012), who explored their use in the learning of reading and writing over a period of three weeks; or the descriptive work by Roskos, Burstein and You (2012), that establishes a typology of the involvement of infant children when reading in this medium on an individual and shared basis; and also the comparison by Sheppard (2011), based on reading a work in printed format and on iPad in a classroom situation where a greater level of involvement is shown, with no parallel increase in school performance, together with a lower comprehension among weak readers, the evaluation of tablets as an element of distraction and the failure to involve the students in offline discussions.

All these works represent and point to significant advances in various lines. However, in parallel, they also call for more research in the field of the reading of digital fiction, on the response of children and adolescents to this new type of production and, more specifically, on the reading of digital literature in the school context – a key area for the training of citizens in information societies.

GRETEL's research project on children's digital literature

In order to contribute results in the field of e-lit for children and adolescents, between 2012 and 2015 the GRETEL research group carried out the R&D project "Literatura infantil y juvenil digital: producción, usos lectores, recepción y prácticas docentes" (Children's digital literature: production, reading uses, reception and teaching practices).[1] The project

[1] The research Project I+D EDU2011-26141, funded by the Ministerio de Economía y Competitividad (MINECO, Ministry of Economy and Competitiveness) of the Spanish government. GRETEL was also given official recognition by the Agència de Gestió d'Ajuts Universitaris i de Recerca (AGAUR, Agency for University and Research Administration) of the Generalitat de Catalunya (Catalonia Government), as a stable research team (2009SGR1477).

pursued three major objectives: to analyse the transformations produced in works by the multimodal forms of narration and by the incorporation of new resources for reader participation; to study the reception of e-lit in terms of motivation, comprehension, interpretation and the ability of emergent readers to evaluate metafictional and metaliterary aspects when engaged in the reading of fictional works, and to observe the impact of fictional reading with electronic devices on school and family reading situations.

With regard to the first of these objectives – the children and adolescent e-lit corpus – work was carried out on the establishment of the digital production typology addressed to children and adolescents and the characterisation of its contributions to the renovation of narrative elements, to the cooperation of languages and to receiver participation. In this framework, it was deemed necessary to first analyse the complex relationships between digital literature and the literature which has so far been addressed to children and adolescents, with focus on the visual, oral and, above all, interactive resources. More specifically, it seemed a matter of urgency to generate knowledge on the typology of children's digital productions that are emerging on the market with special focus on analysing how each main element of the narration in digital format is constructed; i.e., studying how a chronological leap is transmitted or how narrative focalisation is represented through the moving image, sound and interactivity. It was also of interest to establish whether this produced changes in the fictional constructive tendencies and, therefore, if there were variations in the type of proposed fictional experience (the duration of the act of reading and the rhythm of reading, for example, seem to have particular significance in digital fiction).

The second focal point entailed case studies on reader reactions to digital literature by means of different research with students of between nine and fifteen years old and based on the analysis of the discourse content from literary discussions and conversations that were held with small groups of students. This analysis took into account the perception and evaluation of the digital characteristics of the proposed works as well as the interpretive response to each one and was based on the literary and digital aspects that construct literary fiction (Margallo 2013). If the reading of digitised texts on a screen supposes numerous changes with regard to reading skills and strategies in contrast to print reading, then the reading and interpreting of e-lit introduces new factors that transform it into a specific product, and it is therefore of interest to understand the reactions of children and adolescents to this product. Following previous research carried out by our group on the reading response to picturebooks (Colomer, and Fittipaldi eds. 2012), we asked ourselves what interpretive strategies are used by readers when reading digital works, what reading modes are activated and what perception they have of the digital resources that appear in works of fiction.

The third objective refers to the exploration of the effects that the introduction of digital literature into independent reading situations has on student reading practices, preferences and evaluations – all of which are issues that affect decisions on the advisability of integrating this type of literature into the classroom and on the didactic reconsideration of current literary education. Specifically, we observed the effects of the introduction of touchscreen tablets, containing specific e-lit selections, into school and family independent reading practice. The main contexts in which children and adolescents encounter works of digital fiction, in school and in the home, provide favourable settings for the exploration of the reading uses that are activated and produced when encounters with these devices and digital literature take place. In this case these were ethnographic case studies in a natural classroom library situation or in family shared reading situations with children of between two and three years old and children of between eleven and twelve years old on the one hand, and children of up to six years old on the other.

Although the results of these studies will be widely covered in the chapters of this book, we must highlight some of the educational implications that can be deduced from this work as a whole. On the one hand there is the logic and necessity to integrate e-lit into formal literary education in order to respond to the demands of a highly technologised society where literary and digital products are two key aspects for the future of children and adolescents. On the other hand, there is the importance of teaching facilitation for the introduction of the works into quality selections and the incorporation of the analysis and specific evaluation of multimodal resources into literary education. Finally, there is the fact that the continuity of experience and teaching facilitation promote more sophisticated, elaborate analyses on the fictional aspects and artistic resources of digital works.

This book brings together the results of these studies on digital literature for children and its impact on the training of the literary reader. The corresponding previews were initially presented in the framework of the International Symposium "Electronic literature: texts, readers and teaching practices", which was organised by the GRETEL research group and held in October last year in Barcelona.[2] They are presented here in their new, extended and revised versions. Also included is the collaboration from researchers and authors of international renown who were invited to the symposium for their trajectory and influence in

2 For the minutes on the Symposium see GRETEL 2014.

this field, such as Laura Borràs, Bettina Kümmerling-Meibauer, Junko Yokota, Kate Pullinger and Arnal Ballester.

This volume

We have taken these three focal points that influence the transformations in the field of digital literary reading as a point of departure and have structured the book into three central parts – the corpus (Part II, Digital Literature for Children and Young Adults), the reader (Part III, Readers and Digital Literature) and the reading uses in classroom or family situations (Part IV, Educational Practices: Families and Schools) – which are preceded by two chapters as a framework (Part I, Contextualization and Theoretical Framework) and followed by two closing chapters that include the reflections of two agents involved in the production of digital works: an author and an illustrator (Part V, Creating Digital Texts: Two Reflections). The volume is therefore organised into five different sections, focused respectively on the general context of digital reading and the theory of electronic literature (two chapters), the production (three chapters), the readers (three chapters), the uses (three chapters) and the creation of children's digital literature (two chapters).

Given its incipient nature, and beyond the summary presentation provided by this introduction, it was unavoidable to include a section dedicated to digital reading on the one hand, and the current state of the research on e-lit for children and adolescents and the tools available to those who today are engaged in this area of study on the other. It was necessary to establish a state of the art in order to specify concepts and define the bases on which these have been founded and on which the approaches to this expanding literature are based; to determine the aspects that characterise digital literature and draw the lines along which the research is moving and the direction in which it should proceed. And at the same time not neglecting to contemplate unanswered questions and problematise the more complex aspects derived from disciplinary crossroads that can often be stumbling blocks. The initial chapters therefore contextualise digital literary reading and specify the new research framework of digital literature for children and adolescents by, respectively, examining the sociocultural nuclei where these new literary reading practices are located and the theoretical advances in the definition and characterisation of the digital literary product.

Laura Borràs, a renowned international researcher in the field of e-lit, opens Part I. Her chapter "The Reader (in) Digital. Forms of Reading on Screens" provides a global vision, in the context of the relevant social and cultural changes, of what it means to read on a screen. The author sketches the new and multiple media of this reading which is widespread and corresponds to a social reader or to a socialising intention. Focusing especially on children, she identifies a proliferation of digital reading formats, establishes their relationship with book sales and revises some of the works that refer to what she calls *hermeneutics of complexity*.

Lucas Ramada Prieto, a member of the GRETEL research group, completes this initial section. "'Common Places in Children's E-Lit'. A Journey through the Defining Spaces of Electronic Literature" proposes a theoretical interdisciplinary trip through the different knowledge areas that provide the necessary terminology and instruments in order to set out the concept of e-lit applied to children's literature, define its essential characteristics, consider the different classification proposals of the products addressed to children and adolescents, characterise the digital aesthetic and establish the literary potential of this new creative and interpretive paradigm in relation to emergent readers.

After this both general and theoretical introduction to the subject the logical step was to enter into the corpus to provide a global vision of the digital works and their characteristics (Part II). Nonetheless, here it was not only of interest to analyse the new electronic products and reflect on their potential with regard to literary education. Due to the current links and interdependency among them, it also seemed necessary to connect e-lit for children and adolescents with the printed books with which they coexist and to study the nature of the relationships that they have established and continue to establish. Bettina Kümmerling-Meibauer and Junko Yokota, two prominent specialists in children's digital literature and digital production, share this section with Celia Turrión Penelas, a member of the GRETEL research group.

Bettina Kümmerling-Meibauer presents "The Impact of New Digital Media on Children's and Young Adult Literature". Centred on the relationship between the production aimed at the children's market and the electronic medium, this chapter offers a panoramic view of their mutual influences, illustrated with specific works and genres with fan fiction as a highlighted example. The new narrative interactive forms, the innovative genres and changes in content and structure derived from the impact of digital media on children's literature are analysed in parallel with the influence of all of this on literary comprehension and on the drastic reconsideration of the traditional relationship between author and reader.

"The Past, Present and Future of Digital Picturebooks for Children", by Junko Yokota, in contrast, is based on the importance of the facilitators (librarians, teachers and parents) in the selection and evaluation of children's digital literary readings. With the intention of providing effective instruments, the researcher offers a current state of the electronic publication of stories for children in correlation with the world of printed picturebooks and focuses her attention on the ways in which different characteristics of one and the other can affect the comprehension of children readers and influence their responses to this new type of literature.

Celia Turrión Penelas' chapter, "Electronic Literature for Children. Characterising Narrative Apps (2010-2014)", builds a model of analysis for children's narrative apps and applies it to a group of thirty works that appeared between 2010 and 2014. The author thus studies the potential of e-lit for the literary pleasure and education of emergent readers by means of a double formal characterisation: on the one hand that of the current digital corpus conceived for touchscreen tablets and addressed to children and adolescents; on the other, that of the implicit reader which is derived from the essential characteristics of the applications that were studied.

Having established the contextual and conceptual map as well as the panoramic view of the works and their main characteristics, both specifically and with respect to the implied children readers, the book inaugurates the approach to the effective reality of the children's contact with the digital literature that has been designed and addressed to their age group (Part III and Part IV). The comprehensive nucleus of the initial results from the fieldwork carried out by the GRETEL researchers are presented here – all of which was made possible thanks to their R&D project. The first block of contributions (the second of the three central parts after the corpus) focuses directly on the readers in order to study their responses to the literary proposals in the digital products by means of guided reading experiences in different educational centres. The second (third in the nucleus of the book) centres on the family and school uses of e-lit to determine, among other things, what happens when different electronic works are made available to children readers without eliminating printed literature from their environment.

The section dedicated to the readers (Part III) opens with "Traditional Readers and Electronic Literature. An Exploration of Perceptions and Readings of Digital Works", by Mireia Manresa, which provides an analysis of the experiences taken from the literary conversations on five different digital works. This was carried out with three groups of children aged between nine and eleven years old (twelve participants in total) and two groups of adolescents (seven children in total, aged between fourteen and fifteen). There are two focal points by which the children readers' understanding of e-lit and the ways in which they respond to the digital texts (that is to say, how they interpret them) are determined: by interaction and by the interpretation of temporality expressed with digital resources.

"Digital Migrations: Exploratory Research on Children's E-Lit Reading Profiles", by Lucas Ramada Prieto and Lara Reyes López, adopts the perspective of the reader profiles to show the results from the digital reading work carried out in a classroom of students aged between eleven and twelve years old with remarkable literary training but unfamiliar with touchscreen tablets and e-lit. The exploration of their tendencies as digital readers shows the suitability of these works with regard to ludic and exploratory reading attitudes, exposes the ways in which the skills acquired from reading in print are transferred to reading on digital devices and underlines the importance of the selection of a corpus where the expressive digital modes are significant in the construction of the literary text.

Martina Fittipaldi, Anna Juan and Mireia Manresa conclude this part dedicated to the readers with a chapter where they contrast the reading experiences of the same text in print and electronic formats. "Paper or Digital: A Comparative Reading with Teenagers of a Poe Short Story" focuses on the interpretation of "The Tell-Tale Heart" by Edgar Allan Poe by two groups of adolescents in two sessions of literary discussion in order to observe the distinctive characteristics of digital reading (the aspects that form the students' construction of meaning in the work) and to discover to what degree the specific components of e-lit contribute – or not – to this construction.

"iPads, Emergent Readers and Families", by Cristina Aliagas and Ana M. Margallo, opens the part focused on reading uses (Part IV) with the results of longitudinal ethnographic research in a family context with young children. Using the funds of knowledge approach, the changes introduced by touchscreen tablets are explored in the shared reading practices of stories in four homes with regard to four aspects: reading times and spaces, infant digital libraries, techno-literary learning of young participants in relation to adult facilitation and the incidence of multimodality and interactivity in reading experiences.

Next, "Digital Literature in Early Childhood. Reading Experiences in Family and School Contexts", by Neus Real and Cristina Correro, examines the debate on the use of electronic content and devices by young children and provides the results from different observations carried out with children of between two and six years old in four homes and a pre-school. The chapter describes and contrasts the majority uses of the iPad and the digital (literary) preferences of very young readers in both of these spaces and underlines the importance of facilitation in a new type of reading experience which complements analogue literary training in children under seven years of age.

Teresa Colomer and Karla Fernández de Gamboa Vázquez, in "Reading Literature on Screen in a Classroom Library", close the section on reader uses with the results of a piece of exploratory research consisting of the effects of the introduction of digital works in a classroom library in a class of students of between eleven and twelve years old. The chapter explains in detail the resulting reading practices of the group and their preferences with regard to the combination of analogue and digital corpus and exclusively to e-lit; finally it describes the discourse that was collectively constructed by the students on digital reading in order to show its potential, limitations and implications.

After considering the corpus, the readers, and the uses of current e-lit for children in situations of independent reading, it seemed essential to finish by including the reflections of the creators of digital children's works; those responsible for the effective possibility and the development of this new production. The volume therefore closes with a section (Part V) where the floor is given to the authors through the reflections of two renowned names in the English-speaking and Latin American fields: Kate Pullinger and Arnal Ballester.

In "*Inanimate Alice* – How We Accidentally Created a Digital Story for Schools", the London-based Canadian writer tells the story of one of the most popular digital works in the world. Beyond the protagonist and her life journey – which grow in parallel in the same way as the episodes in the work –, and also beyond her own definition of the kind of literature *Inanimate Alice* belongs to, Kate Pullinger focuses this chapter on the general history of a project which, begun a decade ago, has developed intermittently, has been modified according to circumstances and different factors, and so far, does not have an expiry date.

Last but not least, in "Change of Direction", Arnal Ballester tackles the idiosyncrasy of the electronic medium and its influence on the changes of conception in the literary work and the reader. The well-known Catalan illustrator examines the profound social and cultural transformation created by this new paradigm, taking into consideration the relationships between children's print and digital literature and the figure of the receiver, but also videogames and illustration. In short, this chapter proposes a different look at a phenomenon which is already radically modifying our relationships with knowledge and literary creation. In our opinion this provides a very intriguing close to the book in order to continue investigating and reflecting on digital literature for children – on digital texts, readers and educational practices.

Acknowledgements

This volume would not have been possible without the funding from the Ministerio de Economía y Competitividad (MINECO, Ministry of Economy and Competitiveness) of the Spanish government. Neither would it have been possible without the interest shown by the Peter Lang Publishing Group in the project since its very inception. Economic and structural support of this type, which is sadly scarcer today than at other times, is essential in order to be able to carry out research and to reinvest the results of these studies in social and academic development, a situation to which all countries should aspire.

We would also like to make mention of the sustained work of all the members of the GRETEL group over three and a half years; in spite of the difficulties, the obstacles and the innumerable responsibilities, all of them gave their best in order to carry out the research that this book is based on. In direct relation to the results presented here, mention must also be made of the collaboration and enthusiasm of a considerable number of people: first of all, the participants in the different fieldwork carried out in both the educational centres and the homes – students, teachers, management teams, parents, boys and girls –, who provided the essential basis for the effective materialisation of this work; the contributors who do not belong to the UAB research group – Laura Borràs, Bettina Kümmerling-Meibauer, Junko Yokota, Kate Pullinger and Arnal Ballester –, who immediately accepted the proposal to take part in this volume in spite of their multiple commitments and whose chapters have so enriched this book; the friends and external collaborators – Evelyn Arizpe and Tim Mc Quaid – and the members of GRETEL (Cristina Aliagas, Brenda Bellorín, Cecilia Silva-Díaz, Lucas Ramada Prieto and Celia Turrión Penelas) who resolved specific doubts on the English equivalent of specific terminology or, to varying degrees, have directly intervened in the translation of the Spanish original texts and the subsequent revision of the final English version. If this volume constitutes, as we hope, a contribution to the studies on children's digital literature, it is to a large extent thanks to all of them.

Works Cited

Alvermann, Donna E. *Adolescents and literacies in a digital World.* New York: Peter Lang, 2004. Print.

Al-Yaqout, Ghada. "From Slate to Slate: What Does the Future Hold for the Picturebook Series?" *New Review of Children's Literature and Librarianship*, 17.1 (2011): 57-77.

Al-Yaqout, Ghada, and Maria Nikolajeva. "Re-conceptualising picturebook theory in the digital age." *Nordic Journal of ChildLit Aesthetics,* 6 (2015). Web. 16 Feb. 2015.

Arizpe, Evelyn, and Morag Styles. *Children Reading Pictures: Interpreting Visual Texts*. London: Routledge Falmer, 2003. Print.

Bolter, Jay David, and Richard Grusin. *Remediation. Understanding New Media*. Cambridge and London: The MIT Press, 2000. Print.

Borràs, Laura. *Textualidades electrónicas. Nuevos escenarios para la literatura*. Barcelona: UOC, 2005. Print.

—. "Había una vez una app… Literatura infantil y juvenil (en) digital." *Revista de Literatura*, 269 (2012): 21-26. Print.

Cassany, Daniel, and Denise Hernández. "Internet: 1; escuela: 0?." *Revista de Investigación Educativa*, 14 (2012): 128-141. Web. 26 May 2015.

Clark, Dennis T., *et al.* "A qualitative assessment of the Kindle e-book reader: Results from initial focus groups." *Performance Measurement and Metrics*, 9.2 (2008): 118-129.

Coiro, Julie. *Exploring changes to reading comprehension on the internet: Paradoxes and possibilities for diverse adolescent readers*. Ann Arbor: UMI, 2007. Print.

Colomer, Teresa. *La formació del lector literari a través de la literatura infantil i juvenil*. Diss. Universitat Autònoma de Barcelona, 1995. Web. 10 Jan. 2015.

—. *Andar entre libros. La lectura literaria en la escuela*. México: Fondo de Cultura Económica, 2005. Print.

—. *Introducción a la literatura infantil y juvenil actual*. Madrid: Síntesis, 2010. Print.

Colomer, Teresa, dir. *Siete llaves para valorar las historias infantiles*. Madrid: Fundación Germán Sánchez Ruipérez, 2002. Print.

Colomer, Teresa, and Marina Fittipaldi, eds. *La literatura que acoge. Inmigración y lectura de álbumes*. Caracas/Barcelona: Banco del Libro-GRETEL, 2012. Print.

Coll, César, Teresa Mauri, and Javier Onrubia. "El análisis de los procesos de enseñanza y aprendizaje mediados por las TIC: una perspectiva constructivista." *Cómo valorar la calidad de la enseñanza basada en las tic*. Eds. Elena Barbera *et al.* Barcelona: Graó, 2008. 47-61. Print.

Ensslin, Astrid. *Canonizing hypertext. Explorations and Constructions*. London: Continuum International Publishing Group, 2007. Print.

GRETEL. *International Symposium: Electronic Literature: Texts, Readers and Teaching Practices*. 3-4 Oct. 2014, Barcelona. Barcelona: Universitat Autònoma de Barcelona, 2014. Web. 16 Mar. 2015.

Hayles, Katherine. *Electronic Literature: New Horizons for the Literary*. Notre Dame: University of Notre Dame, 2008. Print.

Hutchison, Amy Carter, Beth Beschomer, and Denise Schmidt-Crawford. "Exploring the use of the iPad for literacy learning." *Reading teacher*, 66.1 (2012): 15-23. Print.

Juul, Jesper. "Games Telling Stories? A Brief Note on Games and Narratives." *The International Journal of Computer Game Research*, I.1 (2001). Web. 03 Feb. 2015.

Koskimaa, Raine. *Digital literature. From text to hypertext and beyond.* Diss. University of Jyvaskyla, 2000. Web. 25 Jan. 2015.

Krashen, Stephen. *The power of reading. Insights from the research.* Englewood: Libraries Unlimited, Inc., 1993. Print.

Kress, Gunther. *El alfabetismo en la era de los nuevos medios de comunicación.* Granada: Ediciones Aljibe-Enseñanza Abierta de Andalucía, 2005. Print.

Landow, George. *Hypertext 3.0, Critical Theory and New Media in an Era of Globalization.* Maryland: The Johns Hopkins University Press, 2006. Print.

Lankshear, Colin, and Michele Knobel. *New Literacies Everyday Practices and Classroom Learning.* New York: Open University Press, 2006. Print.

Larson, Lotta C. "Digital Readers: The Next Chapter in E-Book Reading and Response." *The Reading Teacher*, 64.1 (2010): 15-22. Print.

Leveratto, Jean Marc, and Mary Leontsini. *Internet et la sociabilité littéraire.* Paris: Bibliothèque Publique d'Information / Centre Pompidou, 2008. Print.

Liu, Ziming. "Reading behaviour in the digital environment: Changes in reading behaviour over the past ten years." *Journal of Documentation*, 61.6 (2005): 700-712. Print.

Lluch, Gemma. "Jóvenes y adolescentes hablan de lectura en la red." *Ocnos. Revista de Estudios sobre Lectura*, 11 (2014): 7-20. Web. 12 Nov. 2014.

Lluch, Gemma, and Marilu Acosta. "Conversaciones sobre lecturas en la Web 2.0: el caso de Laura Gallego. Análisis discursivo de conversaciones virtuales entre adolescentes." *Lecturas para el nuevo siglo: formación receptora y lector hipertextual.* La Laguna: Servicio de Publicaciones de la Universidad de La Laguna, 2012. CD-ROM.

Mangen, Anne. "Hypertext fiction reading: haptics and immersion." *Journal of Research in Reading*, 31.4 (2008): 404-419.

Mangen, Anne, Bente R. Walgermo, and Kolbjørn Brønnick. "Reading linear texts on paper versus computer screen: effects on reading comprehension." *International Journal of Educational Research*, 58 (2013): 61-68. Print.

Manresa, Mireia, and Ana María Margallo. "New technologies make new readers? Network reading practices which are transforming young people's access to literature." *The Child and The Book 2013. Ninth Annual Conference* 21-23 March 2013.

Margallo, Ana María. "Cuestiones metodológicas en torno a la investitación de las respuestas lectoras a álbumes ilustrados." *Cultura & Educación*, 25.4 (2013): 467-478. Print.

Miall, David S., and Teresa Dobson. "Reading hypertext and the experience of literature." *Journal of Digital Information*, 2.1 (2001). Web. 5 Apr. 2015.

Moreno, Isidro. *Musas y nuevas tecnologías.* Barcelona: Paidós, 2002. Print.

New London Group. "A pedagogy of multiliteracies: Designing social futures." *Harvard Educational Review*, 66.1 (1996): 60-92. Print.

Nikolajeva, Maria, and Carole Scott. *How Picturebooks Work.* London: Routledge, 2001. Print.

Pahl, Kate, and Jennifer Rowsell. *Literacy and Education: The New Literacy Studies in the Classroom.* London: Sage, 2005. Print.

Prensky, Marc. "Digital Natives, Digital Inmigrants Part 1." *On the Horizon*, 9.5 (2001): 1-6. Web. 15 Feb. 2014.

Roskos, Kathleen, Karen Burstein, and Byeong-Keun You. "A Typology for Observing Children's Engagement with eBooks at Preschool." *Journal of Interactive Online Learning*, 11.2 (2012): 47-66. Print.

Ryan, Marie-Laure. "Beyond Myth and Metaphor. The case of Narrative in Digital Media." *Game Studies: The International Journal of Computer Game Research*, 1.1 (2001). Web. 15 Jan. 2015.

—. *Narrative across Media: The Languages of Storytelling.* Lincoln: University of Nebraska. 2004. Print.

Silva-Díaz, María Cecilia. "Libros que enseñan a leer: álbumes metaficcionales y conocimiento literario." Diss. Universitat Autònoma de Barcelona, 2005. Web. 14 Feb. 2015.

Sheppard, D. "Reading with iPads – the difference makes a difference." *Education Today* 3 (2011): 12-15. Print.

Stichnothe, Hadassah. "Engineering Stories? A Narratological Approach to Children's Book Apps." *Nordic Journal of ChildLit Aesthetics*, 5 (2014). Print.

Street, Brian. "What's "new" in New Literacy Studies? Critical approaches to literacy in theory and practice." *Current Issues in Comparative Education*. London: Teachers College 5.2 (2003): 77-91. Print.

Turrión, Celia. "Álbumes ilustrados en pantalla." *Cuadernos de Literatura Infantil y Juvenil*, 256 (2013): 6-12. Print.

—. "Multimedia Book Apps in a Contemporary Culture: Commerce and Innovation, Continuity and Rupture." *Nordic Journal of ChildLit Aesthetics*, 5 (2014). Web. 12 Mar. 2015.

Turrión, Celia, and Lucas Ramada. "Los caminos hacia la actuación del lector implícito en la literatura infantil y juvenil digital. Microestructuras y macroestructuras narrativas." *International Symposium: Electronic Literature: Texts, Readers and Teaching Practices*. 3-4 Oct. 2014 Barcelona. Barcelona: Universitat Autònoma de Barcelona, 2014. Web. 16 Mar. 2015.

Unsworth, Len. *E-literature for children. Enhancing digital literacy learning*. New York: Routledge, 2006. Print.

Yokota, Junko. "From print to digital? Considering the future of picturebooks for children." *Bologna: Fifty years of children's books from around the world.* Ed. Giorgia Grilli. Bologna: Bononia University Press, 2013. 443-449. Print.

Part I

Contextualization and Theoretical Framework

The Reader (in) Digital

Forms of Reading on Screens

Laura Borràs

Universitat de Barcelona

Only if we are able to inhabit can we build.
Martin Heidegger

Inhabiting the digital space: this is what we have been devoted to with stubborn determination since 1998 when Manuel Castells identified the technological revolution that we were living at the time (and have not stopped living since), and an information-based revolution (Castells 2006). And if reading allows us to make a more habitable world, it has also been necessary to explore the possibilities of reading (in) digital in order to inhabit this kind of reading and make it habitable. The *network society* as defined by Castells refers to a type of life in which social behaviours are organised around electronically processed information networks; and Matthew A. Zook and Mark Graham (2007) have used the concept *DigiPlace* to refer to this new spatial environment in which we interact in an interconnected way, in a network, through a potentially unlimited virtual flow of information. Readers have found in this virtual space called the Internet a scenario in which to project our vision of the reading reality in a network. In the course of these pages, we will try to account for the different ways of reading on screens, between screens. We will try to trace, in short, a vantage point from which to see the spectacle of constant creation and modification of an area of collective bargaining which does not stop changing.

Digital reading map

Me encanta utilizar la palabra Red para referirme a Internet. Creo que es porque me parece asombroso que una realidad tan vasta pueda ser nombrada con un nombre tan corto. (I love using the word Net to refer to the Internet.

I think it's because it seems astonishing to me that such a vast reality can be given such a short name.)[1]

Vicente Luis Mora

In 1570 Flemish cartographer Abraham Ortelius published a book with several world maps entitled *Theatrum orbis terrarum*. Ortelius used the Greek definition of *theatron* (theater) to define the map as a place from which to watch a show. Maps are artistic, scientific, ideological objects, closely related to systems of power, but perhaps they are also poetic objects as metaphorical devices. It is true that as people of letters, we always read the world around us in search of meaning, but maps could in fact be interpreted as metaphors to the extent that they imaginatively carry or transport us from one place to another, as do the rhetorical figures in poetry. And depending on how we look at it, maps can also be viewed as stories, for any map specifies a way to understand the stories of the world it represents. In any event, there is a very clear etymological link between the act of mapping and literature, since geography is – literally – the writing (*graphos*) of the earth (*gea*). Maps, therefore, constitute for a cartographer a complex scenario of challenges and opportunities in the work of creative interpretation of the space they want to represent: the challenge of building a graphic document that contains a certain image of the world, both visual and textual, and the opportunity to show the world, to *re-present* it, to *re-create* it, somehow, because a certain worldview ends up conforming a specific map and because a map defines the very worldview of the culture that gives birth to it, as evidenced by Jerry Broton in his fascinating book *A History of the World in 12 Maps*. Experts call it "symbiotic alchemy", where particularly complex elements are involved such as the *perspective* (of what is mapped), the *projection* (of the known cultural reality) and the *imagination* (that the cartographer is prepared to deploy).

It is a fact that the emergence of the digital world (a technological revolution focused on information) has led to substantial changes in the way we have created, received, shared and studied literature in the last fifteen years. The irruption of the digital paradigm – the standardisation of the use of the Internet and ICT – in literature is challenging in a context that has remained relatively stable and impervious to change. Indeed, the world of books has always lived, and – to be frank – comfortably, installed in the previous paradigm, that of Gutenberg and the printing press. However, once the comfort and stability zones represented by the book have been abandoned from both the technological and sociological point of view, the reading map opens up new and multiple paths and platforms

[1] English translations of all quotations in other languages have been provided by Tim Mc Quaid.

in the digital age. Reading today adopts the shapes of an expanded reading that corresponds to a social reader, or at least to a socialising intention.

The widespread impact of the digital effect on reading has substantially modified the status quo. Nobody can ignore that with the advent of the Internet we have experienced a radical transformation which affects and modifies most components of the reading ecosystem, almost in their entirety in fact. We have seen the change in reading devices (from the mobile phone to tablets, from computers to digital readers, i.e. e-readers); transmission channels (we can potentially carry a library in our pocket); content editing and presenting processes, and forms of marketing, reception and consumption. And the very business model of the publishing companies has been affected. Readers' behaviour has changed significantly with the potential of new devices: they are increasingly active and creative. We talk, for instance, about *prosumption* and *prosumers* to refer to activities located between *pro*duction and con*sumption* on the Internet. The interaction between authors and readers has been significantly modified and we have witnessed the weakening, the overlap or confusion of boundaries between leisure, work and learning, which in addition involves, as an overall result of all these changes, a significant change in the way we read.

According to the law of exponential growth of information, reading today is marked by an expansive nature. And expansive reading corresponds to a social reader, or with a socialising intention.[2] Nowadays we can speak of three reading practices in our daily lives: *shared reading* (it is difficult to imagine a more key moment for the socialisation of reading, of large-scale dialogic reading such as viral reading on social networks or with the recent phenomenon of *booktubers*, young readers who make literary criticism in video format and share a channel created for this purpose on YouTube), *fragmented reading* (the studies on today's type of reading reveal that we approach texts in a fragmented – not necessarily sequential in a broad sense –, discontinuous, fugacious way) and *transmedia reading* (that flows between different devices and platforms, combining various modes of narrative from cinema, television, networks, comics, advertising, literary texts, etc.). Because it is certain that we have never before read so much as we do now. What has occurred is that the spectrum of reading has been expanded in order to decode increasingly complex texts which require new literacies.

2 We can identify other expansive moments in history, such as in the Middle Ages, for example, with the reading aloud of *romans* or in the field of scientific reading, which involved scientist readers intervening in texts with annotations such as scholia, glosses, marginalia, etc.

Much of this text decoding takes place in the field of social networks. And in the last ten years these networks have matured and chaos seems to have mutated into strategy. Facebook was born in 2004, YouTube in 2005, Twitter in 2006. Today, their aggregate number of users would convert them into the most overpopulated countries on earth. And in this decade the content explosion has taken place. We have gone from the obsession of attracting followers to fostering the loyalty of users, a loyalty based on content. The Internet opens the way to the hypercustomisation of the media experience. And the figures show that young people choose the mobile phone as their main user device: 45% of users between eighteen and twenty-four years old against 12% of users between forty-five and fifty-four years old. So mobile phones modify media consumption and, therefore, the reader of the new generations ("Els joves i la informació" [Young People and Information] 2014).

If we analyse the behaviour patterns of people who use the mobile phone as a tool for basic information, we realise that they wake up with their mobile phone alarm (not an alarm clock) and before setting foot on the floor they have already consulted the latest messages of their WhatsApp threads, comment notifications or posts on Facebook and Twitter, as well as checking new emails (news headlines included) and, in order to know what to wear, the weather, too. Before getting out of bed! Such a start to a day gives us the perfect pattern of behaviour towards the device. Not surprisingly we are talking about generations that, despite the different names they have received – which have been collected by Ariadna Fernández-Planells and Mònica Figueras Maz (2014) –, are: *The Net Generation* (Tapscott 1998); *Millenials* (Howe, and Strauss 2000); *Digital natives* vs *Digital immigrants* (Prensky 2001); *Generation Millenium* (Oblinger 2003); *Generación Internet* (Internet Generation) (Tubella *et al.* 2008); *Echo Gen Y* (Macnamara 2009); *Digital residents* vs. *Digital visitors* (White 2011); *Generació @* (@ Generation) (Feixa 2012), and *Generació #* (# Generation) (Feixa, and Nofre eds. 2013).

Our young people – terminologies aside – are hyperconnected young adults, with teenagers between fourteen and seventeen (according to Consultant IAB Spain) being those who have the highest degree of penetration in social networks. Those who have teenagers at home will have seen that they study by using WhatsApp, or Snapchat or Hangout or video, that is, the same tools they use to socialise, to connect with the world. Logically, the emergence of new environments corresponds to new reactions which proliferate and often range from FOMO (the acronym for Fear Of Missing Out), i.e. the anxiety of missing something in the digital world, to JOMO (the acronym for Joy Of Missing Out) which, in turn, expresses our need to disconnect, to turn off the devices, to return to the "real" world.[3] It goes without saying, however, as Castells (2006) points out all reality is perceived virtually since we always apprehend the world through a set of signs and symbols. The society-network represents a new communication system that generates what Castells calls *real virtuality*: an integration of material reality in a virtual image.

Platforms and readers in digital

> La science et la technologie se multiplient autour de nous. De plus en plus, elles dictent les langages dans lesquels nous parlons et pensons. Nous pouvons adopter ces langages, ou nous taire. (Science and technology multiply around us. They increasingly dictate the languages in which we speak and think. We can either adopt these languages or shut up.)
>
> J. G. Ballard

An overview of reading taken from the most recent data (IDESCAT 2014) allows us to identify a proliferation of digital reading formats and their increasing relationship to book sales. Notably, as mentioned above, the mobile phone is the primary reading device for many young people. In this regard UNESCO have published a report entitled "Reading in the Mobile era" with their conclusions about the benefits of mobile phone reading which show some of the myths about reading and how digital literacy has become essential (UNESCO 2014).

Young women are those who read the most on the mobile phone, and usually for convenience, comfort and portability. It is also interesting that the UNESCO report that one in five mobile readers becomes a frequent reader. Such data help debunk some myths about reading today, one of which claims, for example, that people used to read better and more in the past. The data do not corroborate this. After all, reading is more a matter of education and training than of devices and platforms, although some digital literacy is required to achieve the skills needed to ensure an improvement in reading ability. With the exercise of reading, the way of looking grows and choices become more assertive because reading broadens perspectives and the ability to make decisions, to select, to choose. Another interesting piece of data is the revelation that there is a continuous transfer between canonical reading circuits and new media.

3 The obsession with obtaining total and permanent information may be the basis of FOMO. It is characterised by the desire to live all experiences and the will to be informed on everything at all times. The psychological foundation of this syndrome is the fear of being left behind with the comparative feeling that others are having a better time. The sense of loss can be of an experiential nature (missing an event) as well as intellectual (ignoring the trending topics), or can even be technological (anxiety to have a new, updated smartphone). The rise of FOMO is directly related to the popularity of social networks and the technology that allows us to always be connected.

Mediamorphosis

Roger Fidler's (1997) concept of *mediamorphosis* becomes very useful when tracing the transformation process that we are examining here. The Canadian theorist defined it as the transformation of media from one form to another, usually as a result of the combination of cultural changes and the arrival of new technologies. As he states, media do not appear by spontaneous generation or independently. They emerge gradually by means of the metamorphoses of the old media. And when new forms of media emerge, the old ways do not die, but continue to evolve and adapt. Fidler actually lists six steps. *Coevolution*, the time when the emergence of a new medium takes place simultaneously with the development of other coexisting media, without any significant effects at the beginning. *Metamorphosis*, the time when the new medium gradually grows and progressively adopts codes of a preexisting medium; it first imitates to be able to innovate afterwards. *Propagation*: after replicating the characteristics of the preexisting medium, the new medium gradually gains new followers while generating its own expressive code, its own language, a new user's manual. *Survival*, when the new medium reaches the point where it becomes a threat to the others and they start their own adaptation to change in order to avoid extinction. *Opportunity* and *necessity*: to reach this stage, the new medium must have achieved a certain status of indispensability. The new medium has projected itself in different directions and spheres of influence: social, political and economic. Finally, delayed adoption takes place. In this sense, the history of media has shown us to what degree we need a complete generational takeover (approximately from twenty-five to thirty years) to achieve the consolidation of a new medium within society.

Electronic literature

> Literariness is in a crisis of new meaning due to its expanded cultural ground.
>
> Barret Watten

Electronic literature has been long exploring the artistic possibilities offered by this new scenario. At this point I will offer a brief review of some of the works that can be included in what I have called *hermeneutics of complexity*, given that electronic literature is somehow a creative response that reacts to the contemporary discredit of the great narratives. At the time, Daniel Cassany (2012) spoke of digital genres as "transferred" (paper-based texts), "reproduced" (online reproduction of printed documents) and "autonomous" genres which depend on the technical possibilities of the Internet (74). I want to speak about this latter textual typology. With different levels of difficulty, we will start with the typographical animation generated by the 16th century humanist, *Bembo's Zoo*. *Bembo's Zoo* is a recreation of the alphabet based on Bembo's typography where the letters come to life and reproduce the essence of each animal or its most easily recreated feature.

An app that also serves to memorise verses, in the style of a karaoke, is *Poems by Heart*. This app allows you to interact with the great poetry of all times and do so in a playful way, highlighting orality and regaining the pleasure of memorising poems.

Changing reading register, and more addressed to teenagers, we have *Ha perdut la veu* (Lost the Voice) by Jerome Fletcher, a story he wrote as *La Freda ha perdut la veu* (Freda has lost her Voice) and adapted as a digital work for the E-Poetry Festival 2009 in Barcelona, organised by the research group Hermeneia, from the Universitat de Barcelona (University of Barcelona). At that time Fletcher played with tension and complicity between languages. He uses the ellipsis because, besides it being his preferred diacritical sign, it also marks the trace of what has been lost. In his own words:

> *It displays the trace of something lost*, and in the context of the phrase 'ha perdut la veu' (has lost the voice), it constitutes a double loss concerning *the disappearance of those who have lost their voice*. Or perhaps it is causal. It could be read as 'as a consequence of losing their voice they themselves inevitably disappear', leaving only a trace in the form of a triplet of dots. (Fletcher 2011)

When he presented the work in Barcelona, Fletcher claimed:

> I want to give an account of the composition of the work and to introduce – no more than that – via Deleuze and Guattari's reading of Kafka, some thoughts about the cultural location of e-literature. The children's story itself revolves around a place called the Lost Voice Office, which is where you go to retrieve your voice and the two main characters – an irreverent eleven-year-old girl and a pompous classically trained actor – lose their voice on the same day and due to a bureaucratic mix-up at the Lost Voice Office, end up with each other's voices.

Returning to the location and context of the piece, there are obvious, albeit comic resonances, between this children's story and the recent history of a people and a language group which were indeed forced to speak with another voice. That voice was stifled for decades under Franco, as Catalan was banned as the official language of the bureaucracy in favour of the dominant form of Castilian Spanish. At the same time – said Fletcher – I re-read Deleuze and Guattari's *Kafka – Toward a Minor Literature*, remembering that Kafka was a writer who had to deal with the problems of which language to write in as a Czech Jew with German at his disposal.

The use of erasure in the piece, where in order to read it is necessary to erase, is crucial. It is related to the erasure of other languages. But erasure only makes other languages visible. "There is an irony here, in that both the texts I am using are translated", says Fletcher. Translated into what is arguably the most dominant of world languages, English.

This is a reading, therefore, where signifier and signified reach an absolute communion. The content merges with the form, which somehow reinforces the meaning of the text.

Conclusions

After more than ten years of teaching electronic literature and eighteen years of teaching 2.0, having developed reading practices on all kinds of platforms in a permanent state of evolution, I state that we need a hermeneutics of the digital text and its scenarios and reading modes. We have to peremptorily generate reading parameters for the new generations of "mobile" readers. At the end of the day, understanding is always a movement, a departure towards interpretation and, as Nabokov wanted, reading (in) digital is re-reading. I conclude with Marjorie Perloff's reflection: "The 'new techniques' whereby letters and words can move around the screen, break up, and reassemble, or whereby the reader/viewer can decide by a mere click to reformat the electronic text or which part of it to access, become merely tedious unless the poetry in question is, in Ezra Pound's words, 'charged with meaning'" (Perloff 2006).

Works Cited

Primary Works Cited

Bembo's Zoo. Web. 23 Mar. 2015.

Fletcher, Jerome. *La Freda ha perdut la veu: A bilingual digital text work*. Web. 23 Mar. 2015.

Poems by Heart. New York: Penguin Group, 2013. iPad Edition.

Secondary Works Cited

Cassany, Daniel. *En línea_Leer y escribir en la red.* Barcelona: Anagrama, 2012. Print.

Castells, Manuel. *La era de la información. Economía, sociedad y cultura*, Vol. 1, *La sociedad red.* Madrid: Alianza Editorial, 2006. Print.

"Els joves i la informació." Dossier. *Capçalera*, 165 (2014): 34-43. Print.

Feixa, Carles. "Què és la generació @?" Universitat Oberta de Catalunya, UOC, 2012. Web. 21 Apr. 2015.

Feixa, Carles, and Jordi Nofre, eds. *#Generación indignada. Topías y utopías del 15M.* Lleida: Milenio, 2013. Print.

Fernández-Planells, Ariadna, and Mònica Figueras Maz. "Els joves i la informació". *Capçalera*, 165 (2014): 34-43. Print.

Fidler, Roger. *Mediamorphosis*. Thousand Oaks, Calif.; London: Pine Forge Press, 1997. Print.

Fletcher, Jerome. "…ha perdut la veu: Some reflections on the composition of e-literature as a minor literature." *Journal of Writing in Creative Practice*, 4 (1): 53-63. Web. 23 Mar. 2015.

Howe, Neil, and William Strauss. *Millennials Rising: The next Great Generation.* New York: Vintage Books, 2000. Print.

IDESCAT. "Ús de les TIC i del correu electrònic a les empreses 2013-2014." IDESCAT, 2014. Web. 29 May 2015.

Macnamara, D. "Cinc dinàmiques globals per analitzar l'any 2010 i el futur proper." *L'audiovisual local. Una mirada per afrontar el futur*. Barcelona: Xarxa de Televisions Locals, 2009.

Oblinger, Diana. "Boomers & Gen-Xers, Millennials: Understanding the 'New Students'." *Educause Review*. July/August (2003): 37-47. Web. 12 Mar. 2015.

Perloff, Marjorie. "Screening the Page / Paging the Screen: Digital Poetics and the Differential Text." *New Media Poetics: Contexts, Technotexts, and Theories*. Eds. Adelaide Morris, and Thomas Swiss. Cambridge and London: MIT Press, 2006. 143-144. Print.

Prensky, Marc. "Digital Natives, Digital Inmigrants Part 1." *On the Horizon*, 9.5 (2001): 1-6. Web. 15 Feb. 2014.

Tapscott, Don. *Growing up Digital. The Rise of the Net Generation*. New York; McGraw-Hill, 1998. Print.

Tubella, Imma, *et al*. "Internet I la televisió. La guerra de les pantalles." *UOC Papers*, 7 (2008). Web. 25 May 2015.

UNESCO. "Reading in the Mobile Era: A Study of Mobile Reading in Developing Countries." Paris: Unesco, 2014. Web. 29 May 2015.

White, David. "Visitors and Residents: A New Typology for online engagement." *First Monday*, 16.9 (2001). Web. 22 Jul. 2014.

Zook, Matthew A., and Mark Graham. "Mapping DigiPlace: Geocoded Internet Data and the representation of Place." *Environment and Planning B: Planning and Design*, 34, (2007): 466-482. Print.

"Common Places in Children's E-Lit"

A Journey through the Defining Spaces of Electronic Literature

Lucas Ramada Prieto

Universitat Autònoma de Barcelona

Introduction. If we cannot define literature, how can we define electronic literature?

If the field of humanities contains a dangerous activity it is the drawing of definitive boundaries for any of its elements. Let us briefly consider, for example, the idea of literature and the enormous conceptual distance that exists between the mimetic vision of Aristotle, who saw in *poetry* the representation of the possible through language (how many times has this idea been misinterpreted in the history of literary theory!) and the vision of Russian formalist Roman Jakobson who, on defining literature as "organised violence committed on ordinary speech", placed the weight of "literariness" on the evocative and reflexive capacity of the external language form (Eagleton 2008: 2). If we continue to review the history of literary ontology a little further – adding, for example, a Plato or a Barthes to the equation – we realise the impossibility of reconciling all our readings and desist in our search for a clearly defined vision of what literature is. This, however, does not mean to say that literature does not exist. Literature exists and is palpable, and any group of people with minimum knowledge on the subject would be capable of reaching an agreement, with greater or lesser precision, on whether a particular text is or is not literary and would be able to do so thanks to the common places that are shared on this vast ocean that is the literary world.

When we transfer definition-oriented debates to a field such as electronic literature where multidisciplinarity is practically limitless, the need for these common places multiplies exponentially. Hayles (2008) says it better than anybody in her *Electronic literature*: *New horizons for the literary* when she says:

> Electronic literature is a 'hopeful monster' (as genetics call adaptive mutations) composed of parts taken from diverse traditions that may not always fit neatly together. Hybrid by nature, it comprises a "trading zone" [...] in which different vocabularies, expertise, and expectations come together to see what might emerge from their intercourse. (4)

In a field where there is a blend of knowledge areas as diverse as literary theory, sociology, computer programming, new media studies, audiovisual narrative, etc., it is essential to establish some common standards to facilitate a general internalisation of the definition of electronic literature if we are to safely navigate the, as yet, "incunable" intellectual field of children's digital literature studies.

The objective of this chapter is precisely this, to journey through the shared spaces that electronic literary theory has defined to date by means of a comprehensive but non-exhaustive examination of the specific panorama of children's e-literature in order to give an idea that will not only offer us a more precise understanding of the research in literary digitality and the works that lend it meaning, but also to provide a glimpse of the future possibilities that this creative and interpretive paradigm has to offer.

Bell says in her controversial "A [S]creed for Digital Fiction" (2010) that digital fiction is "fiction written for and read on a computer screen that pursues its verbal, discursive and/or conceptual complexity through the digital medium, and would lose something of its aesthetic and semiotic function if it were removed from that medium." The researcher's definition inextricably links the essence of digital fiction to the computer medium, as did Bootz when speaking of "numeric" literature as "any narrative or poetic form that uses the computing device as a medium and implements one or more specific properties of this medium" (2007).[1] However, the image portrayed by the French author's words, albeit vaguely, is especially interesting for its explicit connection with the concept of the literary – an idea that Bell appears to shun – and, although unstable for obvious reasons, demonstrates the general feeling among researchers that literary studies are greatly pertinent to the new paradigm of fictional creation. Hayles (2008), in line with this perception of digital literature, suggests that the future expectations of the digital reader inevitably originate in the world of print and therefore e-lit should "build on these expectations even as it modifies and transforms them" (4).

The Electronic Literature Organisation (ELO) adopts the same approach. This is an independent entity founded in 1999 to promote

[1] English translations of all quotations in other languages have been provided by Tim Mc Quaid.

literary reflection within the digital world among academics and creators. They define digital literature as "work with important literary aspects that takes advantage of the capabilities and contexts provided by stand-alone or networked computers" ("What is E-Lit?"). Rettberg, co-founder of ELO, reflects on the ambiguity of the organisation's definition, pointing out that these words do not merely imply the simple fusion of the concepts of "literature" and "digital", because in the current sociological context which is practically entirely digital, this would include any type of literary activity carried out today. What is truly pertinent to the study of digital literature is the understanding that for literature to be digital, the computer is "in some way *essential* to the performance or carrying out of the literary activity" (Rettberg 2014: 169), or in the words of Hayles, "electronic literature is 'born digital', a first generation digital object created on a computer and usually meant to be read on a computer" (2008: 3).

The search for the identity of children's e-lit in digital humanities

Since its now distant beginnings from among fiction hypertexts, electronic literature has always been an academic and unquestionably minority, artisanal and artistic phenomenon. For this reason the arrival of children's digital literature to the core of mainstream fiction for young people has provoked an instant reaction in the research sector and, it may be said, has highlighted an immediate need to focus on a product that targets emergent readers and therefore requires a deep understanding on the part of the socio-educational framework responsible for its mediation. While it is true that the history of interactive children's literature goes back more than twenty years to the Random House publication in 1992 of *Just Grandma and Me* – the first in a series of enriched multimedia works in CD-ROM format known as *living books* (Schwebs 2014) –, it is unquestionable that the real productive explosion in the children's digital literary panorama came about with the mass arrival of new electronic devices such as smartphones and tablets (Turrión 2014a) and especially since the launch of the Apple iPad in 2010.

Moreover, the experimental evolution in the creation of children's literature in the last fifty years has demonstrated the possibilities that the new digital spaces have to offer the world of children's literature, a fact that electronic literature scholars such as Borràs have rightly pointed out:

> Children's literature also has a reserved space in the digital field and is proving to be one of the areas of greatest impact and literary possibilities for the publishing world; children's formats have always provided an opportunity to reveal the explosion of creativity that has brought books for children with

> their textures, smells, pop-ups, etc. to artisanal print publishing – and this opportunity has now also arrived at the digital space. (2013: 21)[2]

This synchrony with the world of the picturebook is what has led children's electronic literature researchers to attempt to isolate in their considerations what Hayles referred to as "born-digital" works (2008), in other words, to separate the digitised from the purely digital:

> The main difference between the two text production models is that the digitalisation of literature supposes the transfer of the known model, paper and print, to digital format. This is merely a transposition of formats that supposes no change in the essence of the text itself, while digital literature, by definition, cannot be printed as it takes advantage of and exploits the intrinsic possibilities of the medium. (Turrión 2012: 41)

Stichnothe (2013) and Schwebs (2014), for their part, agree on adapting the now classic terminology of Prensky (2001) to the electronic corpus in order to differentiate between *native* and *immigrant* digital (texts) where native means the e-lit pieces that "were designed from the ground up as apps" (Stichnothe 2013) and are differentiated from the mere adaptations of pre-existent printed works. This distinction, however, may be excessively "vague", as transmediations such as *The Heart and the Bottle*, where the use of specific properties of the electronic medium are effectively adapted to a pre-existent story, leads us to consider that the native electronic nature in question possibly has more to do with the poetic manner in which the specific characteristics of the medium are used rather than the "origin" of the fictional material itself.

Despite this, independent consideration of digital works supposes a different research approach to the generalised tendency to analyse electronic literature as a mere evolutionary step-up from the picturebook. In this latter line of study we emphasise the terminological adaptation from children's print literature to the new digital literature implemented by Al-Yaqout and Nikolajeva (2015) who, in an effort to establish the metalinguistic bases of the new children's literary paradigm, neglect the new multidisciplinary paths that this has introduced and also, for example, the significant legacy that has been directly handed down from the world of videogaming (Turrión 2014b). This does not detract from the exercise in systematisation carried out, which seeks to fill a dangerous void in the world of literary teaching guidance today, a world that has been completely overrun by the exponential growth of the electronic corpus and which lacks the tools required to safely navigate the new scenario.

---

2 Not to mention the palpable proximity among the multiple studies that link the world of the picturebook with post-modern aesthetics (Silva-Díaz 2005) and the vision of e-lit by the greater part of the research world as the definitive paradigm of writing that is disruptive, metafictional and lacking in precise authorship (Landow 2006).

Among the tools required, the taxonomic analysis of production is essential if we wish to clearly perceive the complex and heterogeneous world of electronic production. Beyond the simple distinctions between the aforementioned digital and digitised works, we encounter some interesting exercises in this necessary, all-inclusive attempt at classification. One of the first typologies carried out on digital productions within the specific world of children's literature was the classification by Unsworth (2006) which, based on the analysis of CD-ROM-based narrative production, outlined the following categories:

- *Electronic stories for emergent readers.* Written text with added audio and help links.
- *Linear electronic narratives.* Traditional narrative (bimodal or not) presented on-screen.
- *Electronic narrative and interactive content.* Works enriched with paraliterary content.
- *Hypertextual narrative.* Purely linguistic works with hyperlinks.
- *Hypermedia narratives.* Multimodal text with hyperlinks.

We can see how Unsworth gradually orders the works based on two fundamental core concepts: expressive multimodality and linearity in the discourse; this is completely consistent with the studies from the end of the last century on adult digital literature (Ensslin 2007) and with the state of development of children's digital literature at the time, which still lacked a device to facilitate active user participation such as the touchscreen tablet.

Yokota and Teale's (2014) description, for its part, is more continuist in terms of the traditional world of children's literature and establishes four different phases in what they consider to be the digital transition of children's literary works to the new electronic scenario:

> 1) Scanning entire print picturebooks; 2) transforming picturebooks into film-like creations; 3) transforming picturebooks with features unique to the digital world, and 4) adding interactive features, including games, that extend beyond the story. (578)

For these Chicago-based researchers, the rupture from narrative bimodality is the first step in an extensive series of transformations that eventually distances the purely digital work from its traditional structure and the gamification of the fictional experience is the last of these transformations, one that researchers do not always approve of as they consider it disruptive to the "narrative" enjoyment of the reading process (Al-Yaqout, and Nikolajeva 2015).

It seems evident that the perception of interactivity as a determining factor in distancing the essence of electronic narrative from print narrative is a key issue in this case and, moreover, is a view that is shared by the majority of contemporary researchers. This has converted the active participation of the digital reader into the cornerstone of electronic poetics in the few studies that have been published to date. For Schwebs (2014), for example, the tactility of the tablet and the implementation of narrative and aesthetic mechanisms that make use of this tactility are an essential foundation for meaning-making, as he affirms in his specific analysis of the iPad adaptation of the short animation film *The Fantastic Flying Books of Mr. Morris Lessmore* when he states "the tactility of the Lessmore app is associated with a sensuous experience of the materiality of the medium, and empowers a potential for meaning making".

Equally determinant is the capacity for choice and interaction on behalf of the user, according to Stichnothe (2014) who, in one of the most interesting theoretical proposals in the research panorama, classifies electronic stories for children and young people on the basis of the incidence rate of user participation within the narrative structure of the works. Based on the formalist distinction between *fabula* and *syuzhet*, the researcher proposes a differentiation between Multiple Fabula Apps, in which reader activity affects the outcome of the story and Alternative Story Apps, where the user only modifies the external form of the discourse without significantly affecting the essence of the story being told. The proposal of the German researcher is interesting and is in parallel with other studies that have approached the classification of the various types of interactivity within the contemporary panorama of electronic narrations (Ramada, and Turrión 2014), but is excessively enclosed within a research scenario eager for proposals that encompass, to the greatest possible extent, the heterogeneous nature of electronic literature.

Within this aspiration to multidisciplinary rigour that has become essential to the analysis of children's literary digitality, the recent research by Turrión (2014b) has, without doubt, represented a step forward for the theoretical collective. In her exhaustive characterisation of digital narrative for children, Turrión draws from transversal disciplines such as literary and audiovisual narratology, the vast tradition of specific theory on children's literature and textual literary pragmatics, but the basic raw material for her work is comprised of purely electronic academic areas such as hypertextual theory, interactive narratology and game studies. The analysis worksheet used for her exhaustive close reading exercise, although limited to the narrative genre, conveys the complexity of digital works and the affordances and constraints that the electronic medium holds for the world of electronic stories aimed at emergent readers.

Within this same work, on the other hand, and returning to the definition exercise that concerns us here, of special interest is the narratological typology created by the author where she differentiates between:

- *Digital audiobooks*: oral narrations that may or may not be accompanied by other types of expressive substance such as written text, but which do not introduce any type of interactive layer or rupture in the linearity of the discourse.
- *Multimedia narratives*: narratives that employ expressive multimodality and while they may employ interactive elements, do not interrupt the linearity of the work.
- *Hypermedia narratives*: works in which multimodality and the possibility of user choice and participation are structural elements.
- *Cross-media narratives*: works in which the story does not centre on one medium alone, but rather disseminates the narrative material over a variety of spaces via outlets to YouTube, blogs, social networks, etc., that serve to extend the fictional world over different platforms.

Beyond this classification, however, we wish to focus on the theory that transcends and sustains this ordering exercise in order to arrive at the "constructive characteristics of the works that rely on the key elements of the electronic medium aesthetic" (Turrión 2014b: 180) and justify the above typologies. As established by Turrión, digital narrative can be therefore analysed on the basis of three basic characterising elements that are reflected in a gradual and interrelated manner in children's works created for the electronic medium:

- *The combination of languages beyond the written word*. The first paradigmatic modification is the multiplication of expressive substances beyond the written word. The electronic medium is capable of encompassing and combining numerous semiotic channels that are not strictly linguistic, such as image (static and animated) and sound.
- *The presence of structures other than linear*. One of the basic characterising elements of digital narratives is the rupture from the traditional form of linear story creation which is ordered and immutable. Whether it is via the inclusion of interactive layers or narrative structures that bifurcate the discursive paths, the electronic medium naturally tends towards this rupture.
- *The various platforms that are sometimes required in order to access the complete story*. The possibility that the fictional material of a story can be divided over different creative spaces, whether via print and digital or by disseminating the material over

multiple virtual spaces, is one of the most paradigmatic evolutions in contemporary narrative in what has come to be known as transmedia storytelling.

The synthetic characterisation of the constructive properties of digital narrative carried out by the researcher is the result of her perceptive examination of much of the research on electronic literature that has been written to date – Murray, Manovich, Ryan, etc. However, it is precisely this generic precision when establishing a specifically narratological defining framework that differentiates her limited perspective from the one we adopt here. An example of this is the prioritisation of interactivity as a determining factor in the digital narratological aesthetic, in the words of Ryan (2006)[3] – which we cannot extend to our work here as it would significantly condition the assessment that could be made on an entire section of electronic production, such as generative poetry where user participation need not necessarily have any greater significance than it would in printed literature.

With this in mind, and as a precursor to our own characterisation proposal for electronic literature, we will now briefly review some of the descriptive definitions proposed by the digital literature theorists in an effort to pinpoint the common spaces and shared places within the complex world of electronic poetics and allow us to form an idea of the properties that constitute this creative universe.

Characterising the volatile. Anatomy of a digital aesthetic

One of the most interesting proposals in order to begin to understand the foundations of electronic creation is the treatise on the aesthetic of digital art proposed by Holtzman in his *Digital Mosaics* (1997), in which the North American theorist establishes the following properties for defining the digital worlds characteristic of cyberspace art:

- *Discontinuity*. Digital worlds are discontinuous and do not predetermine any path and as such, promote free, interest-based choices and decisions.
- *Interactivity*. The digital experience is not passive. It demands participation. The work is defined by the interaction between the work itself and the user.

[3] "Of all the properties listed above, I regard interactivity as the most important. Not all digital texts are interactive, but those that aren't could usually be taken out of the computer and played by another medium. The term has been under attack by cybertheorists for being too vague […] but when interactivity is associated with narrative, its meaning is unambiguous: it mandates choice for the user." (Ryan 2006: 99)

- *Dynamism and vitality.* Digital works generate a wide range of production possibilities and, as such, require a high level of dynamism for their "interpretation".
- *Ethereal worlds.* There is no *there* to the work, and nothing of any material nature supports it. The focus of attention of the text is enhanced from the traditional two-dimensional written page to three-dimensional space, where it acquires other qualities.
- *Ephemeral worlds.* The experience of a sequence of bits exists only momentarily. It is only when the programme is "executed" that the work manifests itself.
- *Promotion of virtual communities.* The dissolution of the time and space barriers that occurs as a result of people connecting with each other online promotes the creation of virtual communities, thereby generating a new form of global conscience.

Despite the perceptibly abstract nature of Holtzman's characterisation of digital art, the synchrony of his proposal with other descriptive exercises in the field of electronic literary theory is easily discernible: a year later, Simanowski (cited in Ensslin 2007) describes the poetics of fictional hypertext based on six aesthetic criteria: multimediality, technological aesthetics, performance, navigation, hyperlink semantics and computer screen aesthetics; and in her classic *Hamlet on the Holodeck* (1997), Janet Murray defines electronic media as sequential, participative, spatial and encyclopaedic.

The dialogue among the three authors is evident. When Simanowski speaks of "performance" he is characterising hypertextual works in the same way as Murray characterises the electronic media when she refers to it as "sequential", and Holtzman, when he describes "the ephemeral nature" of the execution of the programmed code in digital worlds. The fact is that the "coded" and "programmed" nature of digital artistic output is key in the majority of aesthetic characterisations proposed in the theory of cybernetic literature. The same occurs with interactivity – "participation" in the work of Murray and included in the (elective) poetics of the hyperlink in the case of Simanowski and with the "spatiality" of digital text, a direct consequence of the embodiment electronic works on a "screen" – in reference to Simanowski's "Computer screen aesthetics" – and which transforms it into an "ethereal" space (Holtzman 1997) that is potentially navigable by the reader. The conceptual echo among the three authors is both continuous and meaningful in terms of our beginning to form an idea of the role of digitality in artistic literary creation.

Another descriptive reflection essential to a transversal collection of precedents in the field, and which, in addition, is echoed to a significant degree by Turrión and with which we will finish this brief review of digital poetics, is the proposal that Ryan offers in her 2001 work *Narrative as virtual reality* concerning the properties of the electronic medium as a space for (specifically) literary creation. For the Genevois author, this is characterised by:

– *Text mobility*. The electronic medium reduces the space between text and reader due to the ability of the text to "travel" to the reader via the hyperlink, thereby facilitating the "encyclopaedic" essence of the digital text referred to by Murray.

– *Kaleidoscopic skills*. This concept, also inherited from Murray, refers to "the computer's ability to produce multiple patterns [with] the same elements" (214), in other words, the combinatory capacity of the electronic medium, once again highlighting the importance of sequentiality in the electronic aesthetic.

– *Algorithmical and procedural nature*. "The electronic text is the product of a two-level semiotic system by which the signs flashed on the screen are themselves the output of a computer program" (215). Despite its invisibility, this code is what ultimately determines the appearance and behaviour of the text on the screen.

– *Hypermediacy*. The electronic medium allows the combination of various expressive substances that bring us closer to the dream of "total language". By not employing the term "multimediality", Ryan echoes Bolter and Grusin (2000), who seek to convey the creative heterogeneity of the electronic environment aside from the aspirations to holistic and coherent creation that stems from the idea of "multimodal".

– *Interrupted structure*. The electronic medium breaks away from the linear structure of reading, openly inviting users to take secondary paths.

– *Dynamic animation and display and exploitation of temporality*. With these two properties, Ryan highlights the possibilities of this previously mentioned virtual updating of text on screen which allows it to interact explicitly with space-time, determining, for example, the duration of its display on the screen by making it disappear or by manipulating it kinetically.

Although we could continue to gather descriptive characterisations relating to the creative aesthetic of the digital medium and electronic literary poetics,[4] these would only serve to demonstrate the highly complex

4 As a paradigmatic example of the heterogeneity of the descriptive in the world of digital aesthetics, we might mention the endless list of definitions of hypertext that Borràs outlines in the introductory chapter of *Textualidades electrónicas* (Electronic

heterogeneity of the field and complicate our task of theoretical synthesis. Nevertheless, we believe that the compendium so far referenced outlines a panorama that is sufficiently solid to allow us, finalising our work, to launch a proposal that perhaps is not defining, and is intentionally non-definitive, but which helps us to conceptualise the foundations that constitute electronic literary works and the constructive properties on which they are based, thus allowing us to navigate with greater ease through this new creative paradigm.

Electronic literature as programmed artistic impulse

When we approach the world of literary works created specifically for an electronic medium, we gradually find a series of properties which, in their entirety, configure the constructive map of what we call electronic literature. The first of these, which is key and unnegotiable due to the fact that it contains the essence of digital literature, is its *programmed nature*. In other words, regardless of the external form in which it manifests itself to the reader, there will always be an underlying programmed computer code that must be executed by means of a computational environment. We understand that the ephemeral substance that constitutes this code is not specifically a constructive property in its own right, but rather a raw material that ultimately conditions the configuration and final interrelationship of all the properties and, therefore, is the foundation on which the essence of literary digitality is based. As Murray (1997) says, "Authorship in electronic media is procedural. Procedural authorship means writing the rules by which the texts appear as well as writing the texts themselves" (152), from which we can clearly understand the qualitative modification that the creative exercise in digital environments supposes; the idea is not only to create artistically textual meaning but rather to design a performative architecture in the work on the basis of electronic textuality (Borràs 2005).

In order to understand this more easily, let us consider a children's digital work created for interactive tablets such as *My little story factory*. In this combined-format literary text the user encounters a micro-narrative fragmented into four pieces (Figure 1), each of which responds to a basic syntactic function that allows for the permutation of the pieces while maintaining coherence of meaning. In each reading the work begins randomly, making the experience different on each "execution". In addition, the user can also add their own narrative blocks to the system so that they form part of the combinatorial structure, making this one of the

Textualities, 2005), and which, almost in the form of a parody, conveys the inherent difficulty of reaching indisputable affirmations in a field as multidisciplinary as this.

few children's works today that allows for what is known as productive interactivity (Turrión 2014b).

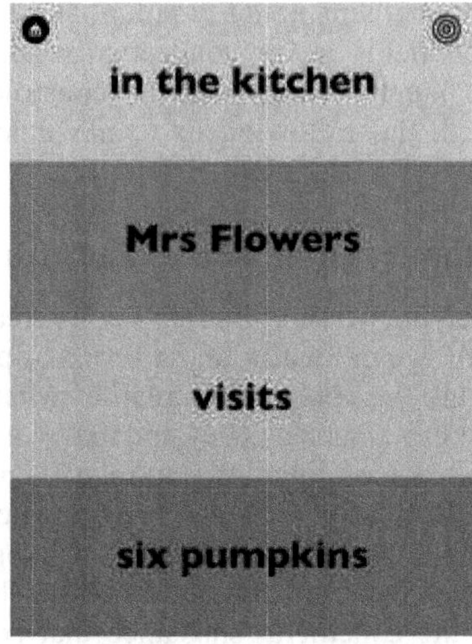

Figure 1. ***My little story factory***

We may arrive at the idea, therefore, that this participation constitutes the central poetic concept of the work, and that the possibility of "shaking" the tablet to randomly create micro-stories based on our own words is its defining characteristic. The true digitality, however, lies in the coded sequence that underlies this behaviour and which determines its textual architecture and all the consequences that this generates. The constructive matter that generates the random mixture of the various pieces of this narrative puzzle each time we shake the tablet is the same matter that allows us to add new blocks and which transforms this binary DNA into a multimedia work of minimalist aesthetic: the code. Furthermore, this code is what determines the gradual nature of the appearance of the remaining properties of the digital work.

However, while we must recognise the essential importance of the code for the conceptualisation of the digital work, we should also be clear that the reader-spectator (Mora 2012) does not connect directly with the code, but rather with its on-screen representation in an adopted virtual appearance which we call *interface*. This constitutes a fundamental element in electronic works, being as it is the mediator between the complexity of pure computer language and the human interpreter.

The interface is that virtually-real space that lies between the text as designed by the author and the mental construction that the reader makes of it (Ryan 2006), and where the paradigmatic modification of the digital work is captured: in the interface the text becomes spatial and navigable and acquires a new temporality that is indifferent (or not) to the reader's rhythms, the expressive substances interweave and, of particular relevance, the text and the reader are offered the opportunity to meaningfully converse, thereby configuring the second of the key properties of the new literary system, namely the possibility of the digital user to *act upon* and interact with the electronic work.

The studies dealing with interactivity in electronic literary theory are both plentiful and considerably heterogeneous in their approaches, although the majority of them skirt around one of the most extended concepts in the complex disciplinary tree covered by studies dealing with digital art, i.e. *ergodicity* (Aarseth 1997). When speaking about ergodic texts the Norwegian researcher sought to define the texts that required "a non-trivial effort" on the part of the user, "to traverse it" (1), which supposed an essential modification within the new "cybertextual" communicative space (trivial effort being, for example, the movement of the eyes over the words or the simple manual turning of the pages).

Beginning with the basic complication that the delimitation of an idea such as interactivity supposes, Aarseth's concept may be too distant from pure literary communication and we are further convinced of this when Murray (1997) refers to action, to the "ability to carry out meaningful action and see the results of our decisions and choices" (126) within electronic environments. Aarseth himself previously made key reference to this interactive loop that is generated between the cybertext and the reader, but we find Hayles' words to be clearer about the true literary significance not just of the reader's action, but of the necessary participative cycle that also involves the machine:

> Electronic literature extends the traditional functions of print literature in creating recursive feedback loops between explicit articulation, conscious thought, and embodied sensorimotor knowledge. [...] While print literature also operates in this way, electronic literature performs the additional function of entwining human ways of knowing with machine cognitions. (2008: 135)

It is precisely this intermediation loop between "[a]uthor and programme, player and computer" (135) that characterises the interactive complexity of the new digital communicative system, and not the mere performance of unilateral actions by the reader.

User participation also affects the third of the constructive properties that mark the definition of digital literature as an artistic system in its own right: *the rupture of discursive linearity*. We have already referred to this modification of the electronic corpus on several occasions – the "interrupted structure" of Ryan (2001), the "discontinuity" of Holtzman

(1997), the loss of linearity of Turrión (2014b), etc. – and the idea that emerges from this consideration is as simple as it is complex: in electronic literature each reading process is different to the previous one as a result of: 1) the possible navigation structures proposed by the author (Ramada, and Turrión 2014); 2) the specific behaviour of the cybertext as a result of its sequential architecture; and 3) the user's own activity within the work.

Consideration of the effect of these three aspects on the multilinearity of electronic text allows us a holistic and comprehensive vision of this modification which is so relevant to the works that target emergent readers. An understanding of how literary communication is affected by the possibility that a reader may be offered hyperlinks to encyclopaedias integrated into the discourse, or that the fictional scenario may change depending on the time of reading, as occurs in *Caperucita App* (Little Red Riding Hood App), or that we are offered the possibility of navigating freely through the literary spaces that make up the world of fiction, as occurs in *The Sailor's Dream*, becomes essential in terms of both research in educational literature and the contemplation of the children's digital literature paradigm.

Neither can we neglect the importance in the construction of a digital work of the possibility of *combining different expressive substances* in the discourse – the fourth and final defining property of electronic literature. However, we wish to relate the multimodal possibilities of the medium with the key importance we are placing on *software* in the configuration of the electronic work and the "permanent extendability" (Manovich 2013) that this allows as a medium capable of coding, via algorithms and data structures, the "wide range of already existing media and those not yet invented" (157). These words harbour both Alan Kay's concept of "metamedium" and the idea that the multimodal nature of digital works is a construct that is constantly evolving and that, while today it continues to revolve around the combinatory possibilities of written language, static and moving images and audio content, we are ever watchful for technological innovation in the pursuit of what has often been labelled total fiction.

In short, and to conclude this defining exercise, we can state that when we speak of electronic literature we are referring to a programmed computer product that is capable of coding multiple semiotic substances in order to construct its discourse and, in addition, allows for the inclusion of the reader as an active participant in the discursive structure, the reading of which tends towards rupture of the traditional linearity of printed text. Four constructive core concepts that tend to present themselves gradually and in an inter-related manner to configure a product that, despite its strangely heterogeneous nature, we believe constitutes a new form of literary creation whose prospects would appear to be, to say the least, exciting.

Works Cited

Primary Works Cited

Flesser, Simon, and Magnus Gardebäck. *The Sailor's Dream*. Malmö: Simogo, 2014. iPad edition.

Jeffers, Oliver. *The Heart and the Bottle*. New York: Penguin Group, 2011. iPad edition.

Mistral, Gabriela, *Caperucita App*. Ill. Paloma Valdivia. Santiago de Chile: Amanuta, 2013. iPad edition.

Gilbert, Bruno. *My little story factory*. Paris: e-Toiles éditions & Autrement Jeunesse 2013. iPad edition.

Secondary Works Cited

Aarseth, Espen J. *Cybertext: Perspectives on Ergodic Literature*. Baltimore: Johns Hopkins UP, 1997. Print.

Al-Yaqout, Ghada, and Maria Nikolajeva. "Re-conceptualising Picturebook Theory in the Digital Age." *Nordic Journal of ChildLit Aesthetics*, 6 (2015). Web. 22 Feb. 2015.

Bell, Alice. "A [S]creed for Digital Fiction." *Electronic Book Review* (2010). Web. 16 Mar. 2015.

Bolter, Jay David, and Richard Grusin. *Remediation: Understanding New Media*. Cambridge, MA: MIT P, 2000. Print.

Bootz, Philippe. "Les Basiques: La littérature numérique." *OLATS, l'Observatoire Leonardo des Arts et des Techno-Sciences*. Leonardo/ISAST, 2007. Web. 16 Mar. 2015.

Borràs, Laura. "Teorías literarias y retos digitales." *Textualidades electrónicas: nuevos escenarios para la literatura*. Ed. Laura Borràs. Barcelona: UOC, 2005. 23-80. Print.

—. "Había una vez una app… Literatura infantil y juvenil (en) digital." *Revista de Literatura*, 269 (2012): 21-26. Print.

Eagleton, Terry. *Literary Theory: An Introduction*. Oxford: Blackwell Publishing, 2008. Print.

Enberg, Maria. "Digital Fiction." *The Johns Hopkins Guide to Digital Media*. Eds. Marie-Laure Ryan, Lori Emerson, and Benjamin J. Robertson. Baltimore: Johns Hopkins UP, 2014. 138-142. Print.

Ensslin, Astrid. *Canonizing Hypertext: Explorations and Constructions*. London: Continuum International, 2007. Print.

Hayles, N. Katherine. *Electronic Literature: New Horizons for the Literary*. Notre Dame: U of Notre Dame P, 2008. Print.

Holtzman, Steven. *Digital Mosaics: The Aesthetics of Cyberspace*. New York: Simon & Schuster Trade, 1997. Print.

Koskimaa, Raine. *Digital Literature. From Text to Hypertext and Beyond*. Diss. University of Jyväskylä, 2000. Web. 4 Mar. 2015.

Landow, George P. *Hypertext 3.0: Critical Theory and New Media in an Era of Globalization*. Baltimore: Johns Hopkins UP, 2006. Print.

Manovich, Lev. *Software Takes Command*. New York: Bloomsbury Academic, 2013. Print.

Mora, Vicente Luis. *El lectoespectador: deslizamientos entre literatura e imagen*. Barcelona: Seix Barral, 2012. Print.

Moreno, Isidro. *Musas y nuevas tecnologías: el relato hipermedia*. Barcelona: Paidós, 2002. Print.

Murray, Janet H. *Hamlet on the Holodeck: The Future of Narrative in Cyberspace*. Cambridge, MA: MIT P, 1997. Print.

Prensky, Marc. "Digital Natives, Digital Inmigrants Part 1." *On the Horizon*, 9.5 (2001): 1-6. Web. 15 Feb. 2014.

Ramada, Lucas, and Celia Turrión. "Los caminos hacia la actuación del lector implícito en la literatura infantil y juvenil digital. Microestructuras y macroestructuras narrativas." *International Symposium: Electronic Literature: Texts, Readers and Teaching Practices*. 3-4 Oct. 2014, Barcelona. Barcelona: Universitat Autònoma de Barcelona, 2014. 26-36. Web. 16 Mar. 2015.

Rettberg, Scott. "Electronic Literature." *The Johns Hopkins Guide to Digital Media*. Eds. Marie-Laure Ryan, Lori Emerson, and Benjamin J. Robertson. Baltimore: Johns Hopkins UP, 2014. 169-173. Print.

Ryan, Marie-Laure. *Narrative as Virtual Reality: Immersion and Interactivity in Literature and Electronic Media*. Baltimore: Johns Hopkins UP, 2001. Print.

—. *Avatars of Story*. Minneapolis: U of Minnesota P, 2006. Print.

Schwebs, Ture. "Affordances of an App: A Reading of The Fantastic Flying Books of Morris Lessmore." *Nordic Journal of ChildLit Aesthetics*, 5 (2014). Web. 18 Mar. 2015.

Silva-Díaz, María Cecilia. "Libros que enseñan a leer: álbumes metaficcionales y competencia literaria." Diss. Universitat Autònoma de Barcelona, 2005. Web. 14 Feb. 2015.

Stichnothe, Haddassah. "Engineering Stories? A Narratological Approach to Children's Book Apps." *Nordic Journal of ChildLit Aesthetics*, 5 (2014). Web. 24 Jan. 2015.

Turrión, Celia. "LIJ digital: nuevas formas narrativas para niños". *Cuadernos de Literatura Infantil y Juvenil*, 248 (2012): 40-46. Print.

—. "Álbumes ilustrados en pantalla." *Cuadernos de Literatura Infantil y Juvenil*, 256 (2013): 6-12. Print.

—. "Multimedia Book Apps in a Contemporary Culture: Commerce and Innovation, Continuity and Rupture." *Nordic Journal of ChildLit Aesthetics*, 5 (2014a). Web. 16 Mar. 2015.

—. "Narrativa infantil y juvenil digital. ¿Qué ofrecen las nuevas formas al lector literario?" Diss. Universitat Autònoma de Barcelona, 2014b. Web. 29 May 2015.

Unsworth, Len. *E-literature for Children: Enhancing Digital Literacy Learning*. New York: Routledge, 2006. Print.

"What is E-Lit?" *Electronic Literature Organization.* Electronic Literature Organization, n.d. Web. 16 Mar. 2015.

Yokota, Junko, and William H. Teale. "Picture Books and the Digital World: Educators Making Informed Choices." *The Reading Teacher*, 67.8 (2014): 577-585. Web. 18 Mar. 2015.

Part II

Digital Literature for Children and Young Adults

The Impact of New Digital Media on Children's and Young Adult Literature

Bettina KÜMMERLING-MEIBAUER

Universität Tübingen

"Very good! Click on the white button…". This sentence appears in Hervé Tullet's picturebook *Un livre* (A Book, 2010), translated into English as *Press Here* (2011). The storyline consists of requests and comments, complemented by simple illustrations of small circles in red, yellow and blue in different arrangements. Comparable to computer games and interactive picturebooks, the reader is asked to do something before turning the pages, for instance, rubbing the circles, tapping on a specific circle five times, or tilting the book. The subsequent doublespread shows the result of the reader's action, sometimes with surprising effects. Tullet's unusual picturebook obviously refers to the increasing impact of digital media on children's literature, but might also be interpreted as a book that makes fun of these new trends.

Although digital media for children have flooded the international market for several years, there is scant research on the history, the reception and the aesthetic and cognitive challenges of these media formats that definitely scrutinises the further development of children's and young adult literature. This chapter focuses on the question of how digital media influence the content and narrative structure of children's literature and even generate innovative genres and interactive storytelling formats. Moreover, particular emphasis is put on the increasing significance of fan fiction that leads to a new perception of the relationship between author and readers. Finally, it will be shown that these recent developments also impact on the comprehension of children's literature and its intricate relationship between (adult) author and (child) reader.

While Tullet's picturebook is characterised by a neutral attitude towards digital media, the majority of children's and young adult books that address the impact of the computer and social media on people's everyday life describe the negative causes of a society dominated by digital media, especially with regard to the increasing power of Internet companies, such as Google, Twitter and Facebook. The invisible threat of the Internet has been recently addressed in Dave Egger's widely discussed novel *The Circle* (2013), which depicts a society in which an encompassing transparency allows complete social control of its members. Although not specifically written for young people, *The Circle* achieved the status of a crossover novel and has been nominated for the German Prize for Youth Literature in 2015. How social media and the power of the Internet can be misused in order to suppress and manipulate other people has also been impressively demonstrated in young adult novels, such as Suzanne Collins' The Hunger Games Trilogy (2008-2010) and Cory Doctorow's *Little Brother* (2008), which achieved wide acclaim due to their unadorned portrayal of a society governed by injustice, hatred and fear.

However, it cannot be denied that the computer, the smartphone and social media progressively belong to young children's daily routine. It is no wonder, then, that digital media not only impact on the child's cognitive development, but also crop up as topics in picturebooks and children's books. Nowadays picturebooks show children's rooms, classrooms and offices that are equipped with computers and laptops. In detective stories for children, the Internet is already a common toolkit for investigating suspicious people, while the cellphone is a permanent companion of the main protagonists in contemporary children's novels that aspire to render an authentic portrayal of children's modern everyday life. Interestingly, this technical equipment usually does not play a significant role concerning the plot and character development. An exception to this rule is Peter Knorr's picturebook *Der mächtige Max* (Mighty Max, 1991), with illustrations by the caricaturist Hans Traxler, in which the main protagonist, a boy named Max, is a computer nerd and hacks a TV channel in order to manipulate the TV programming. However, it is not a big step from this Swiss picturebook to the dystopian young adult novels mentioned earlier.

Generating new genres and narrative concepts

Whereas e-book facsimiles of renowned children's books usually follow the print version and do not add further playful or informational elements, enhanced e-books have embedded features like audio and video (Armstrong 2008). Children's apps, in turn, can be anything that can be programmed, from a movie to a game and beyond, such as *Alice on the iPad*, released in 2010. William Joyce's *The Fantastic Flying Books of Mr. Morris Lessmore* was first launched as a short animated film in 2011 and received the Oscar Award in 2012. Due to this great success, an official iPad app and a printed version were released in 2012 (Schwebs

2014). Another case in point is the BBC television channel CBeebies that has an online webpage with a large amount of classic and new children's stories, and even a cartoon version of Shakespeare's *A Midsummer's Night Dream*. In the CBeebies adaptations still and moving images are dominant with the written text appearing at the bottom of the screen. The text changes colour as the narrating voices read the sentences. The webpage even allows texts to be inserted in any order, so the users are free to follow the order of the storyline or to subvert it, thus creating funny and unexpected versions. The popularity of this channel influenced the British book market, where an increase in print sales of the children's books presented on CBeebies could be observed.

Even advanced reality technology is entering the field of children's books. When readers hold certain pages of *What Lola Wants... Lola Gets!* (2011), written by David Salariya and illustrated by Carolyn Scrace, to a web cam they see the characters come to life in full 3D animation, accompanied by music (Kümmerling-Meibauer 2015). Julia Neuhaus' *Was ist denn hier passiert?* (What Has Happened Here?, 2015) even goes a step further as the reader meets a funny or strange situation on every doublespread which is expressed in images and texts. By means of an integrated QR-code that can be scanned with a smartphone or a tablet the reader can watch a short animation film that explains the causes for the depicted unusual situations.

Under the influence of postmodernist trends and the rise of video games the still prominent game books saw the light of day in the mid-1970s with Edward Packard's *Sugarcane Island* (1976) and Robert Montgomery's *Journey under the Sea* (1977). Both authors are the initiators of the bestselling Choose Your Own Adventure Series (CYOA) which has been translated into twenty-five languages and reached its peak of popularity in the 1980s. Game books are works of fiction whose narrative is divided into various paths that are marked by numbered pages or paragraphs. The readers take an active part in the development of the storyline: at each relevant narrative turn they are asked to make choices between two alternatives strands, but otherwise this game book type resembles a regular novel. In most game books there is usually only one successful ending, while the other storylines lead to failures. Recently published game books benefit from the further advancement of computer games and the intersection with the Internet, such as Ryan North's *To Be or Not to Be* (2013), which is a choose-your-own path version of *Hamlet*. The reader can choose between diverse characters and is able to stick closely to the plot of the Shakespearean tragedy or explore alternative versions. Each ending in the book is accompanied by a full-page illustration created by different renowned artists, so that each rereading generates new surprising insights which alter the narrative in a significant way.

While game books prevailed on the international book market since the 1970s and have been replaced by sophisticated followers, cellphone novels are quite a new phenomenon whose development goes hand in hand with new medial developments. This term describes a form of entertaining literature for girls and female teens that firstly emerged in Japan at the turn of the millennium, starting with *Deep Love: Ayu no Monogatari* (Deep Love: Ayu's story, 2002) by the author Yoshi. The story centres on seventeen-year-old Ayu who runs away from home where she has been mistreated and abused. She earns her living as a prostitute and falls in love with a young man who is fatally ill. Ayu finally dies from a HIV-related infection. This novel and its followers deal with detailed descriptions of violence, sex, drug abuse, illness and death, but the focus is on romantic and tragic love. Initially belonging to the underground culture, Yoshi's Deep Love Series became surprisingly popular among girls and young women. A printed version came out the same year with over two million seven hundred thousand copies sold. This success encouraged the production of a movie (2004), a TV series (2005-2006) and a manga (2005), so that Yoshi's work entered the mainstream (Tetsuo 2007).

While in the beginning the notion of cellphone novels was solely linked to Yoshi's works, a second boom started in 2005 when mobile portals offered free downloads, for instance, Maho no i-rando (Magic Island). This webpage offers readers the opportunity to write blogs and diaries and to create their own cellphone novels which are uploaded on the webpage (to date more than one million cellphone novels have been registered on Maho no i-rando). Users are invited to comment on these works, thus creating a fan community that keeps the webpage alive.

Since cellphone novels are designed to be read on mobile phone screens, the narratives have short and simple sentences with a dominance of colloquial language, dialogues and surprising twists. Influenced by manga and anime, the texts show a preference for onomatopoeia and interjections, whereas the typography with ASCII Art and emoticons is inspired by the communication forms prevalent in social media. Occasionally, links point to other digital texts. Nevertheless, cellphone novels are conceptualised in the same way as printed books with chapters and page numbers. Readers are able to communicate with the author on an external site which is linked to the cellphone novel. While these cellphone novels are generally short, the popular *Koizora* (Sky of Love, 2006) by Mira, later complemented by a manga, showed that readers are even willing to read a text with more than two thousand pages on the mobile phone screen.

Although the cellphone novel originated in Japan, its popularity has spread to other countries, such as China, Germany, South Africa and the

United States. In South Africa for instance, the Shuttleworth Foundation launched a project in Cape Town in 2009, inviting young people to write cellphone novels in cooperation with professional writers. Starting from the premise that young adults very often do not have access to books, but almost everyone possesses a cellphone, this successful endeavour leads to an abundance of cellphone novels which are accessible online (Shuttleworth Foundation 2009). Public portals like Textnovel (USA, 2008) and Handyroman (Germany, 2014) provide readers with cellphone novels written by professional and semi-professional authors, as the Lucy Luder Series (2007ff.), *Handy Girl* (2010) and *lonelyboy 18* (2009), written by Swiss author Oliver Bendel, which delight teenage readers with the hybrid mixture of genres, linguistic styles and intertextual references to popular culture.

The success of the cellphone novel provoked the emergence of related digital texts, like cellphone haikus and SMS fairy tales. The Italian author-illustrator Fabian Negrin transferred the concept of SMS fairy tales to his children's book *Favole al telefonino* (Fairy Tales on the Cellphone, 2010) that consists of abbreviated versions of thirteen Grimms' fairy tales written as SMS with not more than one hundred and sixty characters.

Alan Gibbons' *The Shadow of the Minotaur* (2000), the first volume in the Legendeer Trilogy, and Victor Pelevin's *A Helmet of Horror* (2007), a volume of the Canongate Myth Series, illustrate the intrusion of the computer's hypertext structure into children's books. Conceived as retellings of the Minotaur myth in new shapes, both authors successfully combine references to Antiquity with a critical attitude towards the impact of the computer and games on young people's everyday life. The main protagonist in Gibbons' novel, Phoenix, has moved with his family into a small town against his will. His father, a renowned computer specialist, has been commissioned to develop a new kind of immersive computer game called Legendeer, in which players should assume the role of classical heroes who have to defeat gruesome monsters. When Phoenix is play-testing the game, he gets increasingly sucked into the mythical world the more the game develops, until he is entrapped in a computer-generated labyrinth that resembles the labyrinth in the Minotaur myth. Phoenix gradually becomes aware that the game is not actually a computer game, but a parallel word that is controlled by a malicious Gamesmaster. The only possibility to escape the parallel world is to win all levels of the game by outwitting the beasts and the Gamesmaster at the same time.

By contrast, Pelevin's novel takes place in the cyberspace where eight protagonists who do not know each other are separately locked in rooms with only a screen and a keypad in it. One of them, using the pseudonym "Ariadne", enters into a dialogue by inviting the others to explore the cyberspace. Some of them manage to get outside into a weird surrealist landscape with enigmatic sculptures, buildings and mazes. Here they encounter a fearsome monster that wears the helmet of horror and reveals himself as the Minotaur. His mask resembles a gigantic virtual-reality head-set, but could also be interpreted as a metaphor for the mental construction of the world. The story finally eases into an e-mail exchange about the paradoxes of human perception and visual deception. With its web-symposium format, consisting of short texts appended to strange pseudonyms, the narrative structure resembles a chatroom conversation, thus picking up a convenient communication form of the 21st century.

While Gibbons' novel reveals a more convenient storyline, Pelevin strives for an experimental writing style that takes advantage of the classical myth. The author creates a narrative structure that refers to the labyrinthine topic by meditating on perception, truthfulness and deception. By reinventing the Minotaur myth and transferring it to a modern, media-dominated environment, the books by Gibbons and Pelevin evidently demonstrate that there is an abundance of information that can be achieved by search engines, but that the relevant knowledge is often unattainable. This paradoxical situation mainly contributes to the protagonists' confusion and uncertainty which ensure suspense, but can also be regarded as a universal emblem of modern society on a metatextual level.

Transmedia storytelling

In any case, children today may read a printed and an app version of the same title in different situations and locations, thus using different media formats at a time. Indeed, publishers increasingly launch a media consortium of print version plus children's app that complement each other, following the model of Disney's Kingdom Keepers Series (2005-2014), written by Ridley Pearson, and Scholastic's The 39 Clues Series (2008-2014) written by a collaboration of authors. The seven volumes in the Kingdom Keepers Series follow the adventures of five teens who are holographic hosts in the Disney Theme Park. At night, they fight villains that attempt to conquer the theme park, the Disney Empire and even the world. The series franchise includes an online game and an interactive educational tour offered for school classes in the Youth Education Series, provided by Disney. The 39 Clues Series, however, centres on the adventures of two siblings who are hunting the thirty-nine clues which are the ingredients to a serum that empowers its owner as the most powerful person in the world. As part of tie-in merchandise, each volume includes six cards that lead to an online clue placed on a webpage which readers can open by entering the code on their cards. These cards form an essential part of the story, since readers are only able to solve the puzzle by unlocking the clues given on the webpage. Moreover, the publisher developed an online game called Doublecross in which players must use their cards in order to beat their competitors.

Consequently, such developments certainly change the modes of storytelling in children's literature in the long run, introducing children to transmedia narration which plays an increasing role in contemporary media. Transmedia storytelling is a specific narrative technique of telling a single story across multiple media formats and platforms, including printed books, movies, television, games, webpages and even events, such as conventions and live action role playing (LARP). The aim of this cross-media phenomenon is not only to reach a wider audience, but also to change and expand the narrative itself. However, a story might begin with a character chatting on Facebook or Twitter, then moving to an online game and to a video, and ending up in a graphic novel. Readers might even engage with a story by using user generated content (UGC).

Although transmedia storytelling was initially developed for adult audiences, there are an array of transmedia products that address children and young people, ranging from educational series for pre-school children to sophisticated media products for young adults. In some cases, the transmedia launch starts with a printed book which is complemented by films, apps and online versions, whereas in other cases the sequence is the other way round, beginning with an app or an online version which is followed by a print version. Quite surprisingly, many transmedia products combine a fictive story with non-fiction elements, thus creating stories that serve educational purposes, as in Billy Aronson's *Peg + Cat* (2013) that fosters young children's problem solving capacities by introducing them to mathematics, the *Robot Heart Stories* (2011) which support children's emerging knowledge of geography and maps, or Simon Mayo's *Itch. The Explosive Adventures of an Element Hunter* (2012) that gives an intriguing insight into quantum physics. Kate Pullinger's *Inanimate Alice* (2005ff.) and Sean Stewart's and Jordan Weisman's *Cathy's Book: If Found Call (650) 266-82 33* (2006), however, draw on female teenagers' interest in chatting, writing notes and emphatic communication. While *Cathy's Book* was first printed as a packet with letters, pictures, birth certificates, notes and phone numbers, *Inanimate Alice* started as a digital novel that has been complemented by printed material and films. Both works demand the interactive participation of their readers who can exchange comments among themselves on an Internet platform, but are also given clues that might solve the riddles posed in the texts and visuals. For instance, readers can call the numbers given in *Cathy's Book* in order to leave messages for the book's main characters.

James Frey's and Nils Johnson-Shelton's science fiction novel *The Calling* (2014), the first book in the Endgame Trilogy, causes a sensation, since it is announced that the first reader who is able to solve the riddle in the story wins gold coins worth five hundred thousand dollars. The plot focuses on twelve families who have been chosen by extraterrestrials to fight against each other in the endgame. The only survivor needs to find three keys which decide the fate of humankind. The story of *The Calling* contains a puzzle and is linked to an augmented reality game which can be accessed via the webpage. The narrative structure displays facets of transmediation: six days a week a live actress is accessible online via the webpage Ancient Societies (2015) and other social media. It is her job to propel the storyline by interacting with the readers and players who become active parts of the narrative and contribute to the lore of the Endgame universe.

Fan fiction and other digitised media formats

The emergence of the World Wide Web and of Social Networking Services have facilitated an unpredicted growth in fan communities, where technology enables fans to communicate in forums, to share stories and comments and to influence the creation and evolution of stories they are interested in (Coppa 2006). These sites offer the new kinds of user involvement for online narration foreseen by Ryan (2004). Moreover, these websites allow the development of multiple narrative threads where the participants can interact with a myriad of options in a random order.

Although the potential of online technologies and new social media to support interactions between young people has garnered particular attention in fan studies research, few studies have focused on how children use specific online technologies to create their own stories and artworks, coined as *fan fiction*. *Fan fiction* can be defined as fiction of any length, genre, style and narrative technique which is produced by fans of a wide range of cultural media, such as books, movies, games, TV shows and comics (Hills 2002). Interestingly, the far-reaching significance of this recent trend has not yet been fully recognised by children's literature research, notwithstanding its considerable impact on traditional views on children's literature. So far scholars have more or less concentrated on the adult perspective, given the fact that children's literature and other children's media are usually created, published and bought by adults. Although some scholars parenthetically mention that children also write stories, draw comics and release films, they nevertheless assert that this corpus is negligible. However, in this regard they totally disregard the challenges of the new social media for future trends in children's literature.

A particularly interesting example is Harry Potter fan fiction, as it is produced on several webpages, the largest being Harry Potter FanFiction, followed by MuggelNet and The Sugar Quill. Comics and manga versions of the *Harry Potter* stories, however, are launched on Deviant Art (in English) and Pixiv (mostly in Japanese), where young adults showcase single illustrations inspired by Japanese manga and extensive comic/manga sequences (Noppe 2013). The success of these sites is tightly connected with the overwhelming popularity of Joanne K. Rowling's Harry Potter Series (1997-2007) and its publication history (Orbaugh 2010). The time gaps between the publication of the seven volumes and the excited discussions about the possible outcome of the storyline on different fan sites has led to all kinds of rumours whether – and to what extent – the development of the series may have been influenced by ideas suggested on these webpages. The grassroots enthusiasm stimulated by the Harry Potter hype has not diminished to date, which is proven by the sheer number of fan fiction stories. More than eighty thousand stories are uploaded on Harry Potter FanFiction, approximately six hundred and fifty thousand fan fiction stories are stored on different websites. The stories touch on all genres, often presenting a mixture of genres and styles. Besides sequels, prequels, spin-offs and even parodies, a considerable number of fan fiction stories focus on minor characters which are provided with an individual biography and are involved in adventures that are often loosely connected with the Harry Potter universe. Gaps in the novels and open questions are hooks for developing new sidekicks that lead to considerable changes of the main storyline. Relying on the concept of the butterfly effect, fan fiction writers reflect on the seminal question of what might happen when a single event has been altered or characters behave differently. In this respect, the pairings of characters, for instance Ron Weasley and Hermione Granger and Harry Potter and Ginny Weasley, has been rearranged in order to create some new and even surprising plots. Rowling's confession in an interview that she always thought of Dumbledore as being gay enticed fan fiction writers to develop new stories which focus on the depiction of gay and lesbian couples. This queer reading of Rowling's original novels is typical for *"slash" fiction*, a new genre developed by fan fiction writers.

In addition, the transmedia narratives not only draw on Rowling's novels, but also refer to the film adaptations, interviews with Rowling, other fan fiction and a range of children's books and young adult novels that are intertextually interwoven with the Harry Potter Series. Examples of this crossover phenomenon can be found on FanFiction, a site where Harry Potter is crossed with *Buffy the Vampire Slayer*, *Pokémon*, *The Lord of the Rings*, *Hamlet* and other works belonging to popular culture as well as highbrow culture. Although fans usually revere the authors of the source texts, fan fiction questions the idea of the text as something that belongs to an individual author. Moreover, fan fiction permanently scrutinises the notion of the text as something that is complete and stable, as readers never know how long a particular version of a fan fiction story will remain on a site. The hypertextual structure invites readers to switch between different texts and hyperlinks, thus deferring the linear reading process connected with book reading. Whenever a site is accessed, the stories are rearranged, since new stories are posted or older versions updated. Therefore, users find themselves constrained to use keyword searches or rely on summaries and story titles. Moreover, interactive digital texts offer the potential to change the ways in which narratives are structured (Chandler-Olcott, and Mahar 2003). They also blur the boundaries between the author and the reader, since the latter is able to select between several narrative options, thus facilitating multiple authorship. The concept of updating evidently refers to the idea of the work in progress as a reaction to the fact that most of the fan fiction writers are amateurs who invite other readers to give advice and make suggestions that contribute to the betterment of the narratives (Ensslin 2007).

The interest of fans to seek out new material to enhance and continuously extend a story goes against the need for closure which is central for many theories of narrative (Jenkins 2007). To some extent, the perpetual engagement of fan fiction authors to update their own stories by considering the comments and suggestions of their readers is testament to the enjoyment of rewriting already existing stories. The websites additionally work against closure by calling the user's attention to other sites, a process which stresses the dynamic character of fan sites (Douglas 2001). This level of interactivity often contributes to the creation of spiralling rather than sequential and linear storylines. The author can still maintain control of the story variables, with a restricted number of possible story endings, but due to the story's non-linearity and complexity, each reading can be unique (Bolter, and Grusin 2000).

If one thoroughly analyses the diverse fan sites devoted to the *Harry Potter* media launch, it is obvious that the users employ these platforms to experiment with unusual artistic and narrative designs (Reynolds 2007). The continuation, transformation and conversion of already existing verbal and visual texts lead to surprising perspectives that touch upon all textual elements, such as plot, characters, point of view and setting. These artistic and literary devices entail novel formats that break down traditional narrative strategies and genre expectations, eliciting transmedia storytelling and the generation of hybrid forms.

What is more, the observation that fan sites are platforms where children and teenagers can upload their own works brings into question the assertion that children's literature is generally written and produced by adults. Now the previously unheard voices of children and young people are accessible online, devoid of any economic and pedagogical restrictions. Although fan fiction is generally not published in print form, its offspring is usually a popular book or book series. That the comments and suggestions made by readers on online platforms hark back to the further development of an ongoing series or media launch is evident, not only in the case of the *Harry Potter* novels. But the impact of children and young adults on the reception and dissemination of children's and young adult literature is not restricted to their ability to critically read and comment on already finished products, since they increasingly seize with both hands the opportunity to create their own stories and visuals. Bearing in mind the powerful impact of canonisation processes that influence the constitution of canonical children's and young adult books and other media, fan fiction notably challenges traditional views on the importance of the canon (Thomas 2007). Since the canon is a permanent subject of historical, cultural and cognitive changes, the significance of digitally produced literature for the development of a new digital canon comes to the fore. One premise of a digital canon is the consideration of fan fiction, whether created by professional authors or amateurs, adults or children. In the long run, this new trend will probably achieve that the ambivalent meaning of children's literature finally comes true: children's literature is literature written for children as well as literature written by children.

Conclusion

Although the possibilities of digitised and transmedia children's literary works are often praised enthusiastically, we do not know much of how children's literacy is shaped by the quickly evolving changes brought about by digitisation. Since contemporary children's texts are accessed via a range of media and are likely to embed images, sound and movement, this has implications for the reading process because children need to navigate quite complex texts and images on the page and on the screen (Mackey 2011). Consequently, these newly launched products challenge publishers and readers in different ways. First, they affect the reading process, which turns from an attentive reading session to a joint, interactive activity. Second, digital and transmedia children's literary works, with their complex format of image, text, sound, film and hypertextual markers, address several senses simultaneously: seeing, listening, hearing and touching (Cahill, and McGill-Franzen 2013; Turrión 2014). Third, children's apps combine diverse media formats, such as film, computer game and audio drama, thus demanding the reader's acquisition of digital literacy or digital competence. This requires the skill to analyse messages in different forms, including complex narrative strategies (Marsh 2010; Levy, Yamoda-Rice, and Marsh 2012). Also belonging to this concept is the capacity to navigate between different levels that add a hypertextual structure to the story. Finally, digital and transmedia children's literary works offer the possibility to change the narrative flow by selecting various sidelines and supplements which extend and expand the story in a considerable way. This combination of reading, playing and learning stimulates children to simultaneously use different reading and comprehension strategies (Dresang, and Kotrla 2009; Simanowski 2010).

It is evident that these new trends challenge the conceptualisation of children's literature posed by digital narratives and transmedia storytelling. In order to investigate these changes, a digital narratology approach must be developed to engage with the processes of production and consumption that are relevant to the understanding of these new narratives (Stichnothe 2014). Therefore, these tendencies demand the emergence of a new theoretical framework in the realm of children's literature research that analyses the visible changes evoked by children's and young adults' growing sovereignty in creating their own artworks distributed in social media.

Works Cited

Primary Works Cited

Alice for the iPad. London: Atomic Antelope, 2010. iPad edition.

Aronson, Billy. *Peg + Cat.* Ill. Jennifer Oxley. PBsKids, 2013. iPad edition.

Bendel, Oliver. *Handy Girl.* Zurich: Swissbook, 2009-2010. Web. 17 Apr. 2015.

—. *lonelyboy 18.* Zurich: Swissbook, 2009. Web. 17 Apr. 2015.

—. *Lucy Luder.* Zurich: Swissbook, 2007-2011. Web. 17 Apr. 2015.

Collins, Suzanne. The Hunger Games Trilogy. New York: Scholastic. 2008-2010. Print.

Frey, James and Nils Johnson-Shelton. *Endgame: The Calling.* New York: HarperCollins, 2014. Print.

Gibbons, Alan. *Shadow of the Minotaur.* New York: Dolphin, 2000. Print.

Knorr, Peter. *Der mächtige Max.* Ill. Hans Traxler. Zürich: Diogenes, 1991. Print.

Joyce, William. *The Fantastic Flying Books of Mr. Morris Lessmore.* New York: Atheneum Books, 2011. Print.

Mayo, Simon. *Itch: The Explosive Adventures of an Element Hunter.* London: Corgi, 2012. Print.

Mika. *Koizora.* Tokyo: Futabasha, 2007-2009 (Manga version). Print.

Montgomery, Robert. *Journey Under the Sea*. New York: Bantam, 1977. Print.

Negrin, Fabio. *Favole al telefonino*. Rome: Orecchio Acerbo, 2010. Print.

Neuhaus, Julia. *Was ist denn hier passiert?* Animation by Till Penzek. Munich: Tulipan, 2015. Print.

North, Ryan. *To Be or Not to Be*. Toronto: Breadpig, 2013. Web. 15 Apr. 2015.

Packard, Edward. *Sugarcane Island*. New York: Bantam, 1976. Print.

Pearson, Ridley. *Kingdom Keepers*. Ill. Tristan Elwell. 7 Vols. New York: Disney-Hyperion, 2005-2014. Print.

Pelevin, Victor. *The Helmet of Horror*. Translated by Andrew Bromfield. New York: Canongate, 2006. Print.

Pullinger, Kate. *Inanimate Alice*. London: The Bradfield Company, 2005ff. Web. 15 Apr. 2015.

Robot Heart Stories. Reboot Stories, 2011. Web. 17 Apr. 2015.

Rowling, Joanne K. Harry Potter Series. 7 Vols. London: Bloomsbury, 1997-2007. Print.

Salariya, David. *What Lola Wants... Lola Gets* Ill. Carolyn Scrace. Brighton: Scribblers Books, 2011. Print.

Shuttleworth Foundation. *Yoza Project*. Cape Town, 2009. Web. 10 Apr. 2015.

Stewart, Sean and Jordan Weisman. *Cathy's Book: If Found Call (650) 266-88 33*. Philadelphia: Runningpress, 2006. Web. 17 Apr. 2015.

The 39 Clues Series. Written by different authors. 11 Vols. New York: Scholastic, 2008-2014. Print.

Tullet, Hervé. *Un livre*. Paris: Bayard Jeunesse, 2010 (English edition. *Press Here*. San Francisco: Chronicle Books, 2011). Print.

Yoshi. Deep Love Series. Tokyo: Stars Publishing, 2002. Print.

Secondary Works Cited

Armstrong, Chris. "Books in a Virtual World: The Evolution of the E-book and Its Lexicon." *Journal of Librarianship and Information Science*, 40.3 (2008): 193-206. Print.

Beckett, Sandra L. *Crossover Fiction: Global and Local Perspectives*. New York: Routledge, 2009. Print.

Bolter, Jay David, and Richard Grusin. *Remediation: Understanding New Media*. Cambridge, MA: MIT P, 2000. Print.

Cahill, Maria, and Anne McGill-Franzen. "Selecting 'App'ealing and 'App'ropriate Book Apps for Beginning Readers." *The Reading Teacher*, 67.1 (2013): 30-39. Print.

Chandler-Olcott, Kelly, and Donna Mahar. "Adolescents' Anime-Inspired Fanfictions: An Exploration of Multiliteracies." *Journal of Adolescent and Adult Literacy*, 46.7 (2003): 556-566. Print.

Coppa, Francesca. "A Brief History of Media Fandom." *Fan Fiction and Fan Communities in the Age of the Internet.* Eds. Karen Hellekson, and Kristina Busse. Jefferson, NC: McFarland and Company, 2006. 41-59. Print.

Douglas, Jane Yellowlees. *The End of Books – or Books without End? Reading Interactive Narratives.* Ann Arbor: U of Michigan P, 2001. Print.

Dresang, Eliza T., and Bowie Kotrla. "Radical Change Theory and Synergistic Reading for Digital Age Youth." *The Journal of Aesthetic Education*, 43.2 (2009): 92-107. Print.

Ensslin, Astrid. *Canonizing Hypertext: Explorations and Constructions.* London: Continuum International, 2007. Print.

Hills, Matt. *Fan Cultures.* New York: Routledge, 2002. Print.

Jenkins, Henry. *Convergence Culture: Where Old and New Media Collide.* New York: New York UP, 2006. Print.

Kümmerling-Meibauer, Bettina. "From Baby Books to Picturebooks for Adults: European Picturebooks in the New Millennium." *Word & Image: A Journal of Verbal/Visual Enquiry*, 31.3 (2015): 249-264. Print.

Levy, Rachel, Dylan Yamoda-Rice, and Jackie Marsh. "Digital Literacy in Primary Classrooms." *International Handbook of Research on Children's Literacy, Learning, and Culture.* Eds. Kathy Hall, Teresa Cremin, Barbara Comber, and Luis Molle. London: Sage, 2012. 333-343. Print.

Mackey, Margaret. "The Case of the Flat Rectangles: Children's Literature on Page and Screen." *International Research in Children's Literature*, 4.1 (2011): 99-114. Print.

Marsh, Jackie. "Young Children's Play in Online Virtual Worlds." *Journal of Early Childhood Research*, 8.1 (2010): 23-29. Print.

Noppe, Nele. "Social Networking Services as Platforms for Transcultural Fannish Interactions: DeviantART and Pixiv." *Manga's Cultural Crossroads.* Eds. Jaqueline Berndt, and Bettina Kümmerling-Meibauer. New York: Routledge, 2013. 143-159. Print.

Orbaugh, Sharalyn. "Girls Reading Harry Potter, Girls Writing Desire: Amateur Manga and Shōjo Reading Practices." *Girl Reading Girl in Japan.* Eds. Tomoko Aoyama, and Barbara Hartley. New York: Routledge, 2010. 174-186. Print.

Reynolds, Kimberley. *Radical Children's Literature. Future Visions and Aesthetic Transformations in Juvenile Fiction.* Basingstoke: Palgrave Macmillan, 2007. Print.

Ryan, Marie-Laure. *Narrative across Media: The Languages of Storytelling.* Lincoln: U of Nebraska P, 2004. Print.

Schwebs, Ture. "Affordances of an App: A Reading of The Fantastic Flying Books of Morris Lessmore." *Nordic Journal of ChildLit Aesthetics*, 5 (2014). Web. 10 Apr. 2015.

Simanowski, Roberto. "Reading Digital Literature: A Subject between Media and Methods." *Reading Moving Letters: Digital Literature in Research and*

Teaching. A Handbook. Eds. Roberto Simanowski, Jürgen Schäfer, and Peter Gendolla. Bielefeld: transcript, 2010. 15-28. Print.

Stichnothe, Haddassah. "Engineering Stories? A Narratological Approach to Children's Book Apps." *Nordic Journal of ChildLit Aesthetics*, 5 (2014). Web. 17 Apr. 2015.

Tetsuo, Matsuda. "Japanese Literature Today: Publishing Trends for 2006." *Japanese Book News*, 51 (2007): 2-3. Web. 10 Apr. 2015.

Thomas, Bronwen. "Canons and Fanons: Literary Fiction Online." *Dichtung Digital*, 37 (2007). Web. 17 Apr. 2015.

Turrión, Celia. "Multimedia Book Apps in a Contemporary Culture: Commerce and Innovation, Continuity and Rupture." *Nordic Journal of ChildLit Aesthetics*, 5 (2014). Web. 17 Apr. 2015.

The Past, Present and Future of Digital Picturebooks for Children

Junko YOKOTA

National College of Education, National Louis University (Chicago)

The digital world has changed what we read, how we read and how the book world operates in virtually every aspect, from publishing to libraries to bookstores to archiving. The pace is dizzying and many "rules of operation" continue to be created and recreated even while the game is in development. Over the past decade, the players have changed, the process has changed and the products have changed. But in the midst of this fast-paced fervour, what is important to keep in mind while considering the present and the future of what have long been known as print picturebooks? From the earliest days of digital features and formats of literature for children, this question has guided inquiry in the field (Glass, and Yokota 2008). Digital books have been called both the most exciting thing and the scariest thing for children and adult picturebook aficionados (Yokota, and Teale 2014). This chapter considers *the past:* print picture book publications from generations ago that clearly played with features of oral storytelling that we now see as standard in digital publishing; *the present:* what is being published as digital materials for children to read/play/interact with; and *the future:* what promises to be successful for future development of digital materials for children.

In this chapter, I briefly address the issue of the types of content for children that are well suited for publication in digital formats, focusing the discussion specifically on digital stories. Discussion about digital books is sometimes posited as an either/or drawing of swords, casting print against digital. We love and admire print-on-paper picturebooks; therefore, are we *for* or are we *against* digital? But asking that question ignores changes over history. Oral storytelling was not replaced with the advent of the printing press; rather, print books coexisted and continue to coexist alongside oral storytelling. In their infancy, print picturebooks were experimental and it was only over decades that the field developed and defined what is now recognised as picturebook theory (e.g., Nikolajeva, and Scott 2001;

Sipe 1998). Today, picturebook theory informs the creation of high of quality books that are aesthetically appealing, intellectually rewarding and emotionally engaging. In sum, picturebooks today are a "pleasing whole" when created well.

First considerations: matching content to form

What type of content is likely to be most useful in digital formats? A possible progression of works that are appropriate for digital worlds might be: 1) reference, 2) informational, 3) chapter books/novels and finally, 4) narrative picturebooks. Why is this so? In matching content with intended use, the preceding list follows a progression from highest need for currently up-to-date materials to less need, the spectrum from visual as reference to visual as art, and the range of need for accessibility features that benefit from digital formats versus those benefitting from print.

Reference materials

Reference materials need to be updated as frequently as possible to remain accurate in light of new developments and discoveries. In print, such updates have usually occurred years apart, if ever. Digitally, updates can happen almost virtually as often as necessary and often without even being noticed. (Think of the virtually overnight changes in reference materials when Pluto was deemed no longer a plant in our solar system or when country boundaries such as South Sudan change.) Perhaps more importantly, reference materials benefit from enhanced features the digital world allows. For example, a digital dictionary can have audio pronunciation guides, allow for personal list-making, link to multimedia materials, etc. Print reference books tend to be voluminous, heavy in amount of print and are outdated almost at the point they are being printed. For these reasons and more, even the venerable Encyclopaedia Britannica (published in print since the 18th century) announced the end of its print version with the 2010 edition. There are not as many reference picturebooks in existence, but even children's atlases and maps quickly went to digital when opportunities arose. Among the compelling reasons digital works well for reference is the non-linear ways in which we typically access the content of reference books.

Informational/nonfiction books

Like reference materials, informational books benefit from being instantly updatable in digital format, and like reference materials, informational texts are often read in sections and non-sequentially. A digital children's book on urban wildlife can link to live webcams that show nests of falcons in cities or examples of coyotes, deer, or other animals that have been spotted. Links to multimedia film materials can enhance how information is conveyed. In print, we rely on table of contents and index to access the approximate location of a particular piece of information; digitally, the search feature can take you directly to where that information is located. These and other features show that informational books are indeed well suited to the digital world.

Chapter books and novels

Books for children such as novels, short stories, or poetry consist exclusively or almost exclusively of text. With these books, the ability to change font size and colour can be a feature to add reading ease and accommodate those with visual impairments. Moreover, being able to carry nearly an unlimited numbers of books within the size of one e-reader is appealing for controlling the weight of physical books. Although book design features are of importance in any book, the loss of illustration or change in design from print to digital is less of a problem for novels than for picturebooks.

Picturebooks

Well-designed print picturebooks were not intended to be transposed to under-the-glass of standardised tablet sizes. Moving something developed for one medium (print book) into another (digital device) requires reconsideration and may not be recommendable in many (or most?) cases. Instead, the development of story apps may take the place of digitising existing picturebooks.

Thus, digital formats can be genuine enhancements to a range of types of books for children. Especially important for my research, however, has been the role of digital technologies in impacting what can be considered the essence of literature for children: picture storybooks. Computer technologies have led to the inclusion of an increasing range of interactive features in stories created for children. The presence, potential impact and evaluation of digital picturebooks for children are examined in the remainder of this chapter.

The past: foundations of stories with interactive features

During my 2013 fellowship at the Berlin Staatsbibliothek, the Prussian Heritage Foundation supported my research in its archival materials to consider what aspects of digital storytelling had roots in earlier published materials. Under the guidance of Director Carola Pohlmann, I was introduced to a treasure trove of old German interactive books. Books from centuries ago show movement and sound through devices such as push/pull tabs, turning wheels, cut-out templates and strings that pull out and retract. Among the most notable developers of such books was Lothar Meggendorfer. In 1890, he published *Gemischte Gesellschaft: ein lustiges Ziehbilderbuch* (Merry Company: a Moveable Toybook). On one set of pages, "Der Herkules" ("The Hercules"), a strong man, lifts and lowers very big weights. But perhaps the most magical page is one on which a young housecleaner is standing on a stepstool and cleaning the upper left side of a mirror and her arm moves the cleaning cloth around on the mirror surface; meanwhile, in the lower right side of the mirror, the image of the matron she works for is seen from the back yet her face reflected in the mirror at an angle depicting nearly three dimensional depth. Examples of other features include *The History and Adventures of Little Henry, Exemplified in a Series of Figures* (London, 1810) – a paper doll whose clothes you can change, which in this case provides varied body poses showing the entire set of clothes worn and a head that is moved from outfit to outfit, showing that no matter the outfit, they are all representing the same child – and *Die Arche Noah* (Noah's Ark, 1925) by Oskar Laske, created in leporello style, a long accordion fold book that stretches horizontally as pages are unfolded. Such a book appropriately shows the journey undertaken by the animal pairs, the building of the ark, the flooding and the end of the rains, all visually depicted in a way that benefitted from the long shape. There are many such examples that show how innovative creators of print books incorporated devices that showed sound and movement, perhaps forecasting a future in which such features could be a norm (Yokota 2013b).

The beginnings of digital storytelling

The current challenge is developing a successful future for digital storytelling. It does not need to compete with oral storytelling or print picturebooks; instead, it needs to define its unique qualities and develop its own strengths. As such, there will be growing pains as we move forward, creating in this new medium as our early attempts at telling stories through this newer format.

With the development of computer technology came the first generation of digital stories in the 1990s: e-books that were basically scanned PDF versions of print picturebooks. Many contained "skeuomorphs" that visually made connections from the original print books to the digitised version by leaving in references to page boundaries, gutters and page-turning animation (Sargeant 2015). Early analysis of digital material consisted of evaluating those materials, comparing the print and digital versions of the same stories (Yokota 2011). The next generation of digital stories added "extras": audio (i.e., audio narration, music, sound effects), panning in film-like close-ups and wide shots as early attempts to embed movement, game features (i.e., puzzles, drawing, matching) and more. In some cases, such interactive animations and "play-based features" have been found to disrupt narrative flow (Sargeant 2013; Yokota, and Teale 2014). Accordingly, the next stage of evaluative analyses focused on how such features were in line with the original intent of the book and whether they added to or distracted from the story's intent (Yokota 2011, 2013a). One example of a digital book created during this era is *The Heart and the Bottle* by Oliver Jeffers. The story is well narrated by Helena Bonham Carter; however, there was no "read to me" option so the reader had to push the audio button on each page. Another button gave "hints" as to what to do on each page and a dotted line appeared to lasso the area in which the action could be activated by touching the screen. Actions varied from moving a tricycle forward to adding flowers to the scene to trying to cut the bottle open. Sound effects were realistic and conveyed the action well. Other than a few options to animate each screen, the tablet interactive book was essentially the same as the print book.

The present: interactive digital storytelling

The arrival of tablets marked a new era in digital storytelling. Touch-based apps were capable of interaction and extended possibilities for customisation. At first, owing to the ability to add numerous fun features, apps had plenty of what on the surface were enticing new aspects; however, the goal primarily appeared to be only to embed in the story features that would engage children and hold their attention. Learning goals, story comprehension and appropriateness for how children learn were not much in evidence. Thus, features that were engaging and motivating became what drove the interactive aspect of the app.

These days, an app might emerge first, later become a film and then, a print book, as in the case of *The Fantastic Flying Books of Mr. Morris Lessmore*. But should the same story be played out in so many different formats? Is there a format that is better suited to the story than another? Is there a format in which the art is more suited than the other? Perhaps these are the questions we should be analysing in terms of how story plays out in different formats. In which format is a particular story *best* conveyed? In what ways are the formats different in how they show story features?

Criteria for evaluating and selecting digital stories for children

The book publishing industry in general and picturebook materials for children in particular have undergone rapid and profound changes in recent years with developments in the digital realm. As a result, teachers, school librarians and literacy researchers have been largely left to their own devices to figure out basic questions related to e-picturebooks such as what works, what does not, what is good and so what? Yokota and Teale (2014) proposed an evaluation and selection framework for assessing digital picturebooks that uses the following elements:

First and foremost, the digital book must adhere to standards for quality picturebooks for children:

- Is the story well told, according to literary standards?
- Is the language of the text skilfully crafted?
- Are illustrations artistically skilful and do they work well with the text to illuminate, extend and/or co-create the story as a whole?

Then, the following questions probe the quality of the *digital* format:

1. Is the story appropriately presented in digital format?
2. Does the story take appropriate advantage of features the digital world allows, beyond what is possible in print?
3. Do the interactive features maintain the integrity of the main story?
4. Do any supplementary features align with the story?
5. Do the features make sense in terms of how children learn to read and learn in general?

As digital materials had entered an already well-established print picturebook world, the traditional sources for book reviews had to adjust to also review digital materials, including apps. Many descriptive reviews appeared, but in general, reviewers had no specific training in what qualities were most important in terms of how children learn to read and learn through reading. Learning to make highly reasoned analysis of digital materials and then evaluating them for appropriate features is important for reviewers as well as for educators.

What is likely to remain best in print format?

As Yokota (2013a) has pointed out, the physicality of the print book – size, shape and other peritextual features – plays a significant role in giving emphasis to specific aspects of story and therefore affects the story experience for child readers. In cases where such aspects are significant in the reader's response, changing from the original design to the uniformity of the digital computer or tablet screen can affect response, making it different from the original version. Physically well-designed print picturebooks, therefore, are likely to continue to have a more salutary reader impact than the digital design. One example of a book in which the size and dimensions have been modified for digital publication is *A Seed is Sleepy* by Dianna Hutts Aston, illustrated by Sylvia Long. The original print book is luxuriously large – 9" x 11" (23 cm x 28 cm) – but a tablet's dimensions are around 9.4" x 6.6" (17 cm x 24 cm), making it necessary to significantly change the vertical proportion of the original to allow the book to be shown as a series of double-spread pages. Therefore, grey bars frame the digital book, top and bottom and the pages are reduced in size so they end up having very small text. Sometimes, the decision to buy a digital format is for convenience, other times for cost as typically, a digital format is a fraction of the cost of the print. In this particular case, digital format, a series of PDF pages are purchased for $6.14 whereas a new paperback is $7.99 and a new hardback is $11.32 on Amazon. Price is not the reason one might purchase a digital book in this case, as the print version offers a better experience.

Print publishers and app developers see their roles differently. Publishers are typically not obvious in the initial glance at a print book; one must look on the title page or spine to figure out who published a print book. The author and illustrator names are featured prominently as the people who created the book. In digital books, the names of the creators are usually hidden and found under a separate click and only the developer company name is featured on the equivalent of a title page, the home page (except in the case of recognisable authors or illustrators such as Dr Seuss, whose name will promote sales).

Peritextual elements – aspects of book design – are an important part of the print book. However, in digital format, such features that are distinct in individual books (including individual books from the same publisher) are standardised to fit the company's branding. Thus, in print picturebooks, the book design as an aesthetic is an inherent part of that literary experience that contributes to the "whole book experience", whereas the goals of the digital experience are for comfort through familiarity and brand recognition to increase "discoverability" in other digital books and apps by the same developer.

A final type of book that is generally more likely to work better in the print format is ones that have strong emotional demands – for quietness, stillness and reflection. With a book like Iwona Chimielewska's *W kieszonce* (In the Pocket), the power of the page turn is likely to make more of an impact on the reader than a swipe. A beautiful artifact of bookmaking, the hand-stitched fabric pockets illustrate the different suggestions for what the item sticking out of the pocket might be, but with a page turn, it shows what is actually there.

What features make the digital format of a print book successful?

Whether it is a case of reconceptualising a previously published print picturebook as a digital book or situations in which creators work initially with digital format in mind, the key to making the digital format successful is maximising the opportunities the (a) shape and (b) features (sound, movement, etc.) of the digital device afford. A successful digital book brings out story elements in ways that make sense, the end result being a reading experience that feels as if the telling of the story has been enhanced by the digital affordances.

Take Pawel Pawlak's illustrations in *L'enveloppe mystérieuse d'Arthur le facteur / The Enigmatic Envelope* (2014) as an example. The book follows a mail carrier as he delivers the daily mail to various customers on his route, interacting with them along the way. This book's visual design is varied, from "spot art" within text-heavy pages, to single pages that depict the interior of a room, to doublespread pages that show street scenes. The inside dimensions of the pages of the print book are 20.5 cm x 28.5 cm, making the proportions approximately 3:4, which transfers to tablet dimensions relatively easily without significant distortion. Moreover, the tablet allows for movement from end to end of the screen, being particularly appropriate for a sense of movement as the mail carrier rides his bicycle across town. When you touch the screen in the app version, the bicycle bell rings. The varied art sizes allow for transitions to room interiors while the double spread moves the story from scene to scene. Postmarks and postage stamps are used as decorative elements throughout the book, but the use of the postage-stamp shape to select the section of the book to "jump to" in the digital version is particularly nice.

Fiete – Ein Tag auf dem Bauernhof (*Fiete – A Day on the Farm*) is an app that follows a distinct narrative flow. The story begins at one end of an island and the time of day is clearly early morning and all is dark. A click on the alarm clock at the base of the lighthouse reveals the inside of the room where the workers are sleeping. Touching the alarm clock makes it leap off of the table and onto the floor, but one must nudge each sleeping worker until his eyes are open and he is awake. When all three are awakened, a check mark is given and that task is accomplished. Moving across the island, one can make choices of the various tasks: shear the sheep, pull carrots out of the ground and put them into a wheelbarrow, gather eggs, chop wood, bathe pigs, feed pigs, pick apples and so forth. Tasks go from straightforward collecting of objects to matching objects to the appropriate delivery truck. As one progresses from left to right on the island, the time of day changes from morning to high sun to twilight.

This is a clever showing of how the time of day progresses. What makes it a bit problematic is that if some of the tasks are left unfinished or skipped by the end of the day, it is necessary to go backwards on the island and finish them (the sun also goes back up into the sky as you go backwards). A better design would be if the reader were not able to progress farther into the time of day until each task is completed, or provide a map of the island rather than the day's progression and allow readers to choose tasks in the order they want.

What features of print books are likely to transfer to production as a successful digital book?

Some books currently available in print have features that make them potentially successful in the digital world, perhaps even more so than in print. For example, the *Taro Gomi's Doodles: A Really Giant Colouring and Doodling Book* (2006) is a sophisticated interactive drawing/colouring/puzzle book with elements that stir children's imagination and invite them to engage with it. The book would transfer well to digital format because children could use their fingertips, select tools (colour, width, texture etc.), save the artwork to the tablet, email it to someone, or simply delete it. Each time the book is accessed digitally, a different user profile could be created. In this way, a one-time use book could have unlimited use, whereas the print book can only be used once per page.

Another feature that has the potential to transition successfully from print to digital is one in which the open-endedness invites children to consider their own ideas. For example, *It Looked Like Spilt Milk* (1947) examines the shapes of clouds in the sky and wonders what they could represent. Simple white shapes against a solid blue background are accompanied by repeated, patterned text, "Sometimes it looked like… But it wasn't…". Children could then contribute their own pages by simply creating a white shape against the blue background and filling in the words within the patterned text.

The future: what has potential to work well in digital?

Successful original story apps

Apps that capitalise on new possibilities afforded by tablet devices are not bound by printing limitations. Creators of such apps often think in both linear and non-linear paths, considering how opportunities can be best capitalised on. They keep in mind how children learn and how they learn to read (and through reading). But most of all, they avoid the pitfall of merely trying to reproduce digitally what was created in the print medium. Instead, if the story app is based on an existing story, the new creation is more new than copied, the original story serving as a source of inspiration rather than a template. If the story app is a new creation that never existed in print, it takes advantage of the digital device's opportunities for storytelling in ways that print alone could not. For such story-focused multimedia creations, I propose the following evaluative criteria:

1. Does the app take advantage of the possibilities of digital storytelling?
2. Do the interactive features align with the app's goals?
3. Does the app expand definitions for digital storytelling?

Take advantage of digital storytelling possibilities

Three-time winner of the Caldecott Award David Weisner, known as a master of visual storytelling through his numerous wordless books, has created a new form of storytelling in his app, *Spot*. Inspired by the tablet's ability for viewers to pinch and drag, swipe and zoom, five distinct yet interconnected worlds offer viewers the ability to make choices about how their version of the story unfolds. Weisner's hand-drawn worlds are: Lower Rügg, a tiny world beneath an armchair; Mekanikos, a world of robots; Oceana Prime, an underwater world; Katzaluna, a world of cats, and an intergalactic space station. This app offers readers the ability to make choices of which of the branches to follow in creating their path that make this interactive possibility well suited to the digital storytelling world. More than a decade earlier, Weisner had already pushed boundaries that were limited by print; his *The Three Pigs* (2001) is a classic example frequently considered to define postmodern picturebooks in which non-linear storytelling is masterfully executed.

Interactive features align with app goals

One such successful example is the much admired *Pierre et le Loup*, a co-production of the Camera Lucida productions, Radio France and France Télévisions. As the title implies, the app is based on the famous music by Sergueï Prokofiev in which a young boy interacts with a duck, a bird and a cat and encounters a wolf and hunters. Each character is represented in the original score by a specific instrument throughout the performance. In this app, the main story is presented as a non-interactive film. Throughout the film, musical notations and alphabet fonts are playfully depicted as visual elements that combine to create the characters or merely float by in space as a decorative element. The music is performed by the Orchestre National de France (National Orchestra of France); the musicians are featured both close-up as well as within the context of their orchestra seating. The close-ups even get close enough to show how an instrument is played. There are numerous add-on activities and each is related to the goals of the app: matching instrument representation to character, "capturing" the wolf using the tablet's camera, etc. Activities and narration are only available in French, but most are intuitively understandable.

Expand definitions of digital storytelling

What is yet to be explored fully is redefining digital storytelling. Some apps do not follow a linear progression for story development that has commonly defined "narrative" in the past. Instead, the conceptualisation of digital storytelling is expanded to newer ways of telling and creating story. Christoph Neimann's *Petting Zoo*, for example, opens with a top hat being drawn by a pencil and a rabbit appearing out of it. Cultural knowledge refers to magicians pulling a rabbit out of a hat. Readers are not given any directions, but with a touch tablet, one begins pulling and pushing around the surface and finds that the rabbit is like rubber and can be changed as if it has elasticity.

Chris Haughton's *Hat Monkey* is targeted for pre-school children to interact with the monkey on screen as someone old enough to read the text reads it aloud to the young child (there is no audio choice, but there are multiple written language options). The text directs the child to do various tasks and interact with the monkey: let the monkey in the door when it knocks, play hide and go seek with the monkey, send the monkey a text, give it a high-five, etc.

On the other hand, there are numerous apps for children which are intended to entertain, engage and perhaps educate, etc. but not necessarily for the purpose of creating or telling a story. Hervé Tullet's *Press Here* is such a case. A series of wiggling dots in yellow, blue and red are categorised under the opening set of dots (which serves somewhat like an activity organiser / table of contents). Other than the name of the activity that sometimes gives clues as to what to do, there are no directions. Children are to explore to try to figure out what the intent of the activity is – or is there an intent? For this adult, many remained unclear as to the purpose, no matter how engaging and entertaining. However, it is clear that the app version of this originally created as a print book is cleverly conceptualised. One wonders how the original board book can compare in holding children's attention.

Final considerations

As we move forward in the digital world, many new ways of representing story are likely to be created. Although I cannot anticipate such a future, I do know that as in every previous era of storytelling, there are predictable ways of considering how to evaluate usefulness and appropriateness of such creations. To begin, *the purpose* of the story suggests the best way of telling it. Next, balancing the *availability of resources* such as the technology itself with access to individual *books and other materials* is important. With new materials, there is often a need to "*beware the glitz*" or the appeal of what's new. Most apps are neither all good nor all bad; but in a world with limited time and resources, the challenge is to make the best decisions for the best experiences possible.

Additionally, what has become increasingly clear is the homogenisation of artistic styles in the short history of tablet apps. Colours, shapes and even human features of many apps seem to have taken on a goal for universal marketing and appeal. Perhaps the ease with which such apps cross cultural and language boundaries is the reason why. Or perhaps app developers assume that children's tastes in the digital world are simplified. In any case, the lack of cultural distinctness in the app space could continue this trend toward homogenisation. What does this mean for the future of diversifying what children are introduced to?

As we engage in this world of digital storytelling, we have much to consider from our past, through our present and into the future. But one thing is clear: we must maintain focus on how to offer children the best story experiences (Sipe 2008) possible, no matter what the format. And we must keep in mind that deeper, richer experiences with story trump any debate on format appropriateness and that, often, those experiences depend on the human factors of adult-child interaction rather than on the format of the story.

Works Cited

Primary Works Cited

Children's Books

Chimielewska, Iwona. *W kieszonce*. Torun [Poland]: Media Rodzina, 2015. Print.

Gomi, Taro. *Drawing Book I.* Tokyo: Bronze, 1990-1992. Print.

Joyce, William. *The Fantastic Flying Books of Mr. Morris Lessmore*. New York: Atheneum Books, 2011. Print.

Laske, Oskar. *Die Arche Noah*. Vienna: Schroll, 1925. Print.

Meggendorfer, Lothar. *Gemischte Gesellschaft: ein lustiges Ziehbilderbuch*. Munchen: Esslingen: J.F. Schreiber, 1890. Print.

Shaw, Charles G. *It Looked Like Spilt Milk.* New York: HarperCollins, 1947-1988. Print.

The History and Adventures of Little Henry, Exemplified in a Series of Figures. London: Printed for S. and J. Fuller, 1810. Print.

Weisner, David. *The Three Pigs.* Boston: Clarion, 2001. Print.

Digital Materials

Fiete – A Day on the Farm. Cologne: Ahoiii Entertainment UG, 2014. iPad edition.

Haughton, Chris. *Hat Monkey.* Berlin: Fox & Sheep, 2014. iPad edition.

Jeffers, Oliver. *The Heart and the Bottle.* New York: Penguin Group, 2011. iPad edition.

Neiman, Christoph. *Petting Zoo.* Berlin: Fox & Sheep, 2014. iPad edition.

Joyce, William. *The Fantastic Flying Books of Mr. Morris Lessmore.* Shreveport: Moonbot Studios, 2011. iPad edition.

Moncomble, Gerard. *L'enveloppe mystérieuse d'Arthur le facteur.* Ill. Pawel Pawlak. Wroclaw: Wydawnictwo Format, 2014. iPad edition.

Tullet, Hervé. *Press Here.* London: Chronicle Book, 2012. iPad edition.

Weisner, David. *Spot.* Seattle: Boston: Houghton Mifflin Harcourt, 2015. iPad edition.

Secondary Works Cited

Glass, Nick and, Junko Yokota. "Scaffolding Children's Literature Experiences with Digital Formats." 53rd Annual Convention of the International Reading Association. Atlanta, GA. May 2008. Presentation.

Nikolajeva, Maria, and Carole Scott. *How Picturebooks Work.* London: Routledge, 2001. Print.

Sargeant, Betty. "Interactive Storytelling: How Picture Book Conventions Inform Multimedia Book App Narratives." *Australian Journal of Intelligent Processing Systems*, 13.3 (2013): 29-35. Print.

—. "What Is an Ebook? What Is a Book App? And Why Should We Care? An Analysis of Contemporary Digital Picture Books." *Children's Literature in Education*, (2015). Web. 5 May 2015.

Sipe, Lawrence R. "How Picture Books Work: A Semiotically Framed Theory of Text-Picture Relationships." *Children's Literature in Education*, 29.2 (2001): 97-108. Print.

—. *Storytime: Young Children's Literary Understanding in the Classroom.* New York: Teachers College Press, 2008. Print.

Yokota, Junko. "Picture Books Go Digital: What Works Where When?" Annual Convention of the American Library Association. New Orleans, LA. May 2011. Invited speech.

—. "From Print to Digital? Considering the Future of Picturebooks for Children." *Bologna: Fifty Years of Children's Books from around the World.* Ed. Giorgia Grilli. Bologna: Bononia UPress, 2013a. Print.

—. "Visual Narratives in Picture Book Design: A Comparison of Print and Digital Formats." Prussian Heritage Foundation. Staatsbibliothek zu Berlin, Berlin. May 2013b. Presentation.

Yokota, Junko, and William H. Teale. "Picture Books and the Digital World: Educators Making Informed Choices." *The Reading Teacher*, 67.8 (2014): 577-585. Print.

Electronic Literature for Children

Characterising Narrative Apps (2010-2014)

Celia TURRIÓN PENELAS

Universitat Autònoma de Barcelona

Introduction

Story producers have found broad scope for creation in the current mediasphere, especially for children. The development of the contemporary media map in the past decades has boosted the expansion of children's narratives in multiple formats and the most recent of these is electronic media. With the birth of the iPad in 2010 and the subsequent extensive use of tablets in the home, new entertainment and educational products have been promoted in the digital market. Among these, new types of stories for children, marketed as so-called *apps*, have appeared. But what challenges do they pose and what opportunities do they open in the context of children's literature studies?

From the perspective of teaching and learning literature it has become important to answer some decisive questions regarding literary education such as the type of stories that are on offer, to what extent producers are aware of the aesthetic possibilities of the electronic formats and how they are actually implementing this potentiality in the existing digital works.

A brief look at the majority of the electronic literary works aimed at children shows four main trends. They relate to the industrial mechanisms of cyberculture,[1] including the ludic and interactive nature of almost all human activity (Pérez Latorre 2013: 227), the tensions between simplicity and complexity and the multiple possible variations regarding the proposed fictional experience. The impending analysis from various perspectives of these new forms is a necessary point of departure to solve diverse problems such as the loss of clarity caused by these new forms in

---

1 A term coined by Pierre Lévy (2007) and used by other researchers in the field (Sánchez-Mesa 2004). It defines the socio-technical-cultural system of advanced post-industrial society.

the field of children's literature, the challenges linked to the assimilation of structural changes alien to literature and the facilitators' lack of awareness of the works themselves.

In order to approach these issues in a systematic manner, a model of analysis of narrative apps for children was created and applied to a set of thirty apps that were developed since the arrival of the iPad in 2010 until December 2014 (see Primary Works Cited).[2] This study is based on the application of a collection of combined theories in order to design an instrument for analysis. In addition to the formal characterisation of the selected corpus, its relationship with the implied reader is also stressed.[3] The results of the analysis offer a primary view of the real capacity presented by already existing narrative apps for literary enjoyment and education.

An analytic tool built at the intersection of theories

As explained in this author's thesis entitled "Narrativa infantil y juvenil digital. ¿Qué ofrecen las nuevas formas al lector literario?" (Children's Digital Narrative Fiction: What Do the New Forms Offer the Literary Reader?, Turrión 2014b), the four tendencies mentioned above form the underlying structure of the model of analysis which was used to study narrative apps in this work.

To begin with, it is interesting for children's literature studies to determine the real impact that extra-literary forces have on apps and the degree to which literary aspects are maintained. Secondly, regarding the omnipresent interactive proposal in the apps, it seems a sensible academic goal to delimit the real action capacity the reader has in the story. In relation to the existence of some tensions between complexity and simplification, we can say that while most apps seem to adhere to the *assumptions of simplicity* listed by Colomer (1998: 141-143), others take advantage of the innovative opportunities offered by electronic devices, thus allowing different types of literary complexity. An account on the real implementation of these pole trends is also required in order to assess the possibilities of popular contemporary digital narrative for

2 To fix the corpus we have included apps recommended by the Spanish children's literature research group GRETEL (see GRETEL 2014ff.) and apps mentioned by scholars to date (Al-Yaqout, and Nikolajeva 2015; Schwebs 2014; Stichnothe 2014; Turrión 2014a, 2014b). We have included film, book, traditional tales and classic tale adaptations, as well as native apps, and we have favoured the inclusion of apps related to the children's print literature system. The aim of the selection was to show a considerable and yet representative variety of forms, structures and fictional proposals.

3 The terms *reader* and *user* are used indistinctly. In each case the chosen term is the one better suited to the context.

literary education. Finally, regarding fictional experience variations, this essay questions whether the integration of interactivity, specific playful elements or filmic modes of representation in digital stories have really removed the traditional reading activity from its central position.

For the study of narrative forms, children's literature scholars have often applied the narrative communication model, as it covers both the structural elements of any narration and the pragmatic figures of a communicative situation and their reflections in the text (i.e. Colomer 1998; Silva-Díaz 2005). Nevertheless, interactive studies have shown the insufficiency of the narratological model for the analysis of works that include the reader's participation proposal. An adjustment to the narrative communication model is therefore required in order to include the structural changes linked to the interactive nature of the medium. It was in that spirit that Aarseth proposed the intrigue model of Adventure Games (1997),[4] where he replaces the concept of *author* for that of *creator* and the notion of *reader* for that of *user* (127). He also distinguishes between *intrigant* and *narrative voice* and establishes three implied figures in the reception process: the *implied user*, the *intriguee* and the *puppet*.[5] Even though the production of children's apps usually avoids truly ergodic aesthetics,[6] these concepts can help the analysis.

Furthermore, the adapted model needs to be combined with several theories in order to obtain a comprehensive tool for the study of children's narrative apps. Among them, we find works of dissimilar origins – original works, traditional tale adaptations, film adaptations, picturebook adaptations and classic literature adaptations –, a variable presence and treatment of the written text, of images, multiple verbal and non-verbal sound displays, different combinations of these elements and interactive and non-linear structural options. The intrinsic hybrid condition of the electronic medium, defined as a metamedium by scholars such as Aarseth (1997), Ryan (2006) and Alan Kay (cited by Manovich 2013), calls for a cross-disciplinary study that includes disciplines such as Narratology,

---

4 *Intrigue* is defined as "a secret plot in which the user is the innocent, but voluntary, target [...] with an outcome that is not yet decided – or rather with several possible outcomes that depend on various factors, such as the cleverness and experience of the player" (Aarseth 1997: 112).

5 Aarseth (1997) defines the *intriguee* as "the target of the intrigue [...] and is parallel to the narratee, to the implied reader of the narratologists, as well as to the main character (or 'puppet') [...]" (113), while the *intrigant* is "the architect of the intrigue [...], the mastermind who is ultimately responsible for events and existents but who is not motivated by a particular outcome" (114).

6 Aarseth (1997) defines *ergodic literature* as a type of literature requiring a non-trivial effort to allow the reader to traverse the text (1). The majority of children's apps avoid this type of complexity, although there are examples such as *18 Cadence* that defy this general premise.

Children's Literature Theory, Picturebook Theory, Adaptation Theory, Film Narratology, Interactive Narratology, Game Studies and Hypertext Theory. All these form an essential part of the model of analysis proposed in this essay, although they have been simplified in order to attain an approachable tool with which to work.

The model of analysis employed proposes a series of categories and subcategories structured, as mentioned before, in four groups corresponding to the four general trends detected. In the first place, the cultural coexistence of diverse media brings about the hybridisation of contents in the nascent forms, also influenced by extra-literary sociocultural factors. This circumstance calls for a detailed study of these aspects in the works themselves and we propose to accomplish this through the study of genres and the formal mechanics of adaptation following Genette's categories (1989) for the traditional adaptation processes and Jenkins' ideas (2008) for the more recent ones. As far as the choice of genre is concerned, we study whether genres typical of the commercial exploitation of children's stories (Colomer 2001: 38; Hutcheon 2013: 52; Zipes 1997: 69), such as adventure, historical, horror or mystery genres are predominant; if educational elements such as non-fictional information or a stress on learning appear in apps, or if genres show an attachment to the aesthetics of interactive products such as the repetitive structures found in videogames.

In order to arrive at a thorough description of interactivity, the tool covers several aspects, relying on theories proposed by the scholars Moreno (2002) and Ryan (2004): the reader's involvement with the story, the position in which the reader is placed, the integration of the interactive proposal with the elements of Story and Discourse (including distinctions such as functional/non-functional actions)[7] and the global design of the interactive proposals.

Regarding the complexity-simplification balance, the model includes four categories: traditional and hypertext narrative structures (Ryan 2006: 101-103),[8] narrative complexity through point of view and distance using Genette's categories (1972: 206-207), *composition* of the different semiotic codes,[9] partially using Nikolajeva and Scott's proposal (2006:

---

7 Barthes' *functional events* are more important than *non-functional* in the hierarchical logic also defended by Chatman (1980: 53). For Chatman both actions and happenings are events (26).

8 Ryan distinguishes traditional structures such as plots as state-transition, interplay of actual and virtual events or interwoven destiny lines, and hypertext structures as the network, the vector with side-branches, the sea-anemone, the tree, the maze, etc.

9 In the electronic medium, *composition* refers to the mixed textual, visual and aural meanings. Kaplan and Moulthrop assert the only chance for integration of these media is their move to the homogeneity of the electronic medium (cited in Delany, and Landow 1993).

14-17) and the possible interpretive complexity derived from the use of these strategies including intertextual parody, ambiguity and temporality alterations.

To define the variations on the fictional experience proposed by the works, the study relies on the analysis of narrative modes (Hutcheon 2013), narrative contracts and the formal disposition of contents in the interface.

a) Entertainment and educational industry mechanics	**Type of adaptation:** reduction, enlargement, franchises, transmedia, other
	Genre choices: entertainment, educational, interactive, other
b) Interactivity	**Type of participation:** internal, external
	Degree of participation: selective, productive
	Interactivity integration: real, simulate, false/in which narrative elements?
	Global interactive design: balance and imbalance
c) Complexity-simplification tensions	**Narrative structures:** traditional or hypertext
	Composition: simple, complex, redundant relations
	Point of view (text/image): zero, internal, external
	Types of interpretive complexity: intertextuality, ambiguity, temporality variations
d) Variations of the proposed fictional experience	**Organisation of the information on the interface:** representation of a page, a stage/screen, free use of space
	Dominant mode: diegetic, mimetic, multimodal, interactive
	Type of fictional pact: narrative, intrigue, explicit pact to facilitate, metafictive alterations

Figure 1. A comprehensive model of analysis for children narrative apps based on four basic market trends

Constructive tendencies in the current narrative app market

The analysis using this model of thirty narrative apps for children provided a detailed picture of the sample regarding the aforementioned trends. Although we found a number of apps that lean more towards their commercial or educational use, we detected a far from negligible representation of apps that attempt to take literary advantage of the innovation possibilities offered by the electronic medium. We will now present the main representative results and interpretations of the application of the model.

Impact assessment of the entertainment and educational industries

First, the study showed a combined presence of commercial/educational genres and non-commercial genres. On the one hand there are entertainment genres such as horror and action which appear together with other commercial brands such as filmic gags. There are inventive western (*Lil' Red and the Lazy Coyote*) or horror adaptations (*Little Dead Riding Hood*) of traditional tales such as *Little Red Riding Hood*, as well as stories that stress the most popular aspect of their hypotext, which has become the main genre in the new work (*The Adventures of Don Quixote*). Other adaptations may have been chosen because the hypotext already has popular genres (the *iPoe Collection* – thriller-horror – or the science fictional *The Numberlys*). The analysis reflected, however, a high presence of other non-commercial genres. Such is the case of a manifold of realistic stories exploring friendship (*The Very Itchy Bear*), death (*The Heart and the Bottle*), poverty (*The Unwanted Guest*), or the parsimony of a journey on which the protagonist embarks for personal reasons (*The Journey of Alvin*). The inner being is also explored through metafictive strategies in *Chopsticks*, making the fictional experience become a literary theme, the same as in *Harold and the Purple Crayon* and *The Monster at the End of This Book*.

Secondly, an integration of apps in a system of cultural franchises with variations on the extent of conceptual reinterpretation of the hypotext was identified. The reinterpretation of existing contents in other formats can be carried out with both poor and creative reworking on the part of the producers.[10] Examples of the first case are *Olivia Acts Out*, which adapts *Olivia* TV show materials by means of a set of screenshots accompanied with texts and a limited interactive proposal, and *Shrek Forever After*, which was created from the original film using the same means. Conversely, *The Monster at the End of This Book* (initially a character from a TV series, then a book and finally an app), *The Journey of Alvin* (a reinterpretation of Lynch's film *A Straight Story*), *Don't Let the Pigeon Run This App* (a picturebook digital version), *The Fantastic Flying Books of Mr. Morris Lessmore* (from a short film) or *My little story factory* (whose hypotext is a flap book) demonstrate a high level of aesthetic revision that takes into account the change of medium – and thus include

[10] Hutcheon (2013) defines adaptations, among other points, as a creative *and* an interpretive act of appropriation/salvaging (8).

integrated and solid interactive proposals – as well as the implied readers' literary, filmic and interactive competences.

Thirdly, examples of creation based on utilitarian criteria, but also with the presence of literary criteria, were found in the majority of the apps. Utilitarian premises can be detected, for instance, in the epitexts' explicit statements of the possible uses of apps. *The Cat in the Hat* promotional text declares that it may serve to "encourage literacy skills with highlighted narration" or "learn new vocabulary with tappable words and pictures". This stress on the educational aspects shows that the construction of the interactive proposal in this app is initially aimed at the teaching and learning of language rather than at the development of literary competence. The epitexts of the award-winning *Four Little Corners* highlight the teaching of "values such as friendship, integration and equality". This last work is qualified by the producers as "ideal to start a conversation about equality with children", pointing out the educational possibilities of the app rather than the literary ones. These criteria are also reflected in the app's internal design: both show a reduction of the aesthetic aspects of the work, using the interactive, textual and visual capacities of the format to develop aesthetically simplistic stories considered suitable for children's minds.

Nevertheless, the majority of the selected apps exhibit a firm literary purpose. Both *The Journey of Alvin* and *Lil' Red: An Interactive Story* focus on the fictional space through which the reader accompanies the main character, as well as on their relationships with the secondary characters they encounter. The interactive proposals of these apps focus on the exploration of the fictional world through the main character, giving the reader the chance to learn, through tapping and interpreting, about the time-space composition of these worlds and the characters' connections and roles.

The metafictional spirit of *The Monster at the End of This Book, Harold and the Purple Crayon* and *Chopsticks* also makes the literary purpose clear, while the gradual and productive participation proposed in *Don't Let the Pigeon Run This App*, *CaperucitaApp* and *My little story factory* is proof of the producer's intentions to focus the reader's attention on the varied possibilities of creating a narrative discourse. Similarly, the interactive and interface design of the Nosy Crow apps *Little Red Riding Hood* and *Jack and the Beanstalk*, as well as *1001 stories* and *The Land of Me: Storytime*, stresses the possibility of the reader's action on the Discourse level, which Stichnothe calls "multiple fabula apps" (2014). Finally, linear stories such as *The Very Itchy Bear*, *Hansel & Gretel*, *The Heart and the Bottle*, *The Unwanted Guest* or *The Adventures of Don Quixote* use textual, visual, aural and interactive elements in order to simulate the reader's intervention on the level of the Story, for example, by helping the characters trigger functional actions in the story or by discovering inner aspects of the characters' descriptions.

Tensions between narrative complexity and simplicity

In the first place, general stylistic extension was discerned; sometimes combined with stylistic and thematic simplification, other times intertwined with the narrative elements providing enriching amplification. The possibility of combining different codes in the electronic medium has led app producers to take advantage of this distinctive feature in order to attract children readers. Traditional literary forms based on the written text are enhanced with other semiotic systems – static or dynamic images, verbal or non-verbal sounds – in order to motivate the implied addressee. These are sometimes mere ornamentation, especially if this operation is associated with stylistic and thematic simplification. Impoverished narrative reductions, particularly digests, are present in some adaptations such as *Shrek Forever After* and *The Adventures of Don Quixote.* These two apps are formed by a simple concatenation of some hypotext episodes with poor elaboration of the new discourse. Aesthetic deterioration due to a visual concision procedure appears in *Four Little Corners* and *Olivia Acts Out*, which shows a displacement of the elaborate visual manufacture of the paper hypotexts in favour of artistic simplification and leads to interpretive simplification. For instance, due to the aesthetic choice of minimalist representation, the *Four Little Corners* app loses a great part of the expressive force provided by the textures and colours in the picturebook: the change in the narrative background in the endpapers, or the narrative parallelisms that the reader may infer through the colour composition in some double pages (i.e. Ruillier 2012: 18-19).

However, a good number of apps in the selection show an enriching amplification through the addition of images and sounds. As mentioned by Al-Yaqout and Nikolajeva (2015), *The Heart and the Bottle* app adapts to the medium and reinforces the narrative message and the "user's affective engagement" through the visual, aural and interactive design adaptation ("The inside", par. 7). Also, *The Monster at the End of This Book* adds movement and sounds to the paper hypotext content, linking this adaptation to the TV series aesthetics and intensifying the reader's empathy with the character, whom the readers can see acting and addressing them, as well as the narrative tension built on the simple turning of the pages represented on the screen. The user's boosting of the character's movements and sounds also adds narrative meaning and highlights the reader's involvement in the story in apparently simple apps such as *The Very Itchy Bear*, *Lil' Red: An Interactive Story* or *Harold and the Purple Crayon*. Key interventions of the reader in the fictional world and the linear – although reader-dependent – main story are shown through the animation of the characters: Bear needs the user to go to save Flea and start their new friendship; Lil' Red needs them to move through the scene, pick the flowers and apples or speak through pictograms with the wolf and Harold requires their interaction to literally draw his story's chronotope (Nikolajeva 1996). In summary, by making the characters move and speak, the user stimulates the unfolding of the different layers that form the linear argument of these stories.

Secondly, a balance between simple narrative and interpretive proposals and the presence of complex narrative and interpretive strategies (in both simple and complex apps) was detected. Half of the analysed set shows simple narrative and interpretive designs, with traditional linear structures, simple and redundant compositions and a lack of complex strategies such as ambiguity, intertextuality or time-space variations. In *Four Little Corners*, texts, images and sounds simultaneously display the same fictional information, sometimes even requiring the reader's participation to corroborate already given facts through the resulting sounds and animations, as in screen 4 where Little Square is sad and tries to change shape. In the Spanish version of *Little Dead Riding Hood* the speaker narrator explicitly states what could have happened if the girl had not arrived at Grandma's house after the wolf, which any child used to the narrative forms of television could infer. Narrative and interpretive complexity is absent – using the aforesaid categories – in *Hansel & Gretel*, *The Cat in the Hat*, *Shrek Forever After*, *The Journey of Alvin*, etc.

Conversely, the other half of the production under study showed a remarkable presence of complex narrative and interpretive strategies, adjusted differently to suit the implied reader's learning requirements. Although *The Very Itchy Bear* is quite simple as a narrative, there is a point of view strategy with the hiding of Flea "behind" the arrow. The character's size is used as an excuse for a metafictional game in which the reader must tap the arrow in order to see the insect and go beyond Bear's broad perspective, thus boosting the reader's complicity. We also find point of view variations in *The Adventures of Don Quixote*, *Olivia Acts Out* and *The Heart and the Bottle*, where the reader has occasional access to the character's inner thoughts and in the case of the former, directly links this operation to the original story's main theme. In *The Unwanted Guest* the visual and verbal point of view equal that of the main character, maintaining the metaphor of poverty unexplained. In *Chopsticks* the perspective alteration goes further, provoking an effect of ambiguity at the end of the story due to the sudden unreliability of the photographs and videos provided by the visual narrator.

Narrative complexity built on the variation of the fictional contract appears, as we have already mentioned, in *Harold and the Purple Crayon* and *The Monster at the End of This Book*, *Don't Let the Pigeon Run This App* and *The Lost Houses*. In this last app, for instance, the help tool typical of the electronic communication between reader and machine is given a literary voice, guiding the reader through the interactive proposal. For example, in the "The Two Houses and… the Other House" tale, the help tool warns the reader to be patient because "all love stories have their twists and turns". The *iPoe Collection* apps show this variation along with temporality alterations: the reader seems to become the assassin in "The Tell-Tale Heart" when his fingertips leave bloody marks on the interface background as he touches the screen.

Lastly, hypertext structures add some complexity to the narrative discourse in *The Land of Me: Storytime*, *Little Red Riding Hood* and *1001 stories*, although it is always attenuated in order to suit non-sophisticated digital readers. For example, in *The Land of Me: Storytime* the stories resulting from the initial elections of characters, motifs and endings are always linear; the *Little Red Riding Hood* elections are limited, closely guided by the *intrigant* (in the text and images) and accompanied in the menu by a visual map of the app structure; *1001 stories* follows a similar pattern to Choose Your Own Adventure books, which causes the users' choices to lose meaning as they can even abandon the very short storylines they open.

A third aspect regarding complexity and simplicity is the presence of a well-defined implied reader in the majority of the works analysed. As in other types of children's literature, the dual audience is patent in these apps, but here, the adult addressee gains relevance with respect to the child addressee in some works. This point can be observed in the lack of moral adjustment of the contents to children's supposed sensitivity (i.e. the character hitting the knight with the reader's help in *The Adventures of Don Quixote*). It can also be perceived in the references to the cultural and popular adult knowledge that appear in *Little Dead Riding Hood*, such as the allusions to the characters of Rambo or Indiana Jones, or the fast-food pun in *Lil' Red and the Lazy Coyote*. Nonetheless, the majority of the apps in the corpus show a precise image of their implied child reader: the dramatic content expurgation in *The Journey of Alvin* seeks to suit children's experiential knowledge, in *Four Little Corners* there is a clear moral lesson aimed at children, *The Heart and the Bottle* and *The Unwanted Guest* adapt hard topics such as death and poverty to a child audience and the three *Little Red Riding Hood* versions reconcile a softened story to the ideal reader through the inclusion of happy endings. Other apps such as *Chopsticks* directly appeal to adolescent popular culture – YouTube pop music videos and Tim Burton films –, which helps to demarcate the adolescent addressee.

The interactive design of narrative apps

In our analysis of interactivity, we first found an essential interactive proposal in all the apps examined, sometimes the design follows a precise line of action, and sometimes it combines several lines that may confuse the role of the user. While some apps show a clear interactive proposal, visibly linked to the literary objectives of the work (i.e. metafiction in *The Monster at the End of This Book*, the pleasure of being in nature of *The Journey of Alvin* or the character's escape task in *Jack and the Beanstalk*), other apps overexploit the interactive resources of the digital format. In *The Adventures of Don Quixote* the accurate interactive proposal regarding the change in the visual point of view from zero to internal becomes blurred because of the addition of other meaningless lines of interaction, such as the shields' quest. This also happens in *The Very Itchy Bear*, where the interactive proposal concerning the character's actions, apparitions and the space exploration, becomes confusing due to the marginal task of picking flowers throughout the app. The common repetitive design of the user's interventions may also affect the narrative effect of the resulting actions on the reader; this is the case with tapping on the characters in *The Cat in the Hat*, *Hansel & Gretel*, *Shrek Forever After*, *Olivia Acts Out* and *Little Dead Riding Hood*. Conversely, apps such as *Lil' Red: An Interactive Story*, the two Nosy Crow apps, *The Monster at the End of This Book* or *The Lost Houses* respect the readers' engagement by offering them either a defined outcome for each tapping, or several results that enrich the story in one way or another.

On the other hand, heavy authorial control is reflected in the interactive and structural limitations, responding to the traditional premises of children's literature. Selective and simulative reader participation are the prevailing types, with few cases of productive participation. *Don't Let the Pigeon Run This App* allows the user to record their answers, thus giving them the chance to partially co-create. Similarly, *My little story factory* leaves blank spaces for the reader to imagine and write phrases for the short stories. Even though these productive opportunities are very limited, they set an undeniable precedent regarding the possible modifications of the role of the reader in digital stories. Likewise, the already commented simple hypertext structures in *1001 stories*, *Little Red Riding Hood* or *The Land of Me: Storytime* show both innovative intention and high authorial control that proves the producers still hold educational concerns regarding the reception ability of children to understand complex structures.

The fictional experience proposed in apps

Regarding fictional experiences, we found a preservation of the reading dynamics and occasional superficial adhesion to book features. Paying homage to printed books seemed to be one of the primary interests of the first narrative apps, as shown in *Alice for the iPad* and *The Fantastic Flying Books of Mr. Morris Lessmore*. Superficial representation of book features is a common method to relate apps with an already existing cultural market, even if it may restrict the numerous fictional experiences that electronic devices are capable of conveying. While the representation of pages in *Shrek Forever After* does not transform the set of film screenshots into a proper book offering a literary experience, the elaborate adaptation of *The Monster at the End of This Book* allows page representation even if the proposed fictional experience is not merely literary, but also interactive.

In contrast to the meaningless representation of book features, a number of apps offer a partially literary experience thanks to the presence of elaborate texts and images, careful composition, creative work with narrative elements or respect for the required reading tempo. Examples are *The Very Itchy Bear*, *The Journey of Alvin*, *CaperucitaApp*, *Chopsticks*, *The Heart and the Bottle*, *Harold and the Purple Crayon*, *Lil' Red: An Interactive Story* and *The Lost Houses*.

In any case, the major fictional experience proposed by the apps we analysed stands between interacting and interpreting through reading and viewing. Even though there are some examples in which diegetic modality still prevails (*The Adventures of Don Quixote*, *iPoe Collection*, *Alice for the iPad*, *Olivia Acts Out*), most apps show a combination of multimodal and interactive modalities: *The Fantastic Flying Books of Mr. Morris Lessmore*, *Chopsticks*, *The Very Itchy Bear*, *Hansel & Gretel*, *Jack and the Beanstalk*, *The Heart and the Bottle*, *Harold and the Purple Crayon*, *The Unwanted Guest* or *The Journey of Alvin*. Film animation and picturebook dynamics are probably influencing these new forms, not only adaptations from existing paper books but also native apps. In fact, some show a meaningful inclusion of audiovisual elements that incline the reception towards a mimetic experience, which is the case of *Lil' Red: An Interactive Story*, *The Land of Me: Storytime*, *Don't Let the Pigeon Run This App*, *The Numberlys* or *The Monster at the End of This Book*.

Finally, the fictional contract of these apps is chiefly traditional and covert, except in the metafictional cases. This contract, however, is combined with a general existence of a facilitating intrigant who helps the user in their tasks but does not normally change the established pact. The intrigant takes different forms, such as the musical notes in *Chopsticks*, the arrows in *The Very Itchy Bear*, the hints in *The Heart and the Bottle* or the character narrators in *Don' Let the Pigeon Run This App*, *The Land of Me: Storytime* and *The Monster at the End of This Book*. One special case is where the intrigant in *The Lost Houses* alters the traditional contract with the peculiar advice he gives through the help tool.

Conclusion

The children app market has been functioning for five years now. Far from what we might expect from a nascent cultural sector, this study shows the existence of representative literary proposals in narrative apps, even if they appear slightly modified by the medium for which they have been devised.

Although it is true that, from a literary perspective, there is still an important representation of weak works, there are some promising trends: commercial and educational influences have not ruined creative variety; narrative complexity appears as a steady option; interactivity is frequently intertwined with the story and some producers are testing the limits of the literary experience they can offer children in electronic format. It is now the role of critics and facilitators to understand in depth and take advantage of the existing digital narrative fiction and integrate it in the literary educational projects for contemporary children, the multi-format adult readers of tomorrow.

Works Cited

Primary Works Cited

Alice for the iPad. London: Atomic Antelope, 2010. iPad edition.

Anthony, Jessica, and Rodrigo Corral. *Chopsticks.* New York: Penguin Group USA, 2012. iPad edition.

Bland, Nick. *The Very Itchy Bear*. South Melbourne: We Are Wheelbarrow, 2012. iPad edition.

Cervantes, Miguel de. *The Adventures of Don Quixote.* Ill. Miguel Calero. Madrid: Touch of Classic, 2012. iPad edition.

Choose Your Own Adventure Series. New York: Bantam Books, 1979-1998. Print.

Cloud Castel. *Hansel & Gretel*. Epic Tales, 2012-2013. iPad edition.

Dr Seuss. *The Cat in the Hat. Dr Seuss.* Encinitas: Dr Seuss Enterprises and Oceanhouse Media, 2010. iPad edition.

DreamWorks Animation. *Shrek Forever After.* Santa Bárbara: iStoryTime, 2010. iPad edition.

Falconer, Ian. *Olivia Acts Out.* New York: Polin 8, 2011. iPad edition.

Gilbert, Bruno. *My little story factory.* Paris: e-Toiles éditions & Autrement Jeunesse, 2013. iPad edition.

Gibson, Alishea. *Lil' Red and the Lazy Coyote.* BearBoat Studios, 2014. iPad edition.

Jack and the Beanstalk. Ill. Ed Bryan. London: Nosy Crow, 2014. iPad edition.

Jeffers, Oliver. *The Heart and the Bottle.* New York: Penguin Group, 2011. iPad edition.

Johnson, Crockett. *Harold and the Purple Crayon.* San Francisco: Trilogy Studios, 2011. iPad edition.

Joyce, William. *The Fantastic Flying Books of Mr. Morris Lessmore*. New York: Atheneum Books, 2011. Print.

—. *The Numberlys.* Shreveport: Moonbot Studios, 2012. iPad edition.

Little Dead Riding Hood. Valencia: ItBook, 2013. iPad edition.

Little Red Riding Hood. Ill. Ed Bryan. London: Nosy Crow, 2013. iPad edition.

Lynch, David and Meikme. *The Journey of Alvin.* Barcelona: Meikme, 2014. iPad edition.

Main, Brian. *Lil' Red. An Interactive Story*. Brian Main, 2013. iPad edition.

Mistral, Gabriela. *CaperucitaApp.* Ill. Paloma Valdivia. Santiago de Chile: Editorial Amanuta, 2014. iPad edition.

O'Rogers, Jacqueline. *The Unwanted Guest.* British Columbia: Moving Tales, 2012. iPad edition.

Poe, Edgar Allan. *iPoe Collection*, Vol. I. Ill. David García Farés. Barcelona: Play Creatividad, 2012. iPad edition.

—. *iPoe Collection*, Vol. II. Ill. David García Farés. Barcelona: Play Creatividad, 2012. iPad edition.

Prap, Lila. *1001 stories.* Liubliana: Mladinska knjiga Založba, 2012. iPad edition.

Reed, Aaron. *18 Cadence.* Aaron Reed, 2013. iPad edition.

Ruillier, Jérôme. *Por cuatro esquinitas de nada.* Barcelona: Juventud, 2012 (french ed.: *Quatre petit coins de rien du tout.* Bilboquet, 2004). Print.

—. *Four Little Corners.* Madrid: Dada Company, 2013. iPad edition.

Serrat, Xavi. *The Lost Houses*. Ill. Anna Obon. Mus. Dani Alegret. Barcelona: Editorial La Tortuga Casiopea, 2011. iPad edition.

Sesame Workshop. *The Monster at the End of This Book.* New York: Sesame Workshop & Callaway Digital Arts, 2011. iPad edition.

The Land of Me: Story Time. London: Made in Me, 2012. iPad edition.

Willems, Mo. *Don't Let the Pigeon Run This App.* Burbank: Disney Enterprises, 2011. iPad edition.

Secondary Works Cited

Aarseth, Espen J. *Cybertext: Perspectives on Ergodic Literature.* Baltimore: Johns Hopkins UP, 1997. Print.

Al-Yaqout, Ghada, and Maria Nikolajeva. "Re-conceptualising Picturebook Theory in the Digital Age." *Nordic Journal of ChildLit Aesthetics*, 6 (2015). Web. 18 Mar. 2015.

Bolter, Jay David, and Richard Grusin. *Remediation: Understanding New Media.* Cambridge, MA: MIT P, 2000. Print.

Chatman, Seymour. *Story and Discourse: Narrative Structure in Fiction and Film.* New York: Cornell UP, 1980. Print.

Colomer, Teresa. *La formación del lector literario: narrativa infantil y juvenil actual.* Madrid: Fundación Germán Sánchez Ruipérez, 1998. Print.

—. "La literatura infantil y juvenil actual: entre la unidad y la fragmentación." *La educación lectora: encuentro iberoamericano.* Eds. Felicidad Orquín, *et al.* Madrid: Fundación Germán Sánchez Ruipérez, 2001. 37-46. Print.

Delany, Paul, and George P. Landow. "Managing the Digital Word: The Text in an Age of Electronic Reproduction." *The Digital Word: Text-Based Computing in the Humanities.* Eds. Paul Delany, and George P. Landow. Cambridge, MA: MIT P, 1993. 3-28. Print.

Genette, Gérard. *Figures III.* Paris: Éditions du Seuil, 1972. Print.

—. *Palimpsestos: la literatura en segundo grado.* Trans. Celia Fernández. Madrid: Taurus, 1989. Print.

GRETEL. "Recomanacions digitals." Universitat Autònoma de Barcelona, 2014ff. Web. 12 Apr. 2015.

Hutcheon, Linda. *A Theory of Adaptation.* Nueva York: Routledge, 2013. Print.

Jenkins, Henry. *Convergence Culture: Where Old and New Media Collide.* New York: New York UP, 2008. Print.

Lévy, Pierre. *Cibercultura: informe al Consejo de Europa.* Trans. Beatriz Campillo, Isabel Chacón, and Florentino Martorana. Barcelona: Anthropos; Mexico, D.F.: Universidad Autónoma Metropolitana – Iztapalapa, 2007. Print.

Manovich, Lev. *Software Takes Command.* New York: Bloomsbury Academic, 2013. Print.

Moreno, Isidro. *Musas y nuevas tecnologías.* Barcelona: Paidós, 2002. Print.

Nikolajeva, Maria, and Carol Scott. 2001. *How Picturebooks Work.* New York: Routledge, 2006. Print.

Pérez Latorre, Oliver. "Apuntes sobre la teoría de la diversión." *Homo Videoludens 2.0. De Pacman a la gamification.* Ed. Carlos Alberto Scolari. Barcelona: Universitat de Barcelona, 2013. 223-252. Web. 18 Mar. 2015.

Ryan, Marie-Laure. "Will New Media Produce New Narratives?" *Narrative across Media: The Languages of Storytelling.* Ed. Marie-Laure Ryan. Lincoln: U of Nebraska P, 2004. 337-359. Print.

—. *Avatars of Story.* Minneapolis: U of Minnesota P, 2006.

Sánchez-Mesa, Domingo, comp. *Literatura y Cibercultura.* Madrid: Arco Libro, 2004.

Schwebs, Ture. "Affordances of an App: A Reading of The Fantastic Flying Books of Morris Lessmore." *Nordic Journal of ChildLit Aesthetics*, 5 (2014). Web. 18 Mar. 2015.

Silva-Díaz, María Cecilia. "Libros que enseñan a leer: álbumes metaficcionales y competencia literaria." Diss. Universitat Autònoma de Barcelona, 2005. Web. 18 Mar. 2015.

Stichnothe, Haddassah. "Engineering Stories? A Narratological Approach to Children's Book Apps." *Nordic Journal of ChildLit Aesthetics*, 5 (2014). Web. 18 Mar. 2015.

Turrión, Celia. "Multimedia Book Apps in a Contemporary Culture: Commerce and Innovation, Continuity and Rupture." *Nordic Journal of ChildLit Aesthetics*, 5 (2014a). Web. 18 Mar. 2015.

—. "Narrativa infantil y juvenil digital. ¿Qué ofrecen las nuevas formas al lector literario?" Diss. Universitat Autònoma de Barcelona, 2014b. Web. 18 Mar. 2015.

Zipes, Jack. *Happily Ever After. Fairy Tales, Children and the Culture Industry.* New York: Routledge, 1997. Print.

Part III

Readers and Digital Literature

Traditional Readers and Electronic Literature

An Exploration of Perceptions and Readings of Digital Works

Mireia Manresa

Universitat Autònoma de Barcelona

Introduction

The exposure of children and young adults to digital texts has strong implications in terms of training competent readers in today's society due to the impact on the reading experience and the comprehension and interpretation skills and strategies that come into play. The results from the studies on how readers read digitally are essential in order to advance in the training of readers in this context. There is abundant empirical research available on digital reading, often comparing comprehension strategies between reading in print and reading in digital formats via the Internet, e-books or tablets. Most of this research has addressed cognitive aspects of visual perception or the effects of the materiality of the text on reading processes; it has mainly been carried out using informative or academic texts, but fewer studies have addressed literary reading.

The research conducted in this area has mainly focused on literary texts in e-book or digital (pdf) formats. From their cognitive perspective, the works of Mangen (2008) and Mangen, Walgermo and Brønnick (2013) are representative of this idea and they include, among others, fictional narrative texts in comprehension tests and provide insights into the differences between reading the same text in print or on an e-book reader; they show the difficulty of immersion and the lower levels of comprehension of texts in digital version as well as the impact of the physical and technical characteristics of the digital interface in the reading process. Some case studies have also focused on exploring the involvement possibilities offered by specific devices such as the Amazon Kindle (e.g., Clark *et al.* 2008 or Larson 2010). Other studies show specific reactions to manipulated texts where some specific digital element is included for observation or comparison such as hypertextuality in Miall and Dobson

(2001), who conclude the existence of the negative impact of hypertext in the characteristic reflective mode of literary reading, or Yilmaz *et al.* 2014, who compare the readings of linear texts in pdf format with reading the same texts in multimedia format via questions in comprehension tests.

The field of the reception of electronic literature originally created in digital format and configured by diverse expressive elements such as audio, image, motion, interactivity, text or hypertextuality – that is, neither manipulated nor digitised – has scarcely been addressed to date. In this study we propose an exploration of the impact of this type of digital fiction on children and young adults through the analysis of the perception and interpretation of digital elements in works in app format or available on the Internet, studied in the context of literary discussions with students of different ages and with no previous experience in reading digital literature.

This study is based on the analysis of literary conversations in line with the research model that focuses on reading responses from examples such as Fry (1985), Meek (1988, 1990) or Sarland (1991) and on more recent models that have studied responses to picturebooks (Arizpe, and Styles 2003; Sipe 2008). In addition, we draw from our previous experience and the investigative tradition of our research team using picturebooks and immigrant children (Colomer, and Fittipaldi eds. 2012) and we continue the educational tradition of the reading response analysis focused on the shared construction of the interpretation of the works.

To carry out the study we chose digital texts of different typologies depending on the type and function of the digital elements and we formed small groups of readers to discuss the book we proposed in each case. The results and examples we will show here correspond to the following reading situations with these works:

a) *The One & Only*. Four children aged nine-ten. Narrative work, multimedia version of a printed picturebook, app format for iPad.
b) *Les aventures de la Lala* (Lala's Adventures). Four children aged nine-ten. Original poetic text in digital web-based format.
c) *The Heart and the Bottle*. Four children aged eleven-twelve. iPad version of a picturebook available in print version.
d) "The Tell-Tale Heart". Three teenagers aged fourteen-fifteen. Digital app format, version for iPad of the Edgar Allan Poe story.
e) *Inanimate Alice*. Four teenagers aged fourteen-fifteen. Series of original chapters in digital web-based format.

All situations included readers with a medium-high level of literary competence and solid reading habits. Furthermore, in all cases the students had no prior experience in reading digital fiction, except in the case of those who read *The Heart and the Bottle* where the participants had access for five months to digital works in a free reading situation. Our aim was to investigate the current reality of the majority of children receiving school education for whom literary reading is still essentially linear (Hillesund 2010) and textual – even though digital formats may be available – and excluding a certain percentage of children from literate environments who are familiar with tablets and those for whom digital stories already form part of the family reading routines since infancy.

As can be seen, a wide range of situations that could be explored separately were analysed, attending strictly to contextual characteristics and to the work in question. However, they all had one aspect in common: they provided the experience of reading digital literature and of transforming traditional forms of reading. The main objective of this study emerges at this point: to isolate and detect the most relevant common denominators in different situations of the reading of digital works.

To meet this objective we proposed to investigate the reading experience using certain digital works. More specifically, we wanted to answer the following questions: Do they conceive the work as a literary product? What is their perception of the digital elements? Do they help them to read or distance them from the fiction? Do they provide clues for interpretation? Do they know how to associate the digital media employed with the construction of the fiction?

Bearing in mind the novelty that the experience of reading digital literary works means to our children and adolescents, this research is seen as an initial panoramic exploration to detect relevant aspects for further analysis in future studies. For this reason the literary conversations were analysed from two complementary perspectives in order to facilitate the proposed exploratory approach and focus on the differential variable of the characteristics of digital texts:

On the one hand we wanted to detect the initial reaction to electronic literature, in other words we analysed the readers' *perception* of the digital elements. For this purpose, in this study we focused our attention on the reaction to interaction, one of the essential characteristics of digital literature.

On the other hand we wanted to analyse how readers incorporate digital elements into the *interpretation* of literary fiction, to discover if they detected and how they interpreted the function of digitality in the narrative configuration of the works. In order to achieve this we focused our attention on how the readers approached the construction of temporality in the works, one of the literary conventions that is most prone to transformation by multimodal resources.

The perception of digitality: the reaction to interactive proposals

Electronic literature offers the reader the possibility to *act* in the work, that is, to exercise different roles to participate in the story. In 1938 Rosenblatt defined literary reading as a transactional relationship between text and reader. Now, with digitality, this inherent characteristic of reading no longer merely belongs to the cognitive plane but manifests itself physically or *materialises*.

Regarding the reading experience that interactivity provides, we wanted to observe to what extent the analogue reader is open to negotiation with the text and collaboration with the author (Modir *et al.* 2012); i.e. to what extent readers are prepared to deal with a particular reading pleasure which is quite removed from the type they are used to. For this purpose, we show here the majority of reactions which emerged from the reading situations observed.

Initial mental blank and disorientation

First, and consistent with other observations (Patterson 2000), we found that the analogue reader is initially confused, disoriented and does not know what to do or how to act when faced with the interactive proposals inserted in the literary stories.

We verified this from three different indications: the observations of the videos that showed the physical reactions of the readers – they were passive and overwhelmed in front of the screen. This was also evidenced during the conversations when the children stated they had not explored some of the possibilities offered by the works – sometimes voluntarily and often because they did not notice the possibility – and via their explicit statements such as that made by one of the young readers of *Inanimate Alice*:

> Silvia: It was hard for me to follow because there were a lot of things telling me to click here, click here… and I don't know, I had to ask for help because I couldn't go forward; I was just sitting there, looking and doing nothing. I was looking at the bike [an interactive puzzle proposal] and thinking, it'll just go away.[1]

Or the comment from one of the Poe readers:

> Mariana: I waited but it was obviously supposed to happen. And then the lantern thing [a scene where the screen darkens] I didn't get it until he showed me. I thought it's more enjoyable this way, having to read in the dark.

1 English translations of all quotations in other languages have been provided by Tim Mc Quaid.

It may seem strange that young people, immersed as they are in the digital culture of the Internet, take mental blanks when faced with interactive proposals. In this regard we must clarify that the observations lead us to state that it was not the abstract interactivity that surprised them, but rather that they felt annoyed when it appeared in a literary proposal and they had to click or act in order to *read* a story.

Interactivity as a parallel game

We only detected certain enthusiasm from very few readers who perceived the possibility to act in the story as a game that provided a break from reading as if it were "play time". In this regard it is interesting to retrieve the words of a boy who defined himself as a poor reader – although academically he was considered a good reader – and as a video game fan and user:

> Jordi: A drawing appeared and I wanted to watch and touch it and so on… The doll was there to be destroyed. [The text] says to rip it apart and then you do it. I like this because sometimes you see so many letters that you get tired, you know? So many letters, letters, letters. And you keep on reading and if you're tired you move the doll or the lantern or whatever. I like it better. Maybe it's because I don't read much or I'm not so classic but it's useful for me to progress. (*iPoe*)

In all the explorations, perhaps because we were dealing with children and young adults with reasonably solid reading habits, we found that they perceived a certain tension between the story and the interactive elements, in such a way that they saw it as a choice: read or play? That is, they questioned whether they should stay focused on reading the story or become distracted with the interactivity which they perceived as a game.

In most cases they tended to prioritise the story, i.e. reading as they were used to doing. One of the teenage girls even tried to theorise by saying that for her all the resources looked like stage directions in a play, in the sense that they are in the margin: "Maria: I see it as something interactive so you don't get tired of reading but also like stage directions" (*Inanimate Alice*).

In search of a function for interactivity

As they progressed through the conversation, the participants in the reading sessions tried to find the meaning and function of the interactivity. We observed that they tended to detect its connection with the construction of the fiction (if it exists), but quite often they were incorrect in the explanations they provided due to lack of training in the possibilities of the resources. The case of *Inanimate Alice* chapter 2 is a clear example where two interactive proposals appear:

On the one hand, when the protagonist is looking for her parents, she intends to leave her house alone at night and has to dress appropriately to keep warm. In this scene the reader must select the pieces of clothing that the character has to put on in a certain order.

On the other hand, when the protagonist misses her parents she remembers the day when she designed a puzzle on her console to be solved by her father as a game before dinner. At this point, the reader is unable to move forward in the story until the bicycle puzzle is solved.

In response to these action proposals the readers wondered what point there was in doing it:

> Silvia: The one about the bike is very strange but the other one makes sense: the trousers, okay, the trousers.
>
> Maria: The one about the bike, what does it have to do with anything?
>
> Pau: I didn't understand the bike one very well.

In fact, the introduction of the bicycle puzzle creates a change of focalisation towards the perspective of Alice's father, i.e. it makes the reader live the experience of solving the puzzle in the same way as the father's character had to and is a means of evoking a pleasant memory of the protagonist. Because the readers understood it as a game, they gave more meaning to the puzzle with the pieces of clothing than to that of the bicycle, the opposite to the functionality they have in the fiction.

In the chapters that our students read of *Inanimate Alice* the interactive proposals are occasionally interspersed as the story progresses and certain actions are required to continue reading. And although they are reasonably integrated within the fiction, the fact that their appearance is occasional made the readers perceive them as a distracting sideline game. However, in another of the reading situations analysed, where the interaction places the reader clearly in the role of the author and not in an occasional way, the students showed much more enthusiasm, perhaps because the work had predisposed them in this regard from the beginning. The Catalan poetic work in question, *Les aventures de la Lala* (Lala's Adventures), involves the receiver being asked to build the text by selecting balloons, each containing a message that is built as they are clicked on. In this case the interaction is the basis of the work and it proposes a type of *constructive* participation on behalf of the reader (Ryan 2001). The analysis shows that the readers felt comfortable with this kind of participation where they were active agents in the construction of the work. However, it is worthy of note that this type of interactive participation primarily focuses on the generation of certain feelings and not on the comprehension of the text (Grillo 2013). This is in agreement with the statements made by some theorists that the expectations of interactive fiction is "the belief that our enjoyment of storytelling will rise to a higher power if instead of listening or watching passively we are able to interact with the story world, play the role of a character, and determine the development of the plot" (Ryan, Emerson, and Robertson eds. 2014: 292-293).

Interaction as a help to enter into the work

In parallel to the initial reactions of mental blank and the perception of the interactivity as alien to literature or as an expendable element, it is remarkable that one of the constants that emerged in the conversations was the feeling that digital resources were there to help to understand and to facilitate the reading because they made "you feel more involved in the work".[2] As a Poe reader commented: "Jordi: You read one thing and then you do it, you understand better". Perhaps the fact that they perceived it as a parallel element promoted this feeling.

Furthermore, when comparing digital literature with the experience of reading in print they showed that they perceived the interactive resource as something that made them live the story more closely: "Adriana: Because it's as if you were part of the story, because when you read a printed book you read and that's all, but here you have to do things" (*The Heart and the Bottle*). And another student confirms this idea by adding: "Sonia: In books you *see* what happens to the characters and what they do but you're not a part of it" (*The Heart and the Bottle*). In this sense, they compare it, correctly, to cinema, to the big screen, where: "Pau: You're inside the story and when the film ends you return to reality" (*Inanimate Alice*), in accordance with the statements of some scholars on the fact that cinema is the most immersive form of representation that exists regarding the representations in space made by the audience (Ryan 2001).

In short, our observations show a common initial reaction of surprise and mental blank at the interactive proposals inserted in the literary works as well as the perception that the interaction is a parallel element to the story and therefore dispensable, or it can play a clear role in helping to better understand or in feeling more involved in the stories. In addition, after some time conversing and motivated by the evidence and novelty of the digital resources, the participants overcame the sense of mental blank and assumed a perspective of seeking the function performed by these interactive proposals in the configuration of the story.[3]

---

[2] The perception that the interaction may help comprehension is complemented by the analysis of other multimodal elements which, according to the participants in all the discussions, signified that these works are aimed at children younger than them precisely because they facilitate reading.

[3] It is important to highlight some coincidences in these reactions regarding another multimodal element which cannot be analysed here due to lack of space. The music

So far we have seen some of the reactions and perceptions of the *traditional* reader regarding the digital elements exemplified in the interaction. Now we will turn our observation around to show how they integrated digitality in the evaluation of the construction of literary works. Do they realise that digitality forms a part of the construction of fiction?

Interpreting how works are built in digital format

Interpreting the meaning of literary works largely has to do with the ability to perceive the function performed by the different elements involved in the construction of the story. Also, the specificity of the digital literary work is based on expanding the resources that make up the story and that collaborate with the aesthetic experience of the subject "reader", the same as with literary conventions which can be modified by multimodal resources.

One of the narrative components most favourable to change in e-literature is temporality in all its various manifestations. In effect, the studies that have examined the differences between reading stories in print and reading them in digital format (e-book) point to this element as that which differentiates comprehension between both types of reading; those who read in digital format are less capable of following temporality in fiction (Mangen, Walgermo, and Brønnick 2013). Let us see how our readers perceived this by reviewing all the cases where they discerned the incidence of digital elements in the temporal construction of the literary works.

Diversion of attention to secondary elements: indications of the period of setting of the story

In the conversation on Poe's "The Tell-Tale Heart" the children showed that they detected the period of setting of the story "from the drawings", but not from the text. They perceived an aspect which is quite evident in the digital version of the tale but is not at all relevant to the story. In this case the digitality confused them, making them focus their attention on an aspect that holds no interest with regard to the sense of the story. In fact, this work is explained from the psychological "logic" of a deranged murderer which is the main interest of the story. The students tried insistently to determine the period of setting of the story, but when stating that it was the drawings that placed them in the temporal context, they

---

and sound effects caused a clear sense of initial discomfort and rejection in all the groups participating in the research because they were perceived as an added element and foreign to their idea of *reading* a fiction story, as well as the feeling that they served primarily to "decorate" and to help the reader feel part of the work, in accordance with one of the functions that they also attributed to the interaction.

added that there were almost no indications to show this, that there was a lack of information. Specifically, their comments were: "Marta: There aren't enough descriptions, some text is missing; the descriptions aren't good. [...] I need much more description to imagine it"; "Emma: So many images get in the way of describing the place, the time, the characters...". Notice that at no time do they contemplate that it is the author's intention not to provide precise information on the given contextualisation because of the intentionality of the story.

This case is an example of how digitality may cause confusion and divert attention towards secondary elements. This is probably the result of a poor transfer of the analogue text to the digital version, but it is also evidence that the transfer of printed book strategies to digital format can lead to misunderstandings and confusion which require teaching guidance.

Digitality as evidence of temporal changes: flashback in digital

In chapter 2 of *Inanimate Alice* a chronological change in the story occurs during a phone call. Our readers found it difficult to point out the signs but they eventually explained that they perceived it from the change in the music (which not only indicates recall but also evokes a change of scenario because "now it's Arabic music"), which is transformed in an obvious way by the zoom effect on the screen and the warm colours of the new Arabic scene as opposed to the colder ones in the narrative up to that point.

This is a case where multimodality helps the readers to place themselves within the parameters of the work. As previously mentioned, the very evident cases of digital resource incidence that are quite clearly indicated by music, as in this case, were detected by the readers.

Detection of resource functionality: the passage of time in the story

In *The Heart and the Bottle* there is a scene where the passage of time and the evolution of the main character are evoked through the interaction which requires dragging the image of the character upwards. This action causes animation of the image, a change in colours, and creates a flashback between two different times: the childhood of the girl protagonist, which is associated with an image of the father sitting in the dining room chair, and the maturity of the girl associated with an empty chair.

In this case, the functionality of the resources was detected and interpreted by the students participating in the discussion which they expressed in the following terms:

Adriana: It's as if she explains better what she's saying. The chair's empty, time goes on and the chair's still empty. The chair expresses the feelings.

Facilitator: The feelings or the passage of time?

Albert: It explains two different things, the fact that everything is darker…

Paula: It shows the feelings but also tells you about the passage of time because it gets darker. And night closes in. You just get the message, here it takes you a bit further… There are shadows, it's all dark… You get more into it, you can think about more things… You get the idea of the change she will make mentally.

It is surely not a coincidence that these students were those who enjoyed their classroom library iPads for five months and were already experts at discussing literary texts. This may mark the difference, but it may also be due to the fact that the application makes a good transition from the printed picturebook to the version with digital resources.

Lack of awareness of the possibilities of the digital resources and shared construction of the interpretation: time outside the story

This is one of the most innovative elements in digital fiction. It is not usual to converge the time of the story and the time of the act of reading through the use of words or to control the reading pace of the reader in printed works. In digital format the author can manipulate this condition much more through technology. Do the readers perceive it? How do they live it?

In chapter 1 of *Inanimate Alice* a coincidence in narrative time and reading time occurs in a scene where two characters in the story, Alice and her mother, travel by car in search of the father. To pass the time and calm her nerves the protagonist writes a list of things she would like to do: the screen shows how she writes them and therefore the reader not only reads the words on the list but follows her writing process. This causes a feeling of reality because the reader accompanies the character while she is performing the action. This also happens later when the protagonist sends photographs of flowers to her father and it is the reader who has to operate the camera to send them. The students discussed these episodes in a shy and insecure way without noticing this peculiarity of digital fiction. It is very difficult to bring this element into play in a printed text and therefore analogue readers are not used to it. Notably, however, they came to see this point indirectly through the reflection occasioned by the misunderstanding of the resource by one of the participants in the discussion. His friends explained to him that it is the author's intention that "you feel like you're in the car, just like the protagonist, looking for your father" (Silvia). While they did not stress the temporality, they did perceive that there were resources in this scene that cause a particular *immersion* in the story when they commented: "Maria: I was getting nervous too when they're in the car looking for the father and the girl's playing with the mobile phone and her mother tells her to stop it". Therefore, they identified with the mother because they had entered into the temporality proposed in the scene, accompanying the girl while she whiles away the time in the car when searching for her father.

These cases show that readers with little experience in reading digital works find it difficult to integrate the multimodality and other characteristics typical of these works in the interpretation of their functionality in the story. In fact, in the same way as occurs in literary discussions on printed works, readers focus more on the elements of the story than on those of the discourse, although it should be noted that digitality can contribute to literary education from the evidence of some of the resources from a metafictive perspective. At the same time it can also cause misunderstandings if there is no mediation to guide readers in detecting specific relevant digital pointers.

Final verifications

Firstly, in the cases analysed we found that the characteristics of digital fiction make it a special product which involves "re-learning to read" again. Even previous digital competences serve no purpose because the readers do not associate them with the function they can perform in fictional works and the same occurs with acquired textual reading skills because they can cause confusion.

In addition to this general finding, other points of reflection suggested by the results of the research include:

Factors favouring the introduction to digital literature

The emotional involvement of introduction to the works (feeling comfortable with the product) and the activation of interpretive competence are linked with some factors that have proven to be influential here:

Firstly, previous reading experience of digital literature, i.e., exposure to the product, predisposes the reader to understand how it works. Indeed, the young adults who read the two *Alice* chapters, at a given moment talked about how they enjoyed the second chapter more because: "Pau: You've already got used to the digital madness". Some of our readers said that printed and text-based literature allowed for the imagination of fictional worlds while digital was too obvious and impeded the activation of the imagination. In contrast, those who had contact for a few months with this type of product were able to perceive the digital contributions: "Valeria: It's true that the text makes you imagine and you see it, but in this one you feel like you're inside the story, it makes you see what happens" (*The Heart and the Bottle*).

Secondly, previous reading experience of other products that have similar characteristics to those of digital fiction – other fiction that includes the e-literature resources used – such as image, and familiarisation with other artistic codes such as music, was another influential factor. For example, our studies show that some of the readers who felt more comfortable with digital literature were those who had experience with video games. This point seems to have importance in the introduction to digital fiction and is consistent with other studies that also show the same relationship between other non-textual fiction and reading in digital format (Mangen 2008: 415).

Thirdly: the aspect of prior literary reading experience (reading habits) and previous interpretive experience. The participants in the literary discussions who were already experts in the analytical reflection of literature were more capable of adopting an interpretive perspective of the meaning of the work by detecting the function and intentionality of the digital elements.

Finally, we also found that the type of text clearly had an impact on the type of response and reading experience, but not as much on the perception of the digitality or on feeling comfortable with the work.

Tendency to transfer print reading habits to the digital device

The word was the element that defined literature for the non-expert readers in digital reading. They even stated that "when a book has more images than text to me it's no longer a book" (Jordi, *iPoe*). This confirms little familiarity with other languages and inexperience at integrating other codes in the reading and interpretation of literary works.

The representations of the literary product were strongly embedded in the children and young adults who participated in our studies and this caused mistrust and especially disorientation as well as strongly rooted reading routines. Therefore, their acquired baggage as analogue readers meant they had a very fossilised concept of what fiction reading is, and did not conceive the experience in digital format as proper reading.

Distancing and adoption of a reflective role

Digital elements caused surprise in the readers and this led to a distancing from the story, to the inability to fully "get into" the reading. But on the other hand we perceived that this situation led them to place themselves in a reflective-analytical position, or at least a questioning one, and therefore with a certain predisposition to reflection on the digital and multimodal elements. Indeed, the contrast between textual literary work and the untrustworthiness caused by the digitality in a literary work activated certain vigilance that fostered an opening towards an evaluative interpretation as long as there was someone nearby to guide and lead them towards it and overcome the possible interpretive deficiencies that turned the reading responses into timid descriptions of little assessment value.

Immersion in fiction

One of the characteristics of literature is the ability to make the reader feel immersed in the fiction, either as immersion in the textual world (spatial) in the narrated tense, or through emotional reactions regarding what happens to the characters (Ryan 2001).

Although the reader who is accustomed to printed literature is distanced from the work by digitality, we also noticed that digital resources cause a sense of involvement with the fictional world in the cases where these resources are very clear and obvious.

In our explorations the readers explicitly stated this feeling of immersion related to digitality at specific moments, caused by the interactive manipulation of a certain element (*The Heart and the Bottle*) or due to the feeling produced by the convergence of certain ambient elements (music, sounds, images and perspective) in clearly defined situations. For example, in one of the scenes in *Inanimate Alice* when the children reported they felt like "going into" the work to tell the protagonist not to risk leaving the house. Or when they said they were scared when Alice was alone in the snow, just like the character – and all of this was caused by the effects of the multimodality.

Educational implications

The fact that literature is still currently textual and linear for most school-going generations should not let us forget the familiarisation of this population with the codes that form part of digital literature in other manifestations and, above all, in everyday virtual communication. Understanding and interpreting the current world involves being able to read and understand messages produced with a variety of codes (text, image, sound, hypertext, etc.) and interactions via the Internet increasingly occur without the need for the written word. In this context, the interpretive richness provided by digitality integrated into literary work highlights how urgent it is to *educate* citizens in the interpretation of the different codes that combine to create the aesthetic construction of the product.

For this reason, and taking into account the findings of this research with inexperienced readers in digital literary reading, we highlight the main reference points for introducing children and young adults to this type of literary product.

It seems necessary that schools should not only expand their range of fictional and artistic resources, but also provide continuous exposure to digital literature as one of the most effective ways to promote familiarity with the conventions of digital literature and for its acceptance as a personal reading possibility that provides a different type of experience to that of the printed text.

Also, effective means should be introduced to facilitate the access keys to multimedia, interactive and hypertext messages and products. Not only through the integration of digital literature in literary discussions – which are currently carried out with respect to printed works – but also through specific activities to provide training to understand the function and possibilities of the integration of music, image, movement, lighting effects, colour and interactivity as conventions for the creation of literary fiction as well as facilitate the integration of non-linearity as future possibilities for emergent readers. In this regard advantage should be taken of the distancing and the reflective role caused by the product to perform an analytical and interpretive reading.

And it seems important from the point of view of teaching guidance to consider the importance of the different reading levels. To overcome the initial confusion, and for digital works to be perceived as reading, requires the introduction of *rereading* and is much more necessary than with printed works.

The main challenge for facilitators is to make it understood that this is essentially a very different product that integrates text, images, movement, music, sound, interactivity, hypertextuality, etc., and that all these elements combine as a whole to tell a fiction story. In short, in the classroom environment it should be borne in mind that e-literature offers a particular reading experience which is possibly more sensorial, more immersive and less demanding with regard to abstraction, but is more focused on the ability to diversify interpretive skills.

Works Cited

Primary Works Cited

Jeffers, Oliver. *The Heart and the Bottle*. New York: Penguin Group, 2011. iPad edition.

Kühne, Catalina. *The One & Only*. Ill. Marco Antonio Fernández. México D.F.: CIDCLI, 2013. iPad edition.

Poe, Edgar Allan. *iPoe Collection*, Vol. I. David García Farés. Barcelona: Play Creatividad, 2012. iPad edition.

Pullinger, Kate. *Inanimate Alice*. London: The Bradfield Company, 2005ff. Web. 15 Mar. 2015.

Rubio Faus, Berta. *Les aventures de la Lala*. Web. 31 Mar. 2015.

Secondary Works Cited

Arizpe, Evelyn, and Morag Styles. *Children Reading Pictures: Interpreting Visual Texts*. London: Routledge Falmer, 2003. Print.

Clark, Dennis T. *et al.* "A qualitative assessment of the Kindle e-book reader: Results from initial focus groups." *Performance Measurement and Metrics*, 9.2 (2008): 118-129. Print.

Colomer, Teresa, and Marina Fittipaldi, eds. *La literatura que acoge. Inmigración y lectura de álbumes*. Caracas/Barcelona: Banco del Libro-GRETEL, 2012. Print.

Fry, Donald. *Children talk about books*. Philadelphia: Open University Press, 1985. Print.

Grillo, Juanita. "Entre la lectura literaria y el juego digital. Respuestas lectores a obres digitales en 5º de primaria." Diss. Universitat Autònoma de Barcelona, 2013. Print.

Hillesund, Terje. "Digital Reading spaces: how expert readers handle books, the web and electronic paper." *First Monday*, 15.4-5 (2010). Web. 12 Apr. 2015.

Larson, Lotta C. "Digital Readers: The Next Chapter in E-Book Reading and Response." *The Reading Teacher*, 64.1 (2010): 15-22. Print.

Mangen, Anne. "Hypertext fiction reading: haptics and immersion." *Journal of Research in Reading*, 31.4 (2008): 404-419. Print.

Mangen, Anne, Bente R. Walgermo and Kolbjørn Brønnick. "Reading linear texts on paper versus computter secreen: effects on reading comprehension." *International Journal of Educational Research*, 58 (2013): 61-68. Print.

Meek, Margaret. *How texts teach what readers learn*. Stroud: Thimble Press, 1988. Print.

—. "Why response?" *Reading and response*. Eds. Mike Hayoe, and Stephen Parker. Milton Keynes: Open University Press, 1990. 1-12. Print.

Miall, David S. and Teresa Dobson. "Reading hypertext and the experience of literature." *Journal of Digital Information*, 2.1 (2001). Web. 01 Apr. 2015.

Modir, Ladan, *et al.* "Appraisal of Reader's Role in Revolutionary Potential of Hypertext Fiction." *Life Science Journal*, 9.4 (2012): 5244-5246. Print.

Patterson, Nancy G. "Hypertext and the Changing Roles of Readers." *The English Journal*, 90.2 (2000): 74-80. Print.

Rosenblatt, Louise M. *Literature as exploration*. New York: Appleton-Century-Crofts, 1938. Print.

Ryan, Marie-Laure. *Narrative as virtual reality: immersion and interactivity in literature and electronic media*. Baltimore: Johns Hopkins University Press, 2001. Print.

Ryan, Marie-Laure; Lori Emerson, and Benjamin J. Roberston, eds. *The Johns Hopkins Guide to Digital Media*. Baltimore: Johns Hopkins University Press, 2014. Print.

Sarland, Charles. *Young people Reading: culture and response*. Milton Keynes: Open University Press, 1991. Print.

Sipe, Lawrence R. *Storytime: Young children's literary understanding in the classroom*. New York: Teachers College Press, 2008. Print.

Yilmaz, M. Betül *et al*. "A comparison of sixth grade students' Reading comprehension on two different digital formats." *2014 World Conference on Educational Media and Technology*, 23-27 June 2014. Tampere: Association for the Advancement of Computing in Education (AACE), 2014. 702-707. Web. 03 Feb. 2015.

Digital Migrations: Exploratory Research on Children's E-Lit Reading Profiles

Lucas RAMADA PRIETO
Universitat Autònoma de Barcelona

Lara REYES LÓPEZ
Universitat Autònoma de Barcelona

Introduction. Context and framework of study

The appearance of digital devices in the literary reading practices of children and young people is a relatively recent event that converts this field of study into a growing new area – a growth that has increased since the arrival of tablet devices early in 2010. This leads us to believe that the generations of children born in the last four or five years will no doubt be digitally trained readers. They will have a digital device for reading and will have lived with it all their lives. They will use it equally or more so than print editions and will know all its possibilities. We need to analyse the type of readers they will be and what effect their baseline digital training will have.

Despite this emergence we find ourselves in a moment of transition in which the students, in spite of their social coexistence with technology, continue to receive an extremely analogue education which may condition the forms of integration, especially with regard to electronic literature, a corpus which is still in its infancy. For this reason our exploratory research takes place in the context of a group of students aged between eleven and twelve years old in a school on the outskirts of a city in the metropolitan area of Barcelona, with an adverse cultural and socio-economic reality and with an adult population that has mainly only completed primary education. This presupposed a very low level of technological familiarisation with electronic devices such as digital tablets, although this was a positive aspect insofar as it enabled us to observe the evolutionary process of familiarisation, opinions and reading comprehension when using digital devices. The students of the group, however, had spent four school years receiving education focused on reading training with the same teacher, a member of the GRETEL research group.

This situation meant that all the students of the group were involved, active readers with consolidated reading habits and good literary knowledge. This starting point was also especially interesting for our study given that we were looking for different approaches from mixed reading profiles regarding the electronic reading experience, but with consolidated reading habits and the ability to discuss the works they had read. We were therefore in a privileged position to explore in depth their tendencies as digital readers.

We introduced five electronic devices containing sixteen digital literary works into the classroom library for a period of five months. From January to June during the 2012/13 school year the students of the group were given the possibility to freely explore the selected apps during the daily half-hour reading period and to comment on these apps in the conversations on the texts they had read during the week.[1]

Research methodology

With the groundwork now completed, we decided to adopt an ethnographic qualitative-descriptive perspective for the study. With this perspective we could centre our attention on the comparison between the analogue reader profile of four students in the group and the first conclusions on their possible digital reader profile. We are aware that the limited size of the sample means our work is exploratory in nature, and also eliminates any wish to establish generalisations or conclusions. Our intention is simply to be able to list tendencies and initial observations in a specific environment using readers with a solid traditional reading base and with some experience with electronic literature. For this reason these partial results must take into account the conditioning factors of this starting point, although it is hoped that these may form the basis for future explorations along the lines of comparing profiles of analogue and digital readers and thus be able to contribute to the didactic orientation of work in the classroom.

With the objective clear and the digital classroom library functioning alongside its printed counterpart, we set about selecting four readers for

1 As well as digitised works and e-books, a selection of sixteen literary apps for iPad were included which made significant use of the specifically electronic properties in their construction of literary meaning. In this way the chosen corpus was made up of works which made use of, for example, narrative bifurcation as a way of implicating the reader in the creation of the story, e.g., *Underground Kingdom*, and others that based a large part of their artistic effect on the creation of immersive environments through the use of sound, and aesthetic proposals such as *iPoe Collection*, Vol. I, etc.

our research. If we used the quantitative standards typically used in reader sociology (Manresa 2013) all the readers in our group would be defined as quantitatively strong, as well as possessing many other discursive and evaluation skills; there did however exist sufficient differences between them to be able to qualitatively differentiate two profiles and make a selection based on this.

The two profiles that we tracked were: the strong reader profile and the weak reader profile. For our research the strong reader profile was assigned to the readers with greater and more diverse reading experience, with more confidence, fluency and solid argumentative ability to explain their opinions on the fictional works they read. The weak profile, on the other hand, was assigned to the readers with a more enclosed and less complex reading experience as far as the typology of the works they had read; they were also less confident and had more doubts and difficulties when it came to explaining their point of view on the fictional works they had read. Once these characteristics were defined we chose four students to take part in the research. Within each profile one student had more command of and/or interest in the digital device and the other had a tendency to reject it.

From this starting point we decided that, in order to achieve substantial exploratory depth, the ideal method based on the needs of the research would be the format of a semi-structured interview recorded on video for subsequent analysis. We also decided to carry out these interviews in pairs to facilitate interaction between the subjects and the interviewer. The first of these was held at the beginning of February after the students had had one month to familiarise themselves with the electronic devices. We decided that on a thematic level this first interview would be based more on the dynamic of how they related to these tablets rather than specifically focusing on the works they contained.

The second interview was arranged three months later with the electronic devices then totally integrated into the dynamic of the class and with a thematic focus much more centred on the constructive properties that define the new digital literary paradigm aimed at emergent readers. Despite the innate heterogeneity of this new corpus of works, their poetics is made up of three basic lines that were taken into account in the creation of the guidelines for this second talk with the research subjects: 1) the loss of linearity in the textual discourse which decisively conditions the reading process (Landow 2006); 2) the incitement of the digital work for the reader to actively participate which reconfigures the pre-existing roles of literary communication (Ryan 2001); and 3) the input of different expressive elements in the digital literary creative process such as sound and moving images, considerably modifying the receptive processes and requirements demanded of the student (Turrión 2014). This breakdown of the literary characteristics of digital texts was used to make the semi-structured script for the second interview, as well as the necessary exercise of the analytical reading of the works to which the students had access in order to focalise the reflections of the subjects with specific texts.

On the analysis of content

As previously mentioned, the purely exploratory intentions of the research, which was not aimed at reaching generalised conclusions but at opening up interesting new roads for future research, entailed making a specific methodological choice: when it came to analysing and collecting the material from the four interviews we opted for a procedure focused on describing with certain flexibility the digital reading profiles of the four chosen subjects and not on creating a fixed and generalised categorisation. The lack of specific studies within the field of the sociology of reading, which does not yet appear to have begun to examine the specific question of the reading of digital literature, meant that we could not use a pre-existing categorisation with which to relate the results we extracted to the area of didactic literary research. Furthermore, the majority of research that analyses the introduction of touch-sensitive devices into school contexts does so from a perspective mainly focused on the study of reading and writing skills (Hutchison, Beschorner, and Schmidt-Crawford 2011).

However, with the intention of trying to fill this theoretical vacuum which overshadowed the interpretive process of the interview transcriptions, we chose to look at the field of Game Studies for research on typologies of users and players. We believe this theoretical twist is justified due to the fact that the new paradigm of electronic literature is becoming unquestionably ludified by the application of "elements and mechanics of games in order to engage a user in a task outside of the game context" (Ferro, Walz, and Greuter 2013: 1) which not only modify the work itself but also the attitudes and behaviours that the reader develops during the act of digital reading.

In this respect, the work undertaken by Clark and Duimering (2006) that collected verbalised game experiences was especially useful for our research. This work showed the relationship between what motivates and feels a virtual player when sharing a game situation with other players, on the one hand, and what motivated our research subjects to read in the company of others and enjoy the reading process socially, on the other.

This attitudinal reflection on the gaming process has also allowed us to use the classic categorisation of videogame profiles as used by Bartle (2003) where, in his study, users are divided up based on their behavioural tendencies. From the initial classification of the North American researcher, after eliminating the underlying inter/intrapersonal competitiveness which can be present in videogames and which as yet does not exist in the world of electronic literature, we successfully took two interesting concepts for our descriptive taxonomy: the idea of the *socialiser* who looks for interaction with others during the activity, and the *explorer* who prefers the exhaustive and individual discovery of the fictional proposal. The use of these categories was not as rigid as seen in Bartle's article; instead we chose to adapt them as a means of characterising attitudes from isolated verbalisations and not as a generaliser of an entire stable profile of digital reading.

We also took advantage of the categorisation table of Poels, de Kort and Ijsselsteijn (2007) for the verbalised experiences of videogame players based on the qualitative analysis of four focus group sessions. This was especially interesting for us due to the correlations found between the Dutch study and our own analyses which was clearly in line with other important studies within the universe of digital literature such as the theory of fictional immersion (Murray 1997; Ryan 2001), the paradigm modification of the digital literary work as a programmed and cybernetic product (Aarseth 1997; Hayles 2008), or the frustrations that digital readers can experience due to design or the disruptive proposals made by the creators (Ensslin 2007; Landow 2006).

This heterogeneous, multidisciplinary background allowed us a certain assurance and confidence when facing the exploratory and descriptive characterisation of the digital reading profiles which we present here.

Descriptive analysis of the profiles

Antonio

As an analogue reader we could define Antonio as a weak reader as regards the variety and typology of texts that he enjoys, despite the quantity of reading that he has accumulated which is slightly below that of his other classmates. His reading pathway is characterised by realist works, with characters very similar to himself and with simple, uncomplicated plots. He finds it very difficult to understand any complex fictional mechanisms. For these reasons he is drawn to read works that contain a lot of illustrations, showing a marked quantitative tendency towards reading picturebooks.

Another of his defining characteristics is his insecurity as a reader. He needs to reinforce and to be reinforced in what he knows in order to move forward towards more complex interpretive stages. On the other hand he tends to gain great benefit from the competence of the others when they express opinions on the books they have read and shows great interest when listening to the answers of the other readers. Precisely one of his potentialities as a reader is due to the curiosity he expresses when presented with something new. The insecurity that he has when expressing what he has understood, lived or felt when reading a work disappears when it comes to his desire to experience everything. In fact he experiences much more than he verbalises, and moreover, he shows no signs of reticence or preconceived ideas although he does normally allow himself to be influenced by the tendencies of the group.

When we begin to analyse the material obtained from Antonio in the interviews and start to try and reconstruct his digital profile, we rapidly become aware of the complexity of the new literary scenario and of the modifications that this implies when considering the new act of reading that interaction with digital literary apps supposes.

Without doubt this was a student with an unquestionable technophile tendency (possibly conditioned by the difficulties he had to access technology in his private life), which only gave rise to negative considerations, and then only in a limited way, towards those works within the corpus that were either simple digitalisations or were texts whose aesthetic elements showed an imbalance towards the purely written linguistic aspect. He was in fact the only subject interviewed who perceived the act of reading digitised books on an iPad as a technical improvement due to the possibilities to manipulate the image offered by the device, such as the zoom option. Even so, as we have already mentioned, his electronic literature preferences were never for e-books and similar devices but were regularly prioritised towards works that tended more to the use of purely digital constructive properties.

This preferred tendency towards more gamified works did not totally eclipse his ways of reading inherited from printed literature, and his inclination towards realist type texts with which the student felt more identified was made evident in his enjoyment of the work based on the question of poverty *The Unwanted Guest*. The expressive equilibrium of the application which cleverly combines moving images, ambient sound effects, oral narration and a powerful story inherited from the Jewish tradition, without doubt helped a reader like Antonio to enjoy a "physically" passive reading such as this with complete devotion. This fact allows us to relativise the sometimes apocalyptic affirmations on the subjugation of the unhurried skills of literary enjoyment in favour of the ludic dynamics of fictional digitality.

Having said this, it was evident that this student looked for works within the available corpus which offered him the possibility of more interactive entertainment, such as *Underground Kingdom*, whose branched narrative structure in a "choose your own adventure" style, offered an unquestionably participative and enjoyable environment:

Antonio: I liked it a lot because you can, you have to get into it, you have to put yourself in the place of the character, you have to put yourself in their shoes, and you have to think up the ending: you have to decide. [...] I decide which page I go to.[2]

His difficulties in stating conceptual explanations do not hide the fact that what caught his attention during the reading of the text is this modification of literary communication in which the reader finds himself involved during the narrative process. The student took this modification on board right from the start and we must consider it a competence achievement, taking into account, as we will see further on in the analysis of the digital profile of Adriana (an outstanding analogue reader), that not all students are able to enjoy, or even understand, the possibilities offered by the new constructive forms of the electronic literary paradigm. This was the case with Antonio who demonstrated the ability to enjoy the socialisation of the interactive reading process (Clarke, and Duimering 2006), showing special interest in sharing the decision-making with his reading classmates:

Researcher: How do you prefer to do it?

Antonio: With someone else.

Researcher: Almost more like a game, right?

Antonio: Yes, because then we both decide. Which page do we choose?

Researcher: Of course, it's almost like a videogame sometimes isn't it?

Antonio: Because it's like it makes you... [he makes effusive gestures of enjoyment and emotion].

On the other hand he also showed what game-based studies have called exploratory desires when wanting to try out all the possibilities the digital world has to offer within its sometimes complex textual architecture, as we see in this interaction during the interviews where the student explains to the interviewer how he navigated through the different pages and branches that made up the complex structure of the aforementioned *Underground Kingdom*.

Researcher: Ah, and did you want to know what had happened in the other part? [Making reference to the other branch of the story.]

Antonio: Yes.

Researcher: And how did you do it? Did you finish one or did you go back and...?

Antonio: I finished one, looked forward to see if there was a number nine and if I saw there wasn't one, I went back and when I saw I had finished number nine I went forward again and continued.

2 English translations of all quotations in other languages have been provided by Tim Mc Quaid.

Researcher: Did you realise that up at the top on the right it told you how many endings you had explored?

Antonio: Yes

Researcher: And would you have liked to have known all the endings?

Antonio: Yes!

In short, Antonio's profile reflects the complexity of the new literary paradigm that adds new opportunities for reading enjoyment; opportunities which fall outside the consideration of traditional education and which we must begin to contemplate and take advantage of in cases such as this where students have an active predisposition towards interaction and literary gamification but also have educational needs and require facilitators to help them go beyond the simple external ludic level.

Celia

Celia is the other weak reader chosen for the research. Her reading speed is very good but her interpretation rarely goes further than the literal; she has little ability for abstraction and connection between works to establish patterns which repeat themselves or become more complex. This difficulty for inferential comprehension means that some literary elements create a "noise" that is difficult for her to overcome and therefore she adopts a strategy to eliminate them. Nevertheless, she chooses the most popular novels in the class, despite the fact that these present a challenge for her and are well above her comprehension abilities, and makes the effort to understand and interpret the essence of the content in order to be able to talk about them during the moments of social conversation on the works. She has difficulties in expressing and defending her opinion about what she has read, although she searches out efficient strategies to overcome these weaknesses such as positioning herself in the role of facilitator. As a reader and a student she has insecurities which unlike Antonio, she does not want to show. This fact frequently makes it difficult for the facilitators to approach and support her.

What is of great interest when we delve more deeply into the consideration of Celia's digital reader profile is the evolution in her attitude between the first interview in February and the second, three months later. Later on we will reflect on the possible causes that brought about this change, but it is especially surprising to observe how she went from total rejection of any type of modification of the "traditional" literary modes to evaluating very positively the interactive scenes and multimodal environments in the apps we offered.

As we have mentioned, during the first interview Celia was totally opposed to any type of proposal that involved the use of a specifically electronic poetics. She constantly compared the printed world to the digital and prioritised the digitised works included in the corpus over the literary apps:

> Celia: For me it's been an experience, it is an experience having the iPads in the classes, well, in the class because, we read digitally but, on paper as well but what I like most is reading on paper because it inspires me more, I feel happier with paper than with the iPad because the iPads distract me because they have effects, the sounds – and it's a bit more difficult for me.

Negative reactions such as these (Poels, de Kort, and Ijsselsteijn 2007) were repeated on up to eight occasions in the twenty-five minutes that the interview lasted. From her words we were able to extract little more than this continuous adverse reaction. As we have seen at the beginning of this section, her desire to belong to the reading group that formed the class environment, added to her interpretive difficulties which on occasions meant she needed to make an extra effort to keep up with the generally high level of the others, was perhaps one of the motives that led her to react against the new threat that the considerable modification of the new digital corpus implied.

On the other hand, during the second and much more fruitful conversation that we had in May, the student's attitude was diametrically opposed. The few criticisms she offered concerning the specifically digital modes of literary creation were all totally justified by the lack of significance that they had for her within the general design of the story – for example, the interactive audio animations in *A Chest Full of Monsters*. She was, however, able to create a complete discussion around the immersive possibilities offered by works such as *iPoe Collection*, Vol. I:

> Celia: Yes, I don't know, I like films like horror films a bit more, books that are more frightening, I like them more and even more now, with the background because you're imagining yourself and you're alone and the background is there. Now you are really in the book, aren't you? You go right inside it and it scares you.
>
> Researcher: Of course, in this case, the music and all that draws you more into the story.
>
> Celia: Yes, because for me without the sound, yes it's okay, this and that happens but so what? I don't get drawn into it.

Accepting the multimodal setting of this work as a strengthening feature of the fictional experience is one of the aspects most emphasised by the student and possibly reinforces the idea mentioned earlier regarding the fear that this new characteristic for literary enjoyment caused her *a priori*. When she enjoyed narratives that made balanced use of this creative procedure, the previous fear or animosity felt towards the works turned into explicit enthusiasm on numerous occasions. And even some of the productions with more radical narrative variations such as the adaptation of *The Heart and the Bottle*, whose interactive layer is integrated into the very construction of the story, were evaluated positively by the student. She even contrasted her evaluations with other apps which in her opinion made a banal use of the same characteristic.

In short, Celia makes us question the importance of the initial emotional confrontation of the reader when presented with an unknown product such as digital literature, but it also shows us the importance of facilitation and the importance of the selection of the corpus when introducing texts that require new reading and decoding skills. It makes us realise that the readers' perception of creative significance is crucial to the integration of diversified corpuses and also multiplies the ways in which these are enjoyed. This also opens the door to reflection upon the possibilities (and dangers) that multimodality presents for the fictional experience of the reader, bringing them closer to, or frightening them off from, the created possible world, depending on factors such as predisposition or the balance in design.

Iván

Iván is a strong reader in terms of the quantity and quality of the works he reads. He reads and tries everything, his tastes are very diverse and he does not confine himself to any one genre. He is a constant reader with an established habit, has a great capacity for synthesis and explaining and justifying his analysis of the works. Discreetly and prudently he formulates and develops interesting debating points on the texts, he favours the multiple reading response and works through many approaches to the texts. He knows in each case how to choose the most relevant literary elements of the work under discussion and also has the ability to help other readers focus on these elements in the works he has read. He is a very social reader and naturally tends to combine both individual and group reading depending on the reading requirements of the moment.

This transversal nature of Iván's reading skills, which go further than a mere specific knowledge of the literary communicative system (which he also masters) and have more to do with his attitudes and ability for diversified enjoyment and the socialisation of the experience, greatly helped him to adapt to this new literary corpus. The interviews showed this desire for knowledge and exploration that he now applied to the digital field and its creative possibilities. We can see certain analogies with Antonio in this technophile impulse, but the big difference between both profiles is Iván's enormous conceptual depth; he was always aware of the quality and literary balance of the works without renouncing the enjoyment that they could provide him:

Iván: I think that in *The Zombie* [refers to *A Chest Full of Monsters*], it's improved, what I mean is it's better, because as the story is also very simple, well the effects, I think that they accompany it because the story is very… I don't know, very childish, well I liked these things, the effects because they also make you laugh more and well…

Researcher: They add a little to it, is that right? Because if not, it would be-

Iván: Because if not the story is… I don't know.

Researcher: But would the effects make you go back two or three times to the tale or – ?

Iván: Well perhaps if I was reading it with someone else yes, but if you are reading it alone, no.

This extract from the interviews shows not only his ability to reflect on the pertinence of the more ancillary properties that make up part of the electronic corpus but also his skill of knowing how to frame each work in appropriate reading situations in order to enjoy them, making the ideal combination for his reading profile, moving easily between socialisation, exploration and fictional immersion:

Iván: Well, I liked reading *The Zombie* [refers to *A Chest Full of Monsters*] with my classmate Álex, because it's more like a fun story that I like to share with someone, because I am… I think I'm quite a fun person and I share my happiness, but on the other hand, *The Unwanted Guest* doesn't have so many special effects, and the story isn't so funny, I prefer to read it myself individually, not with someone else.

This procedural flexibility always linked to the search for enjoyment was also reflected in the exhaustiveness with which he investigated the corpus on offer, not only the works as individual products but as a group. This made him, along with Antonio, one of the students who read the greatest number of apps. Despite being in a school environment where the literary selection is pre-chosen, as previously mentioned, Iván showed no need for "authorisation" to explore the different digital products. He was led by both recommendations from his schoolmates as well as his own initiative:

Iván: Well, I, as I said before I'm guided a lot by my schoolmates but I also really like…, to take a risk, what I mean is: What's this here? What is this book? What's it about? Well that sort of thing.

Researcher: In other words, you would prefer to have a lot of apps even though many of them were bad and then decide yourself, or would you prefer that there were less and… an equal mix, is that it?

Iván: Well, neither a lot nor a few, I think that, maybe, two or three more than the iPad had, which were half and half, like *The Zombie* [refers to *A Chest Full of Monsters*], and other better ones like *The Unwanted Guest* because I like to take a risk and see what the story is like.

This fact, which at first sight may appear superficial, becomes essential in this difficult and gestational area of current electronic literature where the lack of adult mediation is the norm and too often dangerous technophobic prejudices affect the innocent enjoyment to which we all have a right. However, in the educational context superficial fun should never be seen as an aim in itself but instead a starting point from which to influence interpretive depth; this is what differentiates Iván from Antonio, his enormous capacity for analytical precision, the result of highly developed literary reading competences with printed books which allowed him to very precisely evaluate in an explicit way the significant pertinence of the poetic use of the constructive properties of the works. This student, for example, had no difficulty in understanding the diverse forms of integration of the interactive layers (inside and outside the narrative; with and without aesthetic-narrative value), or in criticising examples of a multimodal environment such as those in *Mi vecino de abajo* (My Downstairs Neighbour), which far from bringing the fictional world nearer to the reader, generated a type of uneasy dissonance which makes the reader turn off the sound on the device.

Clearly the definition of a good digital profile would appear to be complicated by the heterogeneity of the proposals and the different layers of enjoyment that these offer (was this not already the case with printed literature?), but we believe that subjects like Iván nowadays have the necessary combination of competences in order to interpret the new literary poetics of the electronic medium.

Adriana

Adriana is the other strong reader chosen for our research sample. She shares with Iván the enthusiasm, determination and passion for entering the literary world. Nevertheless she is more demanding and verbalises that she only wants "quality" printed works, clearly refusing "lesser" literature, considering that they use effects (smells, tabs…) to attract readers but which do not add anything more than this superficiality. She is very self-assured about her choices and her reading history and of her ability to discuss a point of view with solid and well-structured motives. As with Iván, she uses different literary elements to talk about the works and her choice of these tends to be totally in agreement with the most relevant elements of each one. Her depth of analysis, contrast, argument and presentation of the texts is very solid and mature, but at the same time she is a very empathetic reader, capable of listening and changing her point of view as well as being willing to benefit from the competence of others.

In the digital realm, as a natural extension of her analogue profile, Adriana defines herself as an almost liturgical literary traditionalist and this does not allow her to consider reading as anything other than the pre-formed idea she has of it:

> Adriana: Well, I don't know, maybe for some people… We already have the habit of reading and we've got the enthusiasm, and people that maybe didn't have that would be more keen to read because they're reading on an iPad, right? Maybe through this they would also get into it. But, I don't know, I, the truth is I feel a bit uncomfortable reading, because I prefer to read these scanned books on paper because of what I said before and it's just that the other books, well, I don't know, for example, I like the story in *The Unwanted Guest* and I like the special effects as well, not like the zombie one [refers to *A Chest Full of Monsters*] which distracts you [she makes a gesture of touching with her hand], it's just that, and then it just repeats the same sequence, and well I liked that one, but I don't find it the same as real reading, for me reading is reading a book, sitting down and reading a real book… a paper book. For me I don't see the point of the iPad.

As we can see, her technophobia even tends towards romanticism, associating reading with the idea of paper and book, and one could think that she has an irrational rejection towards any type of electronic proposal. However this is not so, and despite continuous criticism and shunning of digital works (there are more than fifteen entries in the transcriptions categorised as negative responses) her attacks are made in a justified discourse based on her unequivocal idea of literature as essentially a solitary act, unhurried and preferably with works of "contrasted" quality, all properties which the digital corpus cannot or does not attempt to offer. Within this argument Adriana rates more highly the works based on more traditional narrations such as *The Unwanted Guest*, whereas the native digital works such as *The Numberlys* or *A Chest Full of Monsters*, suffer full frontal attacks or are rated as non-literary entertainment: "Adriana: Well, the one I liked best was [*The*] *Numberlys*, where you had to make up the story yourself, I didn't see it as a game for entertainment, but neither did I see it as reading".

However it became crystal clear when we talked about the branched narrative of *Underground Kingdom* just how limiting such a restricted literary perspective as that held by this student can be. Compared to a supposedly weak reader such as Antonio, Adriana was unable to understand that the fictional proposal of the work was totally focused on the coexistence of possible worlds and in the exploration of these through interaction and the choice of narrative branches – she did not even realise that there was a counter at the top of the interface that counted the number of endings explored. She focused her activity instead on the search for "the real story", the most coherent and extensive narrative proposal and that which all the other possibilities offered had to be based on, which for her were nothing more than secondary distractions for a different type of reader:

> Adriana: I think so, I think that as well as that, I don't know, they do it so that you understand, well, if you want this ending well fine, here it is, but I got the feeling that there was a story, a normal story, that you couldn't choose and then they added that to add other endings that the reader might like better, but those endings were shorter and more limited, and then you get away a bit from the main story, so what I was trying to do was not get it wrong and to follow the central story all the time.

To perceive exploration within branched narrations as a balancing act where one has to try not to get it wrong is without doubt a perceptive limitation of electronic poetics and something to be taken very much into account when talking about reader profiles that are so attached to the linear (almost novelesque) literary tradition.

If we truly intend to include the competence diversification that this new scenario requires in the reading development of our students, we must make an in-depth analysis of factors such as the attitudinal predisposition towards gamified literary proposals that may make excellent readers such as Adriana not wish to, and thus not be able to, enjoy interesting aesthetic experiences. We are aware that the existing corpus is still questionable in terms of its literary quality, and this conditions many of the conclusions that we could draw, but transversally this study outlines a series of very interesting behaviours for the future of literary didactics, one of the most interesting being the difference in standpoints that Antonio and Adriana exhibit when given a text such as *Underground Kingdom*.

Conclusions

This exploratory research on the comparison between the analogue reader profile and the digital reader profile of primary school children has allowed us to observe their stances regarding this new form of literary reading, the constructive properties of which it is composed and the students' assessment of the children's digital literary corpus. The analysis has allowed us to establish some basic points to reflect upon for future research.

First of all, we can clearly see the transference of traditional metaliterary reflective abilities to the new realm of children's electronic literature. The two children with a strong profile clearly made much more profound comments with respect to almost all the subjects on which they were asked. This predicts an ideal scenario for the coexistence of both types of texts within reading training and underlines the need to study whether, conversely, e-lit can encourage the development of analogue reading competence.

On the other hand we can discern that electronic literature sustains certain more ludic and exploratory attitudes during the act of reading, both for the traditionally strong readers as well as for those that did not see this possibility in the printed corpus. This opens the doors for research into new reading typologies, similar to studies related to the world of gamification; it also alludes to the possibilities of a new digital corpus for a certain type of analogue reader that is more reticent to reflective reading.

Finally, it is essential to select the digital corpus. In this sense, the study shows the need for facilitators to have sufficient tools to identify the inherent constructive elements of this type of literature (music, movement, interactivity, etc.), and to be able to evaluate each work to see if these elements are significant or if they distort the meaning of the story through mere decoration. One of the clear effects that we have been able to show in the analysis is that the reader profiles that are less prepared for literary abstraction become disoriented when confronted with these literary properties, which in general appeared only to serve as entertainment with the pretext of literary text.

Works Cited

Primary Works Cited

Jeffers, Oliver. *The Heart and the Bottle.* New York: Penguin Group. 2011. iPad edition.

Joyce, William. *The Numberlys*. Shreveport: Moonbot Studios, 2012. iPad edition.

Lluch, E. *A Chest Full of Monsters.* Alzira: Bromera, 2012. iPad edition.

Nesquens, Daniel. *Mi vecino de abajo*. Madrid: Ediciones SM, 2011. iPad edition.

O'Rogers, Jacqueline *The Unwanted Guest.* British Columbia: Moving Tales, 2012. iPad Edition.

Poe, Edgar Allan. *iPoe Collection*, Vol. I. Ill. David García Farés. Barcelona: Play Creatividad, 2012. iPad edition.

Underground Kingdom. Visual Baker. 2013. iPad edition.

Secondary Works Cited

Aarseth, Espen J. *Cybertext: Perspectives on Ergodic Literature*. Baltimore: Johns Hopkins UP, 1997. Print.

Bartle, Richard A. "Hearts, Clubs, Diamonds, Spades: Players Who Suit MUDs." *Mud.co.uk*. n.p., 1996. Web. 18 Mar. 2015.

Clark, Delwin, and P. Robert Duimering. "How Computer Gamers Experience the Game Situation: A Behavioral Study." *Computers in Entertainment*, 4.3 (2006). Web. 20 Feb. 2015.

Ensslin, Astrid. *Canonizing Hypertext: Explorations and Constructions*. London: Continuum International, 2007. Print.

Ferro, Lauren S., Steffen P. Walz, and Stefan Greuter. "Towards Personalised, Gamified Systems: An Investigation into Game Design, Personality and Player Typologies." 9th *Australasian Conference on Interactive Entertainment: Matters of Life and Death.* 30 Sept.-1 Oct. 2013, Melbourne. New York: ACM, 2013. 1-7. Web. 20 Feb. 2015.

Hayles, N. Katherine. *Electronic Literature: New Horizons for the Literary*. Notre Dame: U of Notre Dame P, 2008. Print.

Hutchison, Andy, Beth Beschorner, and Denise Schmidt-Crawford. "Exploring the use of the iPad for literacy learning." *The Reading Teacher*, 6.1 (2012): 15-23. Web. 25 Mar. 2015.

Landow, George P. *Hypertext 3.0: Critical Theory and New Media in an Era of Globalization.* Baltimore: Johns Hopkins UP, 2006. Print.

Manresa, Mireia. *L'univers lector adolescent: dels hàbits de lectura a la intervenció educativa*. Barcelona: Associació de Mestres Rosa Sensat, 2013. Print.

Murray, Janet H. *Hamlet on the Holodeck: The Future of Narrative in Cyberspace.* Cambridge, MA: MIT P, 1997. Print.

Poels, Karolien, Yvonne de Kort, and Wijnand Ijsselsteijn. "It Is Always a Lot of Fun!: Exploring Dimensions of Digital Game Experience Using Focus Group Methodology." *2007 Conference on Future Play*. 15 – 17 Oct. 2007, Toronto. New York: ACM, 2007. 83-89. Web. 19 Feb. 2015.

Ryan, Marie-Laure. *Narrative as Virtual Reality: Immersion and Interactivity in Literature and Electronic Media.* Baltimore: Johns Hopkins UP, 2001. Print.

Turrión, Celia. "Narrativa infantil y juvenil digital. ¿Qué ofrecen las nuevas formas al lector literario?" Diss. Universitat Autònoma de Barcelona, 2014. Web. 15 Mar. 2015.

Paper or Digital: A Comparative Reading with Teenagers of a Poe Short Story

Martina FITTIPALDI
Universitat Autònoma de Barcelona

Anna JUAN
Universitat Autònoma de Barcelona

Mireia MANRESA
Universitat Autònoma de Barcelona

Introduction

The impact of technologies on reading processes is a source of interest in international research in line with the current transformations taking place in written production. In this changing context, one of the ideal ways to advance in the characterisation of new forms of reading is to make a comparative study in order to contrast reading in its different formats. This perspective has been explored from different methodological standpoints, dealing with different aspects of the impact of digitisation on textual comprehension (Ackerman, and Goldsmith 2011; DeStefano, and LeFebre 2007; Mangen, Walgermo, and Brønnick 2013; Rice 1994). The results of these studies, regardless of whether they are based on digitised texts or native digital texts on the Web, show higher levels of comprehension among those who read on paper as opposed to those who do so on electronic displays, especially when certain actions are required of the reader or when the texts are long, complex and elaborate (Stoop, Kreutzer, and Kircz 2013). Aspects such as scrolling, the hypertext structure and discontinuity of text affect the cognitive processes involved in comprehension and reading speed.

Nonetheless, previous research has scarcely examined the specific nature of digital literary works. We therefore propose to show some differences found in the interpretation of the work of fiction "The Tell-Tale Heart" by Edgar Allan Poe, in print and digital versions (an iPad app),[1] from two groups of young people that took part in two literary discussions on the tale.

We are concerned, therefore, with literary texts, a field where the production of digital works constructed with non-verbal elements has been mainly confined to two creative processes: adaptations of existing works and *native creations* (Turrión 2014) – products originally created in the new formats. The adaptations of classic works of universal literature (our area of study) hold an important place in the market and have brought about an introduction of this literature to the medium in which many children are used to reading. Some examples of these types of productions are the adaptations for iPad of *Dracula*, *Frankenstein*, *Alice in Wonderland*, *Don Quixote* or the tales by Poe which were chosen for this research for their brevity and suitability to the children at whom they are targeted.

As products constructed on pre-existing works, some iPad adaptations tend to be based on the text and therefore maintain their *bookish nature* (Turrión 2014) which coexists to a greater or lesser extent with non-verbal elements such as multimodality, hypertextuality and the possibility to interact with the work, which are the three basic pillars of digital literature (Bolter, and Grusin 2000; Landow 2006; Ryan 2001a, 2001b). These works aim to find a balance between the original text and the other elements, using the latter in a more or less integrated fashion and introducing different levels of interaction complexity. The trend, however, is to use digitality as a complement in order to enliven and create emotion through sound, touch or movement. We are therefore dealing with re-interpretations of original texts which present us with the paradox of having different works at our disposal but that are basically the same; this allows us to contrast between the reading of the print and digital products as proposed in this study.

The comparison of readings of the same work allows us to observe not only to what degree digital elements help with its interpretation, but also to study what the features of digital reading are – in other words, the elements that this interpretation revolves around and what reading abilities are demanded by these types of works. Here, the proposed contrast is based on the interpretive differences of the works read – two versions with the same common basis, but with their differences – this is the variable on which the comparison is upheld.

This research is a qualitative case study which compares the effects of the application of a particular variable, in this case a digital work, by

1 This work was published by Play Creatividad and received the award for best fiction app in the Publishing Innovation Awards 2013.

analysing what occurs in literary discussions. The chosen comparative methodology pivots on the textual variable and not on the configuration features of the subjects participating in the research. In this way, we have tried to minimise the possible distortion factors in the analysis of the data by choosing subjects with similar characteristics: two groups of three fifteen-year-old adolescents with good academic results, solid reading habits and good levels of comprehension. We also decided to choose teenagers who did not know Poe's works and had not read any digital literature. This affected the interpretation of the results as it seemed to cause an essential difference between both groups due to the inequality in the skills required to read the digital product and the greater level of familiarity of the other participants with printed texts; this confirms that reading digital literature demands different skills from those required to read traditional literary works.

Indeed, reading digital works supposes that readers have the same interpretive keys in order to enjoy this fiction as they would in other formats. In this respect, an adaptation period is necessary in order to become familiar with this new way of telling stories. Although there has been an increase in recent years in digital reading (Rainie, and Duggan 2012) and a greater familiarisation among teenagers with productions that have points in common with digital fiction such as videogames, audiovisual products and graphic narrative, most of the public is still quite unaware of digital literature. For this reason the emergent research on this issue can collaborate with the integration of this type of literary work in educational planning.

The transcriptions of two one-hour literary discussion sessions on Poe's tale were used for analysis. Both groups participated separately in these sessions. Each group read the work and discussed it afterwards with the help of a facilitator – this methodology is used by GRETEL (Colomer, and Fittipaldi eds. 2012; Fittipaldi 2012; Silva-Díaz 2005) and is characterised by its double didactic/research dimension (Margallo 2013). This is important for this research because one of the groups was facing a reading format with which they had no experience and therefore the training dimension required more emphasis than in the other group, although in both cases meaning was constructed and developed during the conversation. We analysed the collective guided response to the literary text immediately after reading. Therefore, we did not study the individual responses to a series of questions, but rather the flow of the conversation from which we separated the nuclei of interest that arose from the tale. Therefore, the analysis of the data came from the text and not from the reader (Margallo 2013) and led to the configuration of categories linked to the constructive elements of the story.

The questions this study intended to detect were:

- What differences and similarities arise in a literary discussion where there is a negotiation of meaning between two groups that read two different versions of the same story?
- What elements affect the interpretation of the printed work and the digital work?
- What differences emerge regarding the interpretation of the function of the literary conventions that give meaning to the work?

As already mentioned, the literary work is the focal point of this research. It is therefore important to analyse its characteristics.

Printed work

"The Tell-Tale Heart", published by Edgar Allan Poe in 1843, is a story told in the first person of the obsession with the diseased eye of the old man with whom the narrator lives. This obsession leads him to plan in detail and to carry out the murder of the old man whose body he hides under the floorboards in the living room. When the police arrive, alerted by a neighbour, the murderer goes from being calm to becoming nervous and gives himself away when he hears the heartbeat of the old man which sounds ever more strongly in his imagination.

"The Tell-Tale Heart" is a brief but complex tale because it obliges the reader to bring various interpretive skills into play. There is a premonitory aspect in the title which invites the reader to make predictions and points out the symbol which will lead to the outcome of the story. The figure of the narrator around whom the story develops is a murderer, an anonymous character who attempts throughout the tale to demonstrate his sanity before his listeners.[2]

The structure of the tale can be summarised as follows:

- an initial argument in which the narrator attempts to justify his own sanity by telling the story in the present tense and addressing the readers;
- the chronological account of what happened and the narration of the murder which is presented in the past tense from the murderer's perspective;
- the return to the present where the narrator explains the outcome of the story and in so doing makes his paranoia clear.

[2] For the reading of the printed version we used Julio Cortázar's Spanish translation (Poe 2012; see also Ciudad Seva, n.d.). In Cortázar's translation the narratees are discursively referred to as "*ustedes*" [polite form of you plural] who "take [him] for a madman".

The divergence between the tense of the discourse and the tense of the story (present tense for the narrative and past tense for what has been narrated) denotes the compositional nature of the tale and underlines the plane of discourse which recounts the events that take place in flashback and emphasises how these are experienced by the narrator/protagonist. He makes the objective of his confession clear from the beginning: to prove his sanity before the conviction of all others. The text seems to be woven around the dichotomy of "sanity/madness" in terms of how both of these ideas are understood and related to each other.

According to the narrator's discourse, sanity is associated with the idea of control, which is how the murderer behaves at the start. However, what others understand as madness is, for the protagonist, nothing more than "an acute over-awareness of the senses". His most exacerbated sense is hearing and it is his auditory perceptions (sometimes imaginary) that become the milestones of the tale: hearing the old man's heartbeat which is associated with his imminent death: "The old man's hour had come!"; hearing the ringing of the bells which announces the arrival of the police; hearing the heartbeat of the dead man under the floorboards, a hallucination which becomes ever stronger and finally hastens the outcome of the story.

As the story advances the protagonist loses control and his passions come to the fore: he admits that he has become a prisoner of "instinct" and of "fury", of an uncontrollable horror. He then goes from his initial feeling of "triumph" at managing the situation to a subsequent breakdown due to the imaginary sound which drives him insane and obliges him to confess: the sound of the heartbeat of the murdered old man.

Digital work

The digital version of the tale forms part of the app which contains several of Poe's most disturbing tales.[3] Together with the complete text, the remediation proposes a set of multimodal elements that explore new ways of storytelling. Illustrations, sounds, music, background textures, graphic use of fonts and animated images with which the reader can interact, all strive to configure a product where the transition to the screen has an influence on the telling of the story. But on what aspects of Poe's text do these multimodal elements have an effect?

The initial app stimuli are visual and audio. On the title page the reader already hears sombre music of rising tension that is present throughout the story, providing indications as to the tone and genre even before the text

[3] "The Oval Portrait", "The Tell-Tale Heart", "The Masque of the Red Death" and "Annabel Lee".

has begun to be read. The screen background, which evokes a yellowing page, affects the bookish nature of the app and offers clues to the period in which the tale was written and when the narrated events took place.

The visual and audio resources characterise the classic version in an attempt to show some elements that are not mentioned in the text. The inclusion of images at certain key points in the story attempts to represent the scenario of the characters and show both the atmosphere and the period in which the story takes place; the audio resource, used in cinematographic style, attempts to underline the exacerbation of the narrator's sense of hearing and also underlines the points of greatest narrative tension. Therefore, we can hear the old man's breathing when he feels he is being observed in the darkness, we hear his heartbeat and scream of horror before dying, and we perceive the sound of the bells which announce the arrival of the police. These resources, together with the change in tone and rhythm of the music, direct and conduct the reading rhythm and help the reader to enter into the tale, making it possible to feel some of the sensations experienced by the narrator. The different animations also attempt to affect this latter aspect. Many of the moving images – some of which can be activated by the user – are intended to place the reader in the narrator's perspective and therefore help to enter into the story. The reader's participation, however, is secondary. There is no relation between narrative development and user interaction, although there are three cases in which the interaction – beyond wishing to situate the reader in a given perspective – also has a discursive purpose: the animation of the lantern with which the reader discovers the text where the narrator tells how he observed the old man with a lantern for eight nights; the animation of the clock, which shows the time when touched and with it the arrival of the police and the emergence of the passions and loss of control of the protagonist; the animation of the eyes which underlines the obsessive character of the protagonist and his ability to distort reality by placing the faces of the policemen, disfigured by his obsession, in the foreground.

Therefore, the multimodal elements of the app play on some of the aspects implicit in the original print version and are complex for the adolescent reader to interpret. The illustrations, textures, audio resources, animations and even in some cases the pictorialisation of the text, all aspire to fill some of the voids in Poe's text in an effort to contribute to the comprehension of the tale. The result is a product in which the context, genre and tone are initially more noticeable than in the original. And this aspect brings us to a key question: to what degree do the variations introduced in the digital version facilitate or make more difficult the comprehension of Poe's tale?

How the children build meaning: prominent elements in digital and print reading

From here onwards we will focus on the aspects of the story that both groups emphasised in the discussion. Initially, the most important element might be – as we have said – that while the readers of the print version only had to focus their attention on the words, the app readers were faced with a large amount of multimodal stimuli which might have distracted them from the text and diverted their attention towards other components. The difference between the two versions created divergences in the way both groups interpreted the story and these appeared on both global and specific levels of comprehension. We will now explain the most important aspects.

Inferential reading

As we have pointed out, one of the key elements in the tale is the type of focalisation selected in order to tell the story and the implications that this decision entails in both the act of narrating and in the act of reading. Poe introduces multiple unspoken elements in the plane of expression which play with the written text and must be stimulated by putting into operation the inferential ability of the reader. Those who read the print version not only made inferences while they were reading and recognised the places where these inferences were possible (regarding, for example, the motive of the murderer, the setting, the features of the narrator or the identity of the narratees), but they also realised the importance of the voids in the tale. In fact, they pointed this out as a key aspect in the text: "Ada: The text works because you ask yourself things"; "Eugenio: Yes, that's the potential of the story. The more things you ask yourself the more you come to imagine".[4]

The readers of the digital version, however, suggested that the multimodal elements prevented them from imagining in the same way as when reading in print because the app "does it all for you". But although these visual, audio and kinetic stimuli seemed to demonstrate the unspoken elements in the text, the readers affirmed that there was a lack of information (especially referring to spaces and characters) and they did not see the voids as structuring elements in the tale but as a narrative defect: "Mariana: There is a lack of description and too many illustrations". This general perception led them to consider the experience as more recreational than creative, distancing them from what they understood as literary reading, leaving aside inferential reading and

4 English translations of all quotations in other languages have been provided by Tim Mc Quaid.

linking the experience to that which they normally had with audiovisual media.

Use of metalanguage

Perhaps for this reason, while the readers of the print version were attached to the text and continually went back to it to explain their arguments using quite sophisticated literary metalanguage ("internal narrator", "protagonist", "linear storyline", "flashback" and "secondary characters"), those reading the digital version did not share this requirement. It would seem that the product they were using was so remote from what they considered literature that they did not perceive the need to use metalanguage (they did so on few occasions and in a very basic way) and, as we shall see, this even led them to leave out some central paratexts such as the title.

Reader involvement

This difference in the perception of the product has implications with regard to the elements that all the readers involved considered important in order to enter into Poe's fiction. Those who read the print version coincided that the narrator has the ability to introduce the reader into the story from the first paragraph and they linked this with the method selected for telling the story. Leo made reference to the language used, underlining the importance of the repetitions, the constant appeals to "you", the poetic use of the language and the fact that the narrator's feelings are present throughout the tale, helping the reader to enter into the story: "Leo: The feeling he shows also helps you to put yourself in his shoes. The emotion, the obsession, the 'breathlessness' is how you get into it". Eugenio pointed out the detail with which the narrator explains the events and Ada underlined the importance of the clues left by the narrator throughout the tale in order to comprehend both what he says and what he leaves unsaid: "Ada: He leaves clues in the middle of the story [...]. As if it were a puzzle, he doesn't explain everything, he doesn't give you much information, but he gives you key information".

The readers of the app version, on the other hand, initially did not share a single opinion regarding whether it was easy or not to get into the story. While for some the format was a help (especially due to the audio resources, the illustrations and the interactive proposals such as the lantern), for others it was an impediment. Emma claimed that the format put her off and many of the multimodal resources distracted her: "Emma: I didn't like it [the music] because it distracted me from reading, [...] when I was reading and those things appeared [animated images], they put me off [...]. There were a lot of things that distracted me and I couldn't go back to reading because the format confused me a little."

Jordi, who describes himself as a non-classic reader (by "classic" he understands a reader of print novels), expressed that the audio, visual and animation resources helped him to put himself in the narrator's situation. In spite of the differences, all the readers ended up pointing out the role of the multimodal resources in the creation of the atmosphere and although they recognised that these helped them to enter into the story, they shared the feeling that they become repetitive elements that tire the reader and underline the foreseeable nature of the tale.

Type of story

One of the aspects perceived differently by the readers of the print and digital versions is the nature of the story. While the readers of the print version stressed its capacity to cut short the reader's expectations, the readers of the digital version pointed out that the text is totally foreseeable, similar to the American films where simply by seeing the beginning you know how it is going to end. It is interesting that the readers of the print version explained the unpredictability of the text by referring to how "different" it is compared to what they normally read, the lack of definition of good and evil, the ambiguity of the "truths" it conceals, the doubts it leaves the reader with on finishing the reading and the complexity of the construction of the main character, while the readers of the digital version based their arguments on the predictability of the story by describing the plot (which they only remembered vaguely) rather than reflecting on how the story is constructed.

Recommendations

These differences led both groups to respond differently to the question of to whom they would recommend the tale. Those who read the print version decided to recommend it to more experienced readers who would be capable of reaching a better understanding than them and who would enjoy experimentation and less classic forms of storytelling; the readers of the app version thought of younger readers who would enjoy multimodal elements or of "less classic" readers who would not be interested so much in narrative complexity (which they did not see anywhere) such as multimodal resources that could take them away from the monotonous reading of printed books where you only find "black words on a white background" (Jordi).

As the conversation developed, the reading focused on different elements regarding the construction of the work of fiction. We shall now see some of these and how they were described by the students.

Genre and framework

Regarding the genre, the readers of both the print and digital formats categorised the story as mystery fiction. Nonetheless, while the latter group suggested that the storyline came close to being a "thriller" because it keeps the reader hooked until the end, the group that read the app version considered that the tale could fall within the "horror" genre since the atmosphere created by the imagery and sound seemed to adhere to the Gothic. These elements gave the latter group an idea of the setting; as Emma states, "we know what we know from the images because he doesn't describe very much". The readers of the print version were also aware of this lack of information on the framework and, although they could imagine the "cold" and gloomy atmosphere of the story, they realised that there is a deliberate uncertainty, an intended choice not to give information because what interests the narrator is something else: "to prove that he is not insane" (Leo).

Structure

We will now revise how both groups reflected on aspects of the structure of the tale such as the title, the distinction between the tense of the story and the tense of the discourse and on how the story ends.

The readers of the print version made reference to the title of their own accord and at the beginning of the conversation, while those who read the digital version only realised the existence of the title towards the end of the second session and this was due to the intervention of the facilitator who proposed that they investigate its possible meaning.

The title is therefore one of the first elements that attracted the attention of those who read the print version. This group considered it a key element due to its capacity to anticipate and condense the nucleus of the story: the obsession of the protagonist who ends up giving himself away because he hears the imaginary heartbeats which perhaps, as Leo states, are simply those of his own heart:

> Leo: He feels worse and worse. He starts to remember more, sees the images more clearly, he gets more paranoid thinking that they're laughing at him… And his own tell-tale heart that continues to go thump, thump, thump, thump, and in the end he says: it was me! […] He gives himself away, so it is his heart that is the tell-tale.

The readers of the app version, on the other hand, did not notice the title and, when asked by the facilitator, said that they had not seen it. This could be linked with the readers' sense of removal from the medium in which they were reading; with the feeling they seemed to have that they were not reading literature. When thinking of the title, they also recognised the nucleus and anticipation functions, although they did not manage to clearly specify the former and considered the latter to be a weak point in the text because it made the story foreseeable: "Jordi: It already tells you that the heart is a tell-tale […]. The title is already giving away the ending".

The temporality construction is another aspect underlined by the readers in the discussion. Both groups perceived temporal shifts in the story, however the readers of the print version were better able to explain the framework structure of the story and used appropriate metalanguage to do so: "Eugenio: […] [I]t's done in flashback, he goes back in time to tell what he did every day".

The readers of the print version seemed to recognise – albeit implicitly – the existence of both planes (story and discourse) because they reflected on what was written and on how and for what purpose it was written. This recognition of both planes was not so clear in the case of the readers of the app version, although they showed their awareness of the different tenses using body language and phrases such as this one from Mariana: "as though it already happened and he's explaining it now".

The ending is another element on which there seemed to be contradictory opinions between both groups. Those who read the print version pointed out its unpredictability and reflected on its open nature as one of the strong points of the story due to the "small amount of information you have to summarise" on finishing the text. Also, "it makes you part of it and at the same time distances you from the truth", and allows you to reflect that "maybe there is no truth at all" (Leo). This complexity, based on the choice of point of view, went unnoticed by the readers of the app version; they showed their dislike and lack of understanding of the ending and thought it was abrupt. The contributions regarding this element showed that the illustration in the digital version where the murderer appears with the old man's bleeding heart in his hand was read literally by the students, leading them to wrongly believe that the heartbeats came from the heart of the old man. The subsequent conversation on this point allowed them to become aware of this and analyse how the image prevailed over the words and led them to read in a particular way.

Narrative tension

Narrative tension runs throughout "The Tell-Tale Heart" and comes to a climax at the end of the tale when the murderer admits he is guilty and shows the place where the body is hidden. Although this element was recognised by both groups, the readers of the app version considered that this was *crescendo* and more due to the typographical and audio resources etc. than to the verbal language. It is interesting to note that these students paid more attention to the animations but that they understood them to be "marginal notes" more than resources with a clear discursive function, perhaps because in the app they saw these as serving more as a means of providing atmosphere and entertaining the reader.

Also, as we have seen, when evaluating this intensification, the repetition was seen negatively by the readers of the screen version: "Mariana: It tired me because it was very repetitive. He was constantly saying that the noise was annoying him and it kept getting louder and louder. And then I thought: I understood that the first time you said it".

Focalisation

The internal focalisation is a fundamental element in the story as it leads us to observe the events from the perspective of the murderer. Although they did not refer to it as such, those who read the print version underlined this aspect and pointed out that perhaps it is this that allows the reader to enter into the story more quickly. In the discussion, they also stated that the choice of this point of view meets a discursive objective: the need of the narrator to demonstrate his sanity.

> Leo: He justifies that he isn't mad by explaining what happened. I say this because of the beginning, because he's the one who starts by saying: now listen, I'm not mad, because a mad person doesn't do things so carefully. He's kind of justifying what happened as if they were accusing him of everything, maybe he's accusing himself.
>
> Eugenio: Yes, he wants to use the story to explain that he isn't mad.

The readers of the app version also recognised the narrator as the protagonist who attempts to convince everyone of his sanity, but they did not point out this type of focalisation as a deliberate choice in order to explore certain effects.

When addressing the subject of the possible narratees, those who read the print version repeated the importance of the hypothesis construction and considered two possibilities: one of these, suggested by Leo, is that the narrator explains his version of events to another part of himself; in his madness he builds a monologue in which he seems to split himself in two. The other, defended by Ada, suggested that he is explaining his story to real people in a police interrogation and before a psychiatrist who has diagnosed him as insane. During the discussion, students worked on these hypotheses and mentioned how interesting they found this complexity, this "void" created on purpose so that the readers can create their own ideas:

> Eugenio: This is one of the interesting parts of the story because he makes you have two points of view. You don't know if he's telling it to someone or if he is talking, as Leo says, with two imaginary parts of himself. Then you think:

Is he talking to someone? Is he talking to someone in his imagination? This part of the story is difficult to understand.

When hypothesising on the narratees, the readers of the app version seemed to randomly float ideas, referring to "family members or friends" of the narrator (Mariana), to the police (Emma) or to the readers (Jordi), which also showed the confusion in this group between the planes of story and discourse.

Conclusions

One of the main conclusions of this case study is the confirmation that the readers of the print version achieved a more profound interpretation of the meaning and a greater understanding of the structural threads of the story since their assertions via the comments in the discussions made explicit the function of the key elements of the tale.

Although the adolescents in both groups were unable to precisely state the central importance of the character's psychology, there were notable differences between the two. It was observed that the readers of the screen version showed greater confusion when dealing with key aspects of the work such as the function of the narratee or the indeterminacy of the framework – elements to which they did not seem to give importance – or the misrepresentation of the ending by presupposing that the old man's heart was still beating without questioning the version of the deluded narrator-murderer. On the other hand, those who read the print version clearly perceived the nature of the narrative voice, the functionality of the narratee in the story and they reflected in a discerning manner on the ending. Therefore, the readers of the digital version seemed to remain on a more storyline level than those who read the print version.

The reason for the inadequate interpretation of the function of the discursive elements may be related to the construction of the digital device where aspects such as the framework or the ending, for example, are manipulated and transformed in the app, mainly by visual elements. The images which aim to immerse the reader in the story actually show aspects which are of little importance in the original story and cause misinterpretation. The fact that the app readers' attention must focus on many more stimuli other than the written word can cause, for example, the indeterminacy or the importance of the narratee to go unnoticed in Poe's story. The digital readers did not seem to observe the multimodality as part of the discourse, perhaps because the digital resources in the app do not always function discursively. Nonetheless, when they did observe this aspect, the students perceived them as secondary issues and in some cases they were even misleading.

Moreover, both groups showed differences regarding inferential reflection, the use of metalanguage and the understanding of the author's intentional use of indeterminacy in some aspects of the story. Those who read the print version activated their literary competence and applied it to their reading while those who read the app version did not fully manage to do so. The latter seemed to be obstructed by the distracting display of non-verbal elements and by the prejudice with which they approached the work by not considering it a literary product that should be read using the *same* keys as printed literary stories. For example, rereading did not take place in order to argue their theories – which did occur in the case of those who read the print version. The readers of the app sometimes seemed like learner drivers, more aware of the material aspects of the device than the act of reading itself.

One of the questions that arises from these results and requires more research is whether this difference is due to the readers' lack of training or familiarisation with the construction of multimodal fiction or if it is the multimodality that eclipses or distorts the principal purpose of the work. In this regard we suspect that there is a need to modify the foundations of the reading processes applied to works of fiction.

In light of this evidence, one might ask if the digital readers made the most of the reading experience offered by the app. As observed in the analysis, the students perceived the music and sound as immersive elements in the story but did not experience the same with the images, the movement and the possibility of interaction with some of the resources; these latter elements made following the story difficult and led them to think they were resources to make the story easier for inexperienced readers. In fact, we may be led to believe that the digital readers were embarking on a type of reading which required them to pay special attention to elements that, for them, were *alien* to literary works. Their disorientation when faced with a work that they were unable to put into any category known to them led to a lack of overall activation of their literary competencies. This explains the differences regarding the construction of meaning and it positions the reading experience within the normal parameters in the familiarisation process with digital production. This study confirms the need for children to be afforded more time and greater exposure to the reading of digital literature.

Works Cited

Primary Works Cited

Alice for the iPad. London: Atomic Antelope, 2010. iPad edition.

Cervantes, Miguel de. *The Adventures of Don Quixote.* Ill. Miguel Calero. Madrid: Touch of Classic, 2012. iPad edition.

Poe, Edgar Allan. *Cuentos completos*. Trad. Julio Cortázar. Barcelona: RBA, 2012. Print.

Poe, Edgar Allan. *iPoe Collection*, Vol. I. Ill. David García Farés. Barcelona: Play Creatividad, 2012. iPad edition.

Shelley, Mary. *Frankenstein*. Ill. Miguel Calero. Madrid: Touch of Classic, 2012. iPad edition.

Stoker, Bram, and Dan Pilditch, adap. *Dracula*. Toronto: Padworx Digital Media, 2010. iPad edition.

Secondary Works Cited

Ackerman, Rafeket, and Morris Goldsmith. "Metacognitive regulation of text learning: On screen versus on paper." *Journal of Experimental Psychology: Applied*, 17.1 (2011): 18-32. Print.

Bolter, Jay David, and Richard Grusin. *Remediation. Understanding New Media.* Cambridge and London: The MIT Press, 2000. Print.

Ciudad Seva. "El corazón delator", n.d. Web. 15 Apr. 2015.

Colomer, Teresa, and Marina Fittipaldi, eds. *La literatura que acoge. Inmigración y lectura de álbumes*. Caracas/Barcelona: Banco del Libro-GRETEL, 2012. Print.

DeStefano, Diana, and Jo-Anne Lefevre. "Cognitive load hypertext reading: A review." *Computers in Human Behavior*, 23.3 (2007): 1616-1641. Print.

Fittipaldi, Martina. "La categorización de las respuestas infantiles ante los textos literarios. Análisis de algunos modelos y propuesta de clasificación." *La literatura que acoge. Inmigración y lectura de álbumes ilustrados*. Eds. Teresa Colomer, and Martina Fittipaldi. Caracas/Barcelona: Banco del Libro-GRETEL, 2012. 69-86. Print.

Landow, George P. *Hypertext 3.0: Critical Theory and New Media in an Era of Globalization.* Baltimore: Johns Hopkins University Press, 2006. Print.

Mangen, Anne, Bente R. Walgermo, and Kolbjørn Brønnick. "Reading linear texts on paper versus computter secreen: effects on reading comprehension." *International Journal of Educational Research*, 58 (2013): 61-68. Print.

Margallo, Ana María. "Cuestiones metodológicas en torno a la investigación de las respuestas lectoras a álbumes ilustrados." *Cultura & Educación*, 25.4 (2013): 467-478. Print.

Rainie, Lee, and Maeve Duggan. "E-book Reading Jumps; Print Book Reading Declines." Pew Research Center, 2012. Web. 01 Dec. 2014.

Rice, Gary E. "Examining constructs in reading comprehension using two presentation modes: Paper vs. Computer." *Journal of Educational Computing Research*, 11.2 (1994): 153-174. Web. 21 Oct. 2014.

Ryan, Marie-Laure. "Beyond Myth and Metaphor. The case of Narrative in Digital Media." *Game Studies: The International Journal of Computer Game Research* 1.1 (2001a). Web. 15 Oct. 2015.

—. *Narrative as Virtual Reality.* Baltimore: The Johns Hopkins University Press, 2001b. Print.

Silva-Díaz, María Cecilia. "Libros que enseñan a leer: álbumes metaficcionales y conocimiento literario." Diss. Universitat Autònoma de Barcelona, 2005. Web. 01 Jan. 2015.

Stoop, Judith, Paulien Kreutzer, and Joost Kircz. "Reading and learning from screens versus print: A study in changing habits: part 1 – reading long information rich texts." *New Library World*, 114.7 (2013): 284-300. Print.

Turrión, Celia. "Narrativa infantil y juvenil digital. ¿Qué ofrecen las nuevas formas al lector literario?" Diss. Universitat Autònoma de Barcelona, 2014. Web. 15 Mar. 2015.

Part IV

Educational Practices: Families and Schools

iPads, Emergent Readers and Families

Cristina ALIAGAS[1]
The University of Sheffield

Ana María MARGALLO
Universitat Autònoma de Barcelona

Introduction

The study of children's reading practices within the family context has a lengthy tradition in studies on early literacy as well as in *The New Literacy Studies*, a line of research that draws from the anthropology of social practices and sociolinguistics. Within these lines of research, shared adult-child reading has been one of the most widely studied phenomena, in particular bedtime story reading. From Heath (1983) and others (Colomer 2005; Wells 1986) we know that the practice of telling and reading stories is an activity that is part of family life and constitutes a space for literary socialisation through which children develop coding-decoding skills in the printed word (Sulzby 1986) while simultaneously developing their literary competence. By means of these interactions they become familiar with book conventions (e.g., authorship, title versus text, chapter structure) and the mechanisms of literary narration (e.g., literary genres, narrator, illustration-text relationship). We also know that the greater part of the learning processes that occur in these interactions are stimulated by the verbal actions of the adult (Kucirkova, Sheehy, and Messer 2014), who poses questions to the child, responds to those verbalised by the child and constructs "helps" to progress in the interpretation of the narration.

1 With the support of the Secretaria d'Universitats i Recerca del Departament d'Economia i Coneixement de la Generalitat de Catalunya (Secretary for Universities and Research of the Ministry of Economy and Knowledge of the Government of Catalonia) and the Co-funding programme of the Marie Curie Actions of the 7th R&D Framework Programme of the European Union (Beatriu de Pinós 2011-A). Moreover, the author is member of the R&D project financed by the Ministerio de Economía y Competitividad (Spanish Ministry of Economy and Competitiveness) for the period 1-1-2012 to 31-12-2014 (extended until 31-5-2015): "School 2.0: Digital literacy practices. Materials, classroom activity and online linguistic resources" (EDU2011-28381), directed by Daniel Cassany at Universitat Pompeu Fabra (Pompeu Fabra University) (see sites.google.com/site/ies201x1/home).

In this chapter we reflect on the transformations that the practice of shared adult-child reading has recently undergone and the prominence that the tablet has acquired in the deployment of children's electronic literature, which affects the ways in which parents and children share stories. The boom in tablets (Apple iPad, Microsoft Surface, Kindle Fire, Galaxy Tab and similar) – the mobile device most often purchased in recent years by families with children up to and including eight years of age (Common Sense Media 2013) – is due to the type of interactivity they provide, offering more possibilities for experimentation with multimodality and forms of reader participation than other e-reader models, the design of which is still dominated by the metaphor of the linearity of the printed book. Bearing these aspects in mind, this study approaches some exploratory questions relating to factors of change in the practice of story reading brought about by the iPad: What transformations are taking place in the practice of shared family reading in the home as a result of the arrival of tablets? What effects do tablets have on the creation of children's e-libraries? What techno-literacy and narrative learning processes do they encourage? What influence does the iPad have on the roles adopted by the adult and child during these interactions? How do multimodality and interactivity influence children's literary experiences?

Our interest in these questions leads us to adopt the *funds of knowledge* approach (González, Moll, and Amanti 2015), which assumes that families and communities provide learning resources for children and youths that are meaningful for education. We are interested in exploring the digital literary experiences that young children are developing in the home as a first step towards learning what connections schools may make with the knowledge and skills that increasing contact with the digital world fosters in children's literary literacy. This interest, which is part anthropology and part literary education, led us to an ethnographic study of children's digital story reading practices in the family context where we documented shared reading events using iPads in four families in Catalonia and Spain (Aliagas, and Margallo in press). In this chapter we present some of the structural changes we have observed in relation to the practice of family story reading as a consequence of the use of the tablet as a reading format.

Children, tablets and emergent home literacies

For middle/upper-class children the home has become the place where they access technology, as opposed to school, which still represents literary values traditionally associated with print literacy despite efforts to innovate and modernise. In this "multi-equipped home" (González-Patiño 2011) new generations grow up surrounded by digital devices and participate in social media practices as part of their play-time from as early as their first months of life (Marsh *et al.* 2005). This means that before children can autonomously decode the printed word they have already accumulated experience in interpreting multimodal texts where the meaning is constructed through the articulation of different modes of semiotic representation (e.g., text, image, movement, sound). This reality is leading new generations to enter the world of literacy in new and complex ways and to develop new meanings through which they acquire an appreciation for literary narration and become readers.

The first decade of the 21st century saw an increase in the number of studies dedicated to the documentation and analysis of what Carrington (2001) referred to as *home literacy practices*, in reference to the techno-literacy activities in which children participate in the home, and described by Cassany (2012) in a Spanish context, to mean playing with videogame consoles, communicating (e.g., SMS, WhatsApp, chat, Skype, social networks), consuming music and YouTube videos and participating in network-based communities and fan forums. These studies bring to technological literary practices the line of research which – based on a socio-cultural approach to early literacy – described what children did with texts outside the classroom in that *text-centric* world that now seems so long ago (Heath 1983; Wells 1986).

Reading electronic stories (e-stories) on tablets is another emergent literary practice that the new generations are developing in the home rather than at school. This practice began in the 1990s in CD-ROM format and in the first decade of the 21st century migrated at a dramatic rate from computers to mobile devices, a fact that has encouraged research from a variety of disciplines. Kurcirkova, Sheehy and Messer (2014) demonstrate that the iPad promotes changes in the parent-child communicative structure when using apps, where interactivity becomes a conversation piece and includes new "helps" focused on tactility. Merchant (2014) identifies three types of corporal movement associated with the use of tablets that accompany these parent-child interactions: stabilising movements (e.g., holding the tablet or supporting it with the knees), control movements, which correspond to the basic operations required to access apps and navigate (e.g., writing with one or more fingers, moving elements), and deictic movements (e.g., pointing, gesticulating). The role that tactility plays in the reading process has also been examined from a multimodality perspective (Simpson, Walsh, and Roswell 2013) and, from the point of view of education, it has been suggested that tablets encourage hybrid narrative products (Turrión 2014) that include both popular children's culture and digital games, an inter-relationship that, according to Verenikina and Kervin (2011), stimulates imaginative and spontaneous play.

The use of tablets, therefore, and the access to content that they facilitate, present a new space for literary socialisation that expands on what children could formerly learn in print story reading events.

Funds of literary knowledge: connecting home and school

Funds of knowledge (González, Moll, and Amanti 2005) is an educational theory that, from a socio-cultural and interdisciplinary perspective, combines anthropological, psychological, linguistic and educational traditions to offer a description of learning as a complex phenomenon. With this theory, the authors distance themselves from the dominant descriptions that assume that the nature of learning is strictly psychological and typically associated with the learning techniques that are only applied in schools. Beginning with the premise that individuals are competent learners outside the educational institution and despite the manner in which this institution attempts to position them on its socio-academic value scale, they argue that people learn through the socio-linguistic interaction that occurs when they participate in social, cultural and work-related practices. It is in these life experiences that they accumulate funds of knowledge, in other words, knowledge, ideas, skills and informal ways of learning.

The funds of knowledge theory originated in a socio-educational ethnographic study carried out in Arizona (United States) in which González, Moll and Amanti (2005), on documenting the lifestyles of Mexican-American students in the Tucson district, observed that these acquired significant cultural capital (e.g., agriculture, mining, economics, family management, materials, archaeology, science, medicine, religion) through a complex social exchange network among families and the Latin American community. On the basis of this observation, the funds of knowledge theory argues that the forms of learning that young people acquire via their families, and which they accumulate in the form of cultural capital, resources and literacies, affect the manner in which they subsequently learn at school, and for this reason the researchers defend the idea that this cultural capital should be recognised in the classroom as legitimate knowledge in order that school learning gain cultural relevance.

The influence of technology on children's schooling has been documented by Wohlwend (2009), who observed children between five and seven years old creating smartphones from paper and playing imaginatively co-created videogames in the classroom. These examples demonstrate that the funds of technological knowledge that children develop outside the school environment are present in the classroom whether we want it or not. So, when children arrive at school, they bring to books, be they in paper or digital format, the *funds of literary knowledge* that they have developed with the guidance of their parents, siblings, friends and other adults, and even on their own.

On the basis of these experiences children have also internalised techno-literary exploratory attitudes (Wohlwend 2009) and incorporated new roles as creators, designers and expert interpreters of their favourite narratives (O'Mara, and Laidlaw 2011). However, while children who begin formal education may already be capable of interpreting complex, multimodal narrative texts, what they are asked to learn in the classroom focuses on the acquisition of the written word and text. This family-school discontinuity in children's techno-literary experiences has come to be known as the *digital divide* and, more recently, the *app gap*.

In this study, the theoretical construct of the funds of knowledge (González, Moll and Amanti 2005) allows us to reflect on the continuity and discontinuity of family-school relationships in terms of the literary experiences of the emergent reader. From this perspective we can connect our anthropological interest in describing the practice of family tablet-based reading with the concerns of teachers about the role of technology in literary education in the 21st century.

The study: characterisation of adult-child shared reading practices using iPad

The observations presented here originate from an ethnographic fieldwork in which we documented, over a period of two years (August 2012 - August 2014), the iPad-based shared reading practices of four middle-class families, three from Barcelona and the surrounding area and one from Palma, Majorca.[2] All the families were in possession of their own iPads and a library of e-stories for their children. The participants were female emergent readers of the following ages when beginning the study: Itzel, one year eleven months; Helena, two years five months; Lucía, four years two months, and Chloe, five years seven months. The four families were of mid-level socio-economic status and the parents possessed university-level studies relating to their professions. The fieldwork consisted of observations and partial video recordings of reading and playtime events using the iPad and were complemented with conversations with the participants.

With the aim of offering an overall view of the transformations that the iPad produces in the shared reading activities of the emergent readers in the home, this chapter will present some of the elements of change relating to: i) the time/space of the reading practice in the home, ii) the

2 We are grateful to the participating families for their willing, longitudinal participation in this study.

configuration and use of the iPad children's e-libraries, iii) the techno-literacy learning processes that are constructed from the interaction between the child, the adult and the device, and iv) the effects on the reading experience of some of the multimodal and interactive resources of the apps.

Space-time transformations

As Heath's ethnographic study (1983) showed (with North American families of different social classes), the bedtime story is a practice that is historically constructed in all cultures and manifested in different linguistic-interactional practices that vary in meaning and value depending on the social group. We ask ourselves then, how is the arrival of the tablet affecting the development of this literary practice of sharing children's stories in the family context?

One structural change factor is that two children's libraries now coexist in the home, the digital and the printed, thereby making the same story available in different formats and languages. The fact that the digital library is compiled in a small, moveable device means that its incursion into the family living space does not affect the physical location of the print library. The pacific coexistence of the two libraries appears to keep the two reading modalities alive, digital and paper, which are allocated by means of implicit rules of use associated with space-time factors pertaining to reading.

The specific characteristics of each format lead families to make decisions regarding the location of where the stories are shared. In the case of tablet-based reading, these decisions appear to be greatly conditioned by the desire to control the stabilising movements (Merchant 2014) of the iPad during the shared reading. As a result, the reading of e-stories tends to take place in the living-dining area, generally on the couch or the main table, locations where the adult can "control" the use made of such an expensive and delicate device. In this manner the mobility offered by the tablet is also reduced. Once the adult trusts the child as a tablet user, the couch or the floor would appear to be the favourite places. In contrast there are relatively few rules regarding location or postural behaviour for print reading, with the exception that the practice of bedtime reading is maintained.

Analysis from the perspective of the moment when reading occurs reveals that the coexistence of digital and printed literature conceals a series of redistributions. While digital reading does not substitute print reading, the latter loses presence during the daytime and tends to be reserved for the bedtime story in the child's bedroom. This is the case of Lucía, who, when given the opportunity to read and play on the tablet, includes this option as part of the family leisure activities that took place in the living-dining area (e.g., reading, painting, making cut-outs, watching TV). The following is a "snapshot" that her mother offered us when Lucía was six years old and independent with the iPad.[3]

> Researcher: When and where do you use the iPad? And books?
>
> Mother: The iPad here, in the living room, and the same for books, as sometimes we read in the evening. But at bedtime it's always a [printed] book, in her bedroom.
>
> Researcher: So, in the bedroom it's always a printed book?
>
> Mother: Yes. Sometimes her father goes up to her bedroom with the iPad, but usually when I go I bring a book.
>
> Researcher: And at what point during the day does she most use the iPad?
>
> Mother: In the evening, usually in the evening. That doesn't mean that every day when she comes home from school she goes to the iPad. Some days she does, other days she doesn't touch it.

In this case the iPad did not generate tensions between print and digital reading as the coexistence of the two modalities was implicitly regulated by space-time associations: the iPad was used in the living-dining area for a while after school and over the weekend, while books were read before going to sleep, usually in bed, although they were also read where and whenever desired, and the print library was renovated on a weekly basis with books from the local library. For Lucía, and also for Chloe, the increase in reading autonomy led them both to dissociate literary reading from the iPad which was used for the enjoyment of other narrative and entertainment products. Lucía's father justified the return to the print book that occurred at about six years old on the basis of a gap in the emergent reader market:

> There's a lack of interesting material for someone her age, of more developed material. What there's now is either very simple or it's for when you know how to read and are ten years old. The iPad [in reference to the editorial market accessible via the Apple App Store] does not have sufficient content for this age group. In English yes, but in Catalan there's nothing.

Another change that is evident from the above is the involvement of the father in the shared reading, in contrast with previous studies that depicted the prominence of the mother (Heath 1983). In Lucía's family the introduction of the iPad as a reading option generated a more or less clearly defined distribution in which the iPad was associated with the father and books with the mother (see Image 1 and Image 2), though the

[3] The fragments included have been translated from Catalan and/or Spanish to English. English translations of all quotations in other languages have been provided by Tim Mc Quaid.

bedtime story was an activity that was evenly distributed. In this case the distribution was marked by the fact that the father was the "owner" of the iPad, though he shared it with the other family members. The same occurred with Helena's family.

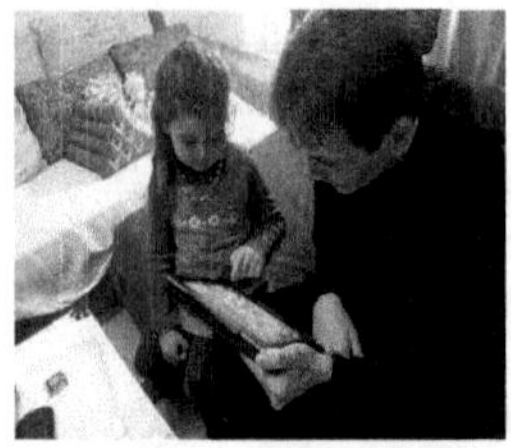

Image 1. Helena (four years two months) reading *The Stolen Stars* with her father in the living-dining area

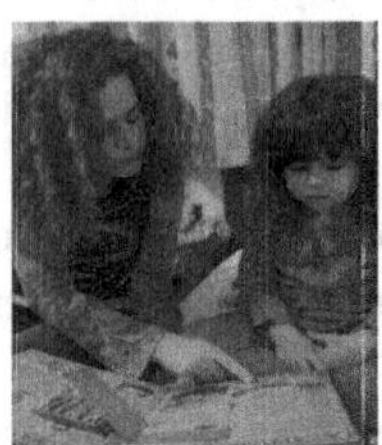

Image 2. Lucía (five years) reading a story with her mother, in bed, before going to sleep

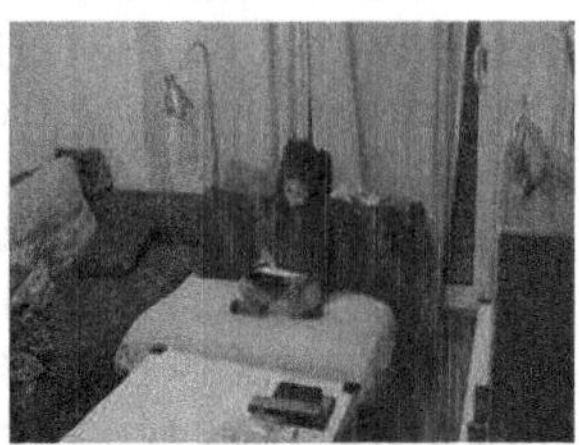

Image 3. Chloe (six years) painting a unicorn using the iPad, in the living-dining area

The reading of e-stories in the living-dining area adds a social dimension to the event, as opposed to the bedtime story which occurs in the bedroom. This change in space and time contributes to making reading in tablet format a less intimate experience. Without a doubt the association of e-reading with shared spaces determines the development of the activity which drowns out ambient noises (e.g., TV, conversations among adults, sibling interruptions), though these on occasion may be integrated in order to enrich the reading experience. An example of this type of integration occurred at the end of the reading of *Snow White*, by Tales Apart, when Helena became frightened by the presence of the stepmother who turns into a witch. The end of the tale – which says "the witch ran away into the forest never to be seen again." – did not satisfy the child, who wanted to know where the witch was "after the story" for fear that she might appear to offer her an apple. To combat this fear, which was expressed in the form of insistent questions by Helena about the whereabouts of the witch, the father incorporated the baby's cries into the reading, interpreting it as a symptom of the same concern: "Look, your little sister doesn't know where the witch is either! Tell her she's gone into the forest". Adopting the role of the elder sister allowed Helena to use the same soothing words that her father had used with her and she calmed down, consoling the baby: "She's gone into the forest! Don't cry. She's gone into the forest". The socialisation of reading allowed her to overcome the fear that the tale generated by transferring it onto her younger sister, and demonstrates how the integration of context into the reading adds new meanings to the experience.

Configuration and use of children's e-libraries on iPad

In the homes we visited the family shares the same iPad and the children's apps are stored in folders bearing the names of the children. Observation of the digital products contained in these folders demonstrates the coexistence of e-stories of significant diversity, and not always literary in nature. The predominant e-stories correspond to what Unsworth (2006) calls *digitally re-contextualised literature*, in other words, traditional stories that have been digitally enhanced, such as *Snow White* and *The Three Little Pigs*.

The children alternate e-stories with games (drawing and painting, ordering and association, thinking and strategy, simulation of everyday practices such as hair styling, makeup, pet care or cooking), music apps and family photograph and video albums. The ease with which they switch from a story to a game demonstrates the similarity that the literary product has with other products intended for educational or entertainment purposes and suggests that the iPad encourages an expansion of the concept of literature. And not only because the repository nature of the tablet favours the coexistence of very diverse products, but also because its open nature, by allowing access to the Internet, expands the range of possibilities for the enjoyment of a narrative product. For instance, during the fieldwork we observed that Chloe independently accessed YouTube and searched for episodes of *Pippi Longstocking*, thereby incorporating an audiovisual reference into the print reading of this children's literary classic that she had embarked on at the time.

The parents' criteria personalises the composition of the e-libraries with apps that respond to one or more of the following factors:

1) *The parents' interests* are projected in the search for apps that stimulate in their children the kind of narrative enjoyment that they themselves value. For example, Lucía's father, a fan of role-playing games, encourages adventure and mystery stories and e-stories where the reader adopts a participative role in the story, or does so by means of an avatar.
2) *The educational or linguistic function of the apps*. For example, Helena's father, in an effort to increase his daughter's linguistic input, expands the e-library with e-stories from Nickelodeon's *Dora's Christmas Adventure* collection, the Spanish version of which incorporates phrases in English. In Chloe's case the e-library is a mixture of stories in Catalan, Spanish, English and French – which is her father's native language and that of the school she attends. Itzel enjoys classic stories like *Little Red Riding Hood* told in Mexican Spanish which connects her with her father's language and culture.

3) *Indications of literary quality*, such as the number of stars displayed in the App Store purchase option. Lucía's father detailed his procedure for navigating a world which he considered limited in the options available in Catalan or Spanish for children from five to ten years old: "What I always look for are the stars. First I look for products for children aged two to five, then the stars. If I don't see any, I don't buy it. If I see four or five stars, that means the story is good". In the case of Chloe's mother, her professional ties to the world of children's literature allows her to access new products from an academic-literary criticism perspective and this is reflected in the careful selection of literary story apps in her daughter's library.
4) *The girls' preferences* in terms of specific stories, characters or interests. The fact that *Snow White* is one of Helena's favourite stories justifies the presence in her e-library of three versions of the story in addition to a princess's hair-styling game. Lucía's love of theatre, an activity to which she dedicates occasional evenings, is also reflected in the purchase of apps that include, as an extra, the possibility of dramatising the story.

New techno-literary learning and the role of the adult as facilitator

Access to e-library content requires the development of technological literacy skills in addition to learning processes related to literary narration:

> The potential for literacy learning when using such an app includes print literacy, visual literacy, app-based literacy (learning the controls of the specific app), and technological literacy, as readers/users/players engage physically and intellectually with the iPad. (Nixon, and Hateley 2013: 35)

These techno-literary learning processes are generally overseen by the adult in a complex process where the child progressively acquires autonomy. The diversity and specific nature of the actions required to navigate the library and each app means that initially it is the parent who carries them out while the children gradually request increased participation in the handling of the device, as can be seen in Image 1 and Image 3: in Image 1 it is the father who holds the device while Image 3 shows Lucía as an independent iPad user. When Lucía was five, her mother told us, she handled the iPad on her own. She would open it and decide what she was going to do. When she wanted to read she chose the audio narration option and only called on the adults when she was unable to resolve a specific problem. As a result, we can establish that the child's desire to control the device stimulates progress in technological competence.

Playing also acquires a training dimension that is simultaneously motor-based, cognitive and narrative. For example, when reading Nickelodeon's *Dora's Christmas Adventure*, Helena quickly overcomes the challenges that require skill in moving around the screen or associating interactive elements. When Chloe "plays" the role of a theatre extra in the Tales Apart *Snow White* app, she is exercising her comprehension of the story, as each screen only allows her to use the puppets-characters that correspond to the scene in question. The different types of playing observed, therefore, offer opportunities to interact in different learning processes while, at the same time, the girls learn to access the narrative space from a variety of conceptual entry points.

Navigation within the digital library also requires familiarisation with a series of consumer regulations, the initiation into which is demonstrated by the following dialogue.[4] Itzel was one year and eleven months old and it was the second time she had interacted with the iPad. After enjoying three apps, her mother suggests returning to the first, but the child prefers to try those she does not know and whose icons appear faded on the screen. The parents explain that, in these cases, in order to play they would have to purchase the apps:

Mother: Shall we go back to these three? We only have these three.

Itzel: No! No!

Mother: Which one?

Itzel: No!

Mother: No, no? OK, not the Koala [referring to an app]. Which one then? You choose.

Itzel: No, this one! [pointing to an app with a faded icon].

Mother: Which one do you want?

Itzel: This one [pointing to an app with a faded icon].

Father: But we have to pay for that one, Itzel.

Mother: We don't have those ones yet…

Children should learn to recognise semiotic indications that distinguish a downloadable app from the potential purchase option and internalise the fact that faded icons on the screen indicate that, despite their apparent availability, these apps are not accessible. Children should also be trained to resist the advertising tactics that incite purchase and that sometimes lead the parents to rapidly take the device from them when they realise they are about to click on the "buy now" button.

4 The exchange takes place in Catalan with the father's intervention in Spanish.

The effects of multimodality and interactivity on the reading experience

Literary reading during the events we observed focused on the fictional apps that the girls preferred and which they wanted to show to the researchers. The stories they read offered a wide variety of multimodal resources (image, movement, music, voices) and forms of interactivity, this being understood to refer to the wide range of relationships that can be established between the text and the reader (Ryan 2006) depending on the internal or external role that this plays in the story and the capacity to transform it or simply "live it". Many of these resources had noteworthy effects on the girls' reading responses (Sipe 2007) which leads us to argue that they influenced the way in which they experienced the fiction. We have selected two types of response, the immersive and the ludic, in an effort to demonstrate how multimodality and interactivity can affect the fictional experience.

The immersive response manifests itself in verbal and behavioural indications that demonstrate the symbiosis of the reader with the story. This process of "fictional absorption" happened to Lucía during the reading of Alpixel's *The Stolen Stars*, an adventure story where reader participation is projected onto an avatar, a narrative strategy that invites permeability between reality and the story and which, according to Ryan's (2006) classification, is the maximum type of interactivity, as opposed to that of external reader/spectator. Lucía experienced certain tension at the responsibility of affecting the fate of her chosen protagonist and insisted that her father make the decisions. When she was finally obliged to select one of the options presented by the narrator she covered her eyes and ran away from the screen, fearful of suffering the consequences of her decision. The captivating power of the excellent, expressive reading of the narrator, combined with the other multimodal resources (images, background music), provoke a dramatic impression that intensifies the reading experience, which in this case was further accentuated by the feeling of making of irreversible decisions.

Helena had a similar physical reaction also brought about by fear, in her case associated with the first appearance of the stepmother in the Tales Apart version of *Snow White*, a classic fairy tale that focuses on the stepmother's desire to kill the protagonist. The character of the stepmother disturbs Helena and she covers her ears throughout the entire reading as a defence mechanism that gives her security. In the culminating moment, when the stepmother disguises herself as an old woman to go and meet Snow White with the poisoned apple, the child asks her father not to continue to the next screen and gets up to distance herself from the device. At the end of the tale Helena feels the need to establish a border between the fictional world and her own reality and initiates the following dialogue, containing traces of meta-literary reflection, with her father:

> Helena: The witch isn't going to come because I've been a good girl. Why is there a witch [pointing to the screen]?
> Father: Why is there a witch? Because that's the way the story goes.
> Helena: But there are no witches here.
> Father: There are no witches here, isn't that right?
> Helena: But why?
> Father: Because we all behave ourselves very well here.

For Helena this immersion in the story leads the two worlds to merge, something we observed previously in the same reading event when, for example, she consoled her baby sister by telling her that the witch had gone into the forest. This adherence to the fiction explains her difficulty in confirming the impossibility that the character who terrifies her cannot invade her reality and also simultaneously explains the call for good behaviour as a safety device to save her in the event that this were not the case, and which her father reinforces in order to make her feel safe.

It is true that indications also appear in the reading of print books that demonstrate the intensity with which children experience the story, as shown in the study by Sipe (2007) concerning the reading responses to illustrated picturebooks in three-to-seven-year-old children. Among other categories, Sipe analysed examples of "transparent response" in which the children merge with the story and experience it as though it were their own. This category also corresponds to the responses of Lucía and Helena that we have just described. While in Sipe's study (2007) this category was a minority (2% of the speaking turns), our ethnographic data suggests that it is more frequent in children's electronic literature reading experiences due to the capacity of the multimodal and interactive resources to create a direct entry into the world of fiction, thereby multiplying the possibilities of merging with the story.

On the other hand the ludic response is associated with pleasure and satisfaction and is expressed in both cheerful behaviour and in the level of concentration with which the children respond to invitations to participate. In general it was the forms of interaction that challenged the reader to participate in the recreation of the story that incited this type of response. One example is the theatre option which allows the recreation of the tale by means of stick puppets that represent the story's characters in an interactive scenario. Another activity that appears in the "extra features" is that of recording one's own voice while reading the story.

The effect of these challenges on the reading experience is revealed in the manifestations of delight and the desire to socialise the experience. For example, Chloe encourages her mother to take part in the recording option by recording each other in turn while reading Itbook's *The Three Little Pigs*, where she manifests nervous delight with laughter and expressive gesticulation. The relationship between Lucía and the "theatrical extra" option found in Tales Apart's *Snow White* illustrates other nuances of the ludic dimension which in this case are experienced on an individual level while the parents chat; the child becomes absorbed in the activity and begins to softly verbalise the words she puts in the mouths of the puppets as she gets them to portray the story. The pleasure that this involvement in the activity causes her to feel, evidenced in her discreet smiles of delight, shows that children take seriously what may appear a mere game or pastime: concentration and the willingness to dedicate significant time to the activity. In short, the forms of interactivity we observed encourage the adoption of an active reader role that offers the child the possibility of enjoying the fiction from a creative perspective, shifting between recreation and imagination.

Educational implications

In order to further develop the educational implications of our study we begin with the conclusions of González, Moll and Amanti (2005) on the need for the new ways of interpreting and creating meanings that children develop within the family context to be taken into consideration in the classroom in order to reduce the technological and literary divide that has distanced the *print-centric classroom* from the *mobile-centric world*. Along these lines, our ethnographic observations on shared digital reading in four families provide information on the reflection of literary education in pre-school and primary education. It is based on previous studies that have explored the educational possibilities of tablets for the development of reading and writing skills (Burnett 2013; Colomer, and Fernández de Gamboa 2014; Lynch, and Redpath 2014).

In order to take into account the *funds of literary knowledge* of children accustomed to tablet-based reading in the home, schools should be aware of some of the characteristics of expanded literary conception promoted by the use of digital devices. For example, the coexistence in the tablet of both digital stories and a wide range of audiovisual products places literary reading in the field of personal enjoyment and shared cultural consumption. This aspect, combined with familiarity with the multimodal and interactive products contained in e-libraries, influences children's expectations with respect to literature, the scope of which has extended to include new ways of narrative fulfilment. It is important for schools to commit to an approach to children's literature that does not restrict the extended representation of the reading matter that emergent readers carry in their school bags when they enter the classroom, but rather enhances it.

Another aspect to be taken into consideration is the set of attitudes that children naturalise through the tablet-based reading experience. The iPad reader is aware of the impact that a story might have on them because they have previously had immersive experiences where the boundaries between the real and fictional worlds become indistinct. Moreover, the diversity of forms in which apps – via games and challenges – allow the reader to participate in the story, have revealed the ludic dimension of the activity to the reader while simultaneously accustoming them to adopting an active and participative role in the recreation options of the story. Schools should offer these digital experiences to those who lack them, without neglecting to provide them with a corpus of stimulating reading matter with activities that enrich and expand the reading experience.

The study presented here constitutes an example of how the observation of techno-literary practices developed outside school may offer guidance for the classroom. Given the increasing influence of technology in the literary socialisation of children and young people, we feel it necessary for research to progress towards knowledge of these practices that can be translated into educational proposals that establish a significant association between the home technological-driven practices and the school.

Works Cited

Aliagas, Cristina, and Ana María Margallo. "Children's Responses to the Interactivity of E-storybooks in Family Shared Reading Events Involving the iPad." *Literacy* (in press).

Burnett, Cathy. "Investigating Children's Interactions around Digital Texts in Classrooms: How Are these Framed and What Counts?" *Education 3-13*, 66.2 (2013): 192-209. Print.

Carrington, Victoria. "Emergent Home Literacies: A Challenge for Educators." *The Australian Journal of Language and Literacy*, 24.2 (2001): 88-100. Print.

Cassany, Daniel. *En línea.* Barcelona: Anagrama, 2012. Print.

Colomer, Teresa. *Andar entre libros.* México: FCE, 2005. Print.

Colomer, Teresa, and Karla Fernández de Gamboa Vázquez. "La incorporación de literatura infantil digital a la biblioteca de aula." *Anuario de investigación en literatura infantil y juvenil*, 12 (2014): 19-36. Print.

Common Sense Media. *Zero to Eight: Children's Media Use in America.* Common Sense, 2013. Web. 16 Jan. 2014.

González, Norma, Luis C. Moll, and Cathy Amanti, eds. *Funds of Knowledge: Theorizing Practice in Households, Communities, and Classrooms*. Mahwah, NJ: Lawrence Erlbaum, 2005. Print.

González-Patiño, Javier. "Rutinas de la infancia urbana mediadas por la tecnología: un análisis visual." *Papeles de Trabajo sobre Cultura, Educación y Desarrollo Humano*, 7.2 (2011): 1-16. Web. 29 Mai. 2015.

Heath, Shirley Brice. *Ways with Words: Language, Life and Work in Communities and Classrooms*. Cambridge: Cambridge UP, 1983. Print.

Kucirkova, Natalia, Kieron Sheehy, and David Messer. "A Vygotskian Perspective on Parent-Child Talk during iPad Story Sharing." *Journal of Research in Reading*, 38.4 (2014): 428-441. Print.

Lynch, Julianne, and Terry Redpath. "'Smart' Technologies in Early Years Literacy Education: A Meta-Narrative of Paradigmatic Tensions in iPad Use in an Australian Preparatory Classroom." *Journal of Early Childhood Literacy*, 14.2 (2014): 147-174. Print.

Marsh, Jackie, *et al*. *Digital Beginnings: Young Children's Use of Popular Culture, Media and New Technologies*. Sheffield: Literacy Research Centre of University of Sheffield, 2005. Web. 29 May 2015.

Merchant, Guy. "Young Children and Interactive Story-Apps." *New Literacies around the Globe. Policy and Pedagogy*. Eds. Cathy Burnett *et al*. Oxon: Routlege, 2014. 120-139. Print.

Nixon, Helen, and Erica Hateley. "Playing and Learning in the Age of Digital Media." *International Handbook of Research on Children's Literacy, Learning, and Culture*. Eds. Kathy Hall *et al*. Oxford: Blackwells, 2013. 28-41. Print.

O'Mara, Joanne, and Linda Laidlaw. "Living in the World: Two Literacy Researchers Reflect on the Changing Texts and Literacy Practices of Childhood." *English Teaching: Practice and Critique*, 10.4 (2011): 149-159. Web. 23 Feb. 2015.

Ryan, Marie-Laure. *Avatars of Story*. Minneapolis: U of Minnesota P, 2006. Print.

Simpson, Alyson, Maureen Walsh, and Jennifer Rowsell. "The Digital Reading Path: Researching Modes and Multidirectionality with iPads." *Literacy*, 47.3 (2013): 123-130. Print.

Sipe, Lawrence. *Storytime: Young Children's Literary Understanding in the Classroom*. New York: Teachers College Press, 2007. Print.

Sulzby, Elisabeth. "Writing and reading: Signs of oral and written language organizations in the young child." *Emergent literacy: Writing and reading*. Eds. William Teale, and Elisabeth Suzby. Norwood, N.J.: Ablex Publishing Corporation, 1986. 50-89. Print.

Turrión, Celia. "Multimedia Book Apps in a Contemporary Culture: Commerce and Innovation, Continuity and Rupture." *Nordic Journal of ChildLit Aesthetics*, 5 (2014). Web. 20 Mar. 2015.

Unsworth, Len. *E-literature for Children: Enhancing Digital Literacy Learning*. New York: Routledge, 2006. Print.

Verenikina, Irina, and Lisa Kervin. "iPads, Digital Play and Pre-schoolers." *He Kupu*, 2.5 (2011): 4-16. Print.

Wells, Gordon. *The Meaning Makers: Children Learning Language and Using Language to Learn*. Portsmouth, NH: Heinemann, 1986. Print.

Wohlwend, Karen E. "Early Adopters: Playing New Literacies and Pretending New Technologies in Print-Centric Classrooms." *Journal of Early Childhood Literacy*, 9.2 (2009): 119-143. Print.

Digital Literature in Early Childhood

Reading Experiences in Family and School Contexts

Neus Real
Universitat Autònoma de Barcelona

Cristina Correro
Universitat Autònoma de Barcelona

Introduction

The use of electronic devices by children under seven years old is a controversial subject. However, recent studies show that with correct supervision and guidance (control over usage times, responsible intervention by adults) the digital device offers undeniable benefits in terms of development in young children. The tablet, in particular, is considered especially suitable as it offers them an object for exploration and learning that has become essential in this technological age. For children of up to two years old, the tablet's exceptional visual, auditory and tactility characteristics present a format that is very close to their own intelligence, while for children from two to six it diversifies their sources of stimulation and develops an incipient digital conscience, non-analogue thought processes and abilities associated with sensorimotor forms of understanding and interaction (Bach *et al.* 2013). The spread of the use of these products in children's environments is, in addition, a social phenomenon that educational institutions cannot ignore, primarily because this expansion is not general to all environments as it is restricted in a way that further accentuates the already existing socio-economic inequalities that have increased in recent years as a result of the economic crisis. This situation, which is difficult to resolve on an individual level, must find a solution in the schools, where the responsibility for democratising an attribute that is essential to the personal and professional development of today's children – digital literacy – cannot be ignored.

From the specific perspective of literary education and children's literature it is impossible to disregard this new electronic paradigm (Borràs 2012; Hayles 2008) as its momentum and level of implementation are already determining factors in the education of literary readers (Stichnothe 2014; Turrión 2014b). At this point, however, we still know little about early childhood, tablets and electronic literature (e-lit) in the contexts of the home and the classroom (Al-Yaqout 2011; Aliagas, and Margallo in press; Roskos, Bourstein, and You 2012; Turrión 2014b; Yokota, and Teale 2014). Consequently, within the framework of the standpoints on the issue, this chapter offers the initial results of a series of observations carried out with children from two to six years old in both contexts. The objective is to address the various uses that can be made of children's digital literature in early childhood and contribute to a reflection on the potential of the electronic medium in the literary training and education of young children by providing descriptions of what happens when we confront them with tablets and literary apps: how do they learn to use them and what does this process entail; what are their preferences and why; how do they read on digital devices; what experiences are most interesting to them; how do tablets influence their reading progress; and what are the corresponding educational implications.

Young children and tablets: standpoints and contributions

The proliferation of touch tablets and the growth in digital output are two growing phenomena in developed countries (Common Sense Media 2013; Ministerio de Industria, Energía y Turismo [Spanish Ministry of Industry, Energy and Tourism] 2014; Gremi d'Editors de Catalunya [Publisher's Guild of Catalonia] 2014). Major toy manufacturers, bookshop chains and shops specialising in childcare and educational games have even created their own devices and content for the under-threes, and while their interests are purely commercial, this reflects the increasing influence of the new digital culture on the lives of young children. However, few studies exist that either endorse or advise against the various uses, encourage in-depth debate or offer guidance to those involved.

Researchers in academic circles assume two basic standpoints: detractors and defenders. The former base their arguments on studies carried out prior to the appearance of the iPad in 2010, such as those of the American Academy of Pediatrics (e.g., Strasburger, and American Academy of Pediatrics 2010; Christakis 2009; Strasburger, Jordan, and Donnerstein 2010). These opinions, subsequently disseminated by large communications companies that created social alarm by expounding their damaging effects (Quencua 2014), are based on the contact that children have with non-interactive devices, such as television and video games. In Europe, in contrast, over the last three years prestigious authorities have published studies that advocate the use of interactive devices in early childhood. One of the first to do so was the Académie Française des Sciences.

Their excellent multidisciplinary book, *L'enfant et les écrans* (2013), postulates the importance of a digital literacy that guarantees access to cyberculture for all children regardless of their social origin. It defends the early use of tablets on the basis of their potential for both cognitive development and the deployment of child sensorimotor intelligence (demonstrated by advances in areas such as neurobiology and medicine) by means of categorisation (shapes, colours, sounds and finger movements), and shows that, in the first years of life, electronic culture can encourage visual and mental agility, interactivity, sensory multiplicity, motivation, imagination, exploration and symbolic play, thereby optimising learning processes and possible aesthetic experiences. It therefore reaches areas that books have never managed to reach and offers endless possibilities for multiple customised readings. And all this while simultaneously insisting on the need to regulate exposure times, incorporate the use of devices into children's activities in a moderate way and accompany learning with training in digital self-regulation (Bach *et al.* 2013).

Despite contributions as relevant as that of the Académie Française des Sciences, its unique nature (further references of this category are scarce) is an indication of the pressing need to increase our knowledge on the subject. In light of this it is gratifying to see a group of more than fifty researchers obtain the IS1410 COST-action in 2015 for the research project entitled "The Digital Literacy and Multimodal Practices of Young Children" (DigiLitEY 2015).[1] Funded by the European Union and headed by Dr Jackie Marsh of the University of Sheffield, the project's aim is to develop multidisciplinary research on an international level to redress the lack of empirical studies dealing with the potentialities of digital devices with children of up to eight years old.

In a scenario thus far lacking a consolidated theoretical framework, international organisms and recognised authorities on children's literature have presented initiatives that encourage the use of digital devices by young children or, given the high degree of social implementation, attempt to provide guidance. For example, following their analysis of the impact of new technologies on early childhood, the North American non-governmental organisation Zero to Three has expressed their support for the reading of digital works, although they insist on suitable facilitation and guidance as well as complementary activities (National Centre for Infants, Toddlers and Families 2014), in a position analogous to that of the Académie Française des Sciences. The German reading foundation Stiftung Lesen recommends the use of this new technology from the earliest possible age, given its benefits to both the promotion of reading

1 The group has participants from more than twenty countries, including two members from GRETEL in Spain.

and the motivation of readers and facilitators, and offers a section on studies and electronic selections on their website (Stiftung Lesen 2014). In France, the Centre national de la littérature pour la jeunesse (Children's Literature National Centre) of the Bibliothèque Nationale, includes a quarterly selection of apps in *La revue des livres pour enfants* (Review of Books for Children) (*La Joie par les livres* 2014). In Spain, the Fundación Germán Sánchez Ruipérez (Germán Sánchez Ruipérez Foundation) has carried out various digital projects and also recommends works on its website ("Recursos digitales" 2014). In Catalonia, the GRETEL research group has created a virtual space with a bibliography, recommendations and links of interest ("LIJ Digital" 2014).

On a more global level, recommendations also come from the work carried out in dissemination and international recognition in the form of several specialised awards such as the Bologna Ragazzi Digital Award, presented by the Bologna Children's Book Fair, and the Prix du livre numérique jeunesse (Youth Digital Book Award), awarded by the Grenoble municipal libraries ("Bologna Ragazzi Digital Award"; "Le Prix du livre numérique jeunesse"). And although they are individual initiatives, we should nonetheless mention the app critiques posted on independent blogs, which serve to illustrate the open, horizontal, knowledge-sharing nature of the new digital ecosystem.[2]

Research on digital uses in early childhood: design and development

Beyond the institutional and individual responses to the social phenomenon of digital devices, recent research emphasises the urgent need to analyse digital works in order to determine what they offer the literary reader (Turrión 2014b) and to study what happens de facto with digital reading (Al-Yaquot 2011; Roskos, Burstein, and You 2012; Sheppard 2011). The specific insistence on the need for analyses of the true impact of tablets on children's literary education, both in the home and in school, and including the youngest family members, was the motivation for this project, the overall results of which are presented here: to introduce tablets featuring literary apps to children of up to six years old in environments where they previously were not present. In order to observe the entire discovery process in both the home and the school and to study the reading uses that were developed using the tablets, an exploratory investigation was carried out based on two longitudinal observations, one of them direct, over a period of two calendar years and with four families,

[2] Some good examples can be found in *CLAAB* 2014; Leveugle, and Leblanc 2012; ScreenKids 2010; and Turrión 2011.

the other based on the monitoring of two school years including direct observation in three pre-school classrooms. The comparison of results in the family and classroom contexts was considered a relevant objective from a didactic perspective as it could offer interesting data on the level and lines of impact of teaching facilitation and guidance focused on literary education.

The Apple tablet was chosen as it offers the widest selection of children's literature in iOS format and because its apps are the most popular (Horne 2012) and of better overall quality. The corpus was delimited to twenty five literary works on the basis of prior categorisation and analysis of those aimed at early childhood readers (Correro, and Real 2014a, 2014b) and the application of the basic selection criteria for children's books (Colomer 2010). The embryonic nature of digital production which is still of limited quality, the necessary adaptation of the apps to the effective reading possibilities of very young readers and the limited range of literary options available (currently far more ludic and educational than artistic), account for a selection that included fictional and non-fictional works that were considered on the whole to be of superior quality; these were notable for a series of unique components and focused on the cultural references that were most familiar to the children.[3]

In order to carry out observation in the family context, in September 2012 a questionnaire was sent to twenty families who had children under six years old and lived in the vicinity of the researchers. Four families were chosen that did not possess tablets, were not acquainted with literary apps and were willing both to participate and to welcome the researchers into their homes one evening a month. Once the families had been selected and the corresponding consent protocols signed, our young research subjects eventually numbered seven, were of both sexes and with similar profiles: four boys and three girls aged two to five from urban environments, middle class and with mainly Catalan-speaking parents with mid to high

3 The final list was: *Lil' Red: An Interactive Story* by Brian Main; *Emma Eats* by Carlsen; *The Forest Waits in Line... To Dine!* by CIDCLI; *Four Little Corners* by Dada Company; *La coccinelle* by Gallimard Jeunesse; *Hat Monkey* and *Nighty Night* by Fox&Sheep; *Rita the Lizard* by Irene Blasco Grau; *The Three Little Pigs*, *Alice's Adventures in Wonderland* and *Puss in Boots* by Itbook; *Saint George and the dragon* by SAU-La Galera; *Little Red Riding Hood*, *Parker Penguin*, *Bizzy Bear on the Farm*, *Bizzy Bear Builds a House* and *The Three Little Pigs* by Nosy Crow; *Fourmi* by Rouergue; *To the Farm!* by Sanoen; *SnowWhite and the Seven Dwarfs* and *Sleeping Beauty Puppet Show* by Tales Apart; *Barefoot World Atlas* by Touchpress Limited, and *Emma Loves Pink*, *The Red Apple* and *In front of My House* by WingedChariot (see Primary Works Cited). Linguistic criteria was not applied to the selection due to the difficulty in finding quality apps in the children's languages (Catalan and Spanish) and to the prior informal verification of how little this factor affects the children's interest in the apps.

cultural levels (three families with two children, each with a two-year-old boy and a five-year-old girl, and one family with a three-year-old boy). In December 2012 an iPad was presented to each family; two families also received an iPad mini in order to observe whether there were different uses depending on the tablet size. In addition to the digital corpus all the devices offered WiFi access to the Internet.

To select the schools we carried out interviews and classroom observations in three pre-school centres in the areas close to where the researchers lived during the 2011/12 school year. One pre-school, Escola Bressol Municipal Can Caralleu de Barcelona (Barcelona Municipal Pre-School Can Caralleu), was chosen for the fact that literary education formed one of the cores of its teaching programme, also regular literary reading practices were offered from the initial education level and, finally, because they were willing to participate in the research. In August 2012 three tablets (two iPads and one iPad mini) containing the twenty-five selected apps were presented to the two higher level two-to-three-year-old classes. A total of thirty-six pupils, their two teachers and the director of the centre participated in the digital replication of the activities usually carried out using printed works: independent reading in a classroom library context (supervised by an adult in order to ensure the safety of the devices) and shared reading events guided by a teacher.

In January 2013 monthly observations of one and a half hours' duration were initiated with the families. In the school, the children's evolution was monitored via ongoing contact with the teaching staff and two morning sessions (each one containing several reading events) were observed in July 2013 (one in each class following a full year using the tablet) and another in December, for purposes of contrast, with a new group of children aged two to three (from the 2013/14 school year). Data was recorded using four instruments: a field notebook, audiovisual recordings, questionnaires and semi-structured interviews. The overall descriptions and findings, organised by subject, are presented below.

iPads in the family context: uses and (literary) preferences of young children

One of the first results of the research in the family context was the confirmation of the expectation and interest that the tablets generate in young children, an observation that is present in all prior research projects. With regard to the apps, all seven children requested the iPad daily (50%) or two or three times per week (50%). They enjoyed discovering and reading the works and preferred to use the device on their own. Fascinated by the possibilities, they preferred the iPad to other activities and were never willing to relinquish them. As a result, some regulations had to be immediately established in all cases. The figure of the adult facilitator (father or mother) was an essential factor in regulating the time spent using and sharing the iPad (to avoid conflicts among siblings). From the third month onwards, use of the tablet stabilised to the same level as other entertainment opportunities but the level of attraction remained throughout the two years of the study, largely as a result of the increased uses provided by the addition of an Internet connection and the availability of options such as painting and writing.

Another notable aspect was the speed with which priority uses of the tablet and preferences for specific digital works were established. After twelve weeks, once the novelty of the device and the apps had worn off and access to the Internet had been discovered, all the children used the iPad for watching their favourite television series and re-reading their favourite apps, in that order. From the beginning the chosen apps were those that allowed them to interact by playing with the protagonists and that also contained comic and scatological elements (e.g., *Nighty Night* or *Emma Eats*) as well as more relevant elements of direct reader action (for example, helping the protagonists swim to escape from their predators, or constructing something, such as in *Parker Penguin* or the Bizzy Bear Series, or offering the possibility of recreating the story by dramatising it, such as in *SnowWhite and the Seven Dwarfs*). The possibility of becoming a co-protagonist or co-author became a highly motivating component and one of the principal factors of the children's preferences, thereby confirming that involvement is promoted by the features in digital tablets and apps that include a strong interactive component (Aliagas, and Margallo in press; Roskos, Burstein, and You 2012; Sheppard 2011).

The adaptations of popular stories, because of the highly ludic nature of their digital remediation and the fact that they were known to the children, constituted the second group of preferences (Itbook's *The Three Little Pigs* being significantly one of the most popular). In third place were the new versions of informative books (such as *La coccinelle*, *Parker Penguin* and *The Forest Waits in Line... To Dine!*) whose success is due to the spectacular expansion of the reading experience which is multi-sensorial and infinitely more comprehensive (Correro, and Real 2014a, 2014b). The fourth place was occupied by apps with a special attraction in terms of identification or personalisation, i.e. those that generate more empathy thanks to the potential of digitality, e.g., *Emma Loves Pink*, with its charming and convincing child's voice which the children loved even though they did not understand English, or those that allow the reader to record the story in their own voice (versions of popular stories by Itbook). Without these elements neither the digital versions of picturebooks nor even the most experimental apps enjoyed much popularity: the children were quick to see the difference between reading on the device and reading in print (if they wished to "play", they chose the tablet and apps; if they wanted "a story", they asked to read a book with an adult).

These uses and preferences changed over the two years of the project. As they got older and became more familiar with the device and the corpus, the children rejected the simpler, more ludic works ("it's for babies", replied one of the children to her father in October of 2014 when he asked her why she no longer chose *The Three Little Pigs* by Itbook when initially she had loved it) in favour of more complex and interesting works such as the multi-linear *Little Red Riding Hood* by Nosy Crow. While they still used the iPad to watch television series, they progressively added video games that they played online or downloaded, initially with the help of the parents and later on their own. This confirms gamification in uses of digital media and the importance of the literary proposal from apps, and facilitators should therefore know how to evaluate them correctly (Al-Yaqout 2011; Aliagas, and Margallo in press; Turrión 2014b; Yokota 2013).

Their preferences having been established, the children returned repeatedly to the apps they were familiar with over a significant but limited period of time (from two to four months) and with generally fragmented readings. While initially they switched from one app to another when a problem appeared that they did not know how to solve or by accident, as their control over both the tablet and their own actions increased, the fragmented nature of the readings continued; they would directly navigate to the scenes that were most entertaining and which offered them particular interactive pleasure, an aspect that should be taken into consideration in the light of the differential nature of digital literature with respect to the printed book, despite their concomitances (Stichnothe 2014; Turrión 2014a) and the level of involvement required (Roskos, Burstein, and You 2012).

The material learning process in the children was very swift – significant changes were observed in just a few weeks and in two years they became iPad experts – and afforded them very significant autonomy in their development stage. The children enjoyed being able to do without the adult to access the apps, a fact that indicates the suitability of tablets for uses identified in numerous studies (Al-Yaqout 2011; Bach *et al.* 2013; Correro, and Real 2014a). Some notable autonomous learning processes were observed. For example, with regard to the linguistic potential of digital literature: the children internalised new structures and vocabulary that they subsequently used in oral exchanges with the adults and repeated words, phrases and titles that they heard in their mother tongue and other languages.

With regard to autonomous uses, the children's preference (especially those under three) for the iPad mini is also relevant. In both families that possessed both sizes of iPad, the larger was immediately rejected as the proportions and lighter nature of the mini version made it more manageable.

Finally, it is interesting to confirm that the initial impulse towards app reading and the subsequent complementary addition of an Internet connection evolved, in 70% of cases in the final phase of the research, towards exclusive interest in the iPad for the purposes of watching television programmes and playing video games. Uses were distributed progressively (after four months' observation) between apps and print. On the one hand through the identification of tablets with pre-existent entertainment proposals (which at this point were used autonomously, like television), or with entertainment proposals discovered via the device by the children, who found them more attractive than the apps (video games); and on the other hand through the identification of printed books with the proposal of "reading a story" under adult guidance. This points to elements that are worthy of consideration in terms of the literary quality of children's digital production, the basic possibilities that this output offers young users today, the ability of these users to perceive the virtues and limitations of the productions and the difference made by adult guidance.

iPads in schools: uses and literary preferences in pre-school

In the Escola Bressol Municipal Can Caralleu de Barcelona (Barcelona Municipal Pre-School Can Caralleu) the children's initial curiosity and keen interest in the tablet were confirmed and, as occurred in the home environment, they began experimenting with the device and discovered its basic operating functions in a short space of time. In the plural context of the classroom, however, significant differences occurred: the children with more initiative and leadership ability, more advanced motor skills and greater prominence in everyday routines and proposals, controlled the use of the iPad in both the independent and shared reading events. The more timid and prudent children would generally remain on the sidelines or require adult intervention in order to take part in the digital literary reading. Intermediate attitudes were also observed, leading to the establishment of three clearly defined groups: primary interactors, secondary interactors and observers.[4]

4 For some years now the term *interactor* has been applied to users of interactive systems (Ribes 2001). Given the active nature of the participation encouraged by the interactivity of the apps referred to here, its use is considered most suitable for the purposes of categorisation.

The plurality of the classroom also explains the occurrence of further conflicts, principally between primary and secondary interactors. This leads us to suggest that, in the classroom (where it is normal that there are more users than tablets due to their cost and student ratios), complementary options for controlling the usage times and organising the individual and shared use of iPads should be considered, such as using a projector to visualise the iPad on a large screen and distributing turns and interactive actions with the apps among the children.

The children's literary preferences coincided with those in the family context. The more entertaining and interactive apps – i.e. playful adaptations of popular classics, non-fictional works that offered multi-sensorial experiences and titles that were notable for either their empathetic appeal or for their inherent possibilities for personalisation – were the selections of the pupils at all times. The same occurred in shared reading events, in which the teachers alternated the possibility of reading a specific app with the collective reading of apps chosen by the children. With regard to the device itself, however, as the months passed the interest in autonomous use declined and, significantly, not because of the shared use of the device with intervention by the teachers – whose guided readings offset the strict playing style that the children opted for when they were on their own. The difference that facilitation and guidance makes to early childhood e-lit reading practices (an aspect that we will return to later) was thus established. As it stands today, it would appear that without facilitation the overall possibilities of digital literary reading are diminished in both qualitative and, increasingly, quantitative terms.

Another notable aspect, and one which once again coincides with the observations in the family context, is the children's pleasure in experimenting with the device and learning to control it. For those who struggle for autonomy on a daily basis (two or three years old), the ability to effectively operate the tablet without assistance, combined with the resulting successive discoveries, constituted a highly attractive element. The children were also attracted to the digital reading experience and found it more personal due to the sensorial and tangible idiosyncrasies of the device and the traits inherent to the primarily tactile, auditory and kinetic nature of children's digital literature. The children's free and unrestricted access to the digital works (they were not reliant on reading thanks to the audio) became a significant aspect as their autonomous reading of children's literature was thus made possible earlier thanks to a specific kind of literature, e-lit, that also offered possibilities which, beyond mere reception, extended to options for direct learning and creation without facilitator intervention. For example, this occurred through the spontaneous repetition of words and phrases (with *To the Farm!* among other apps), the recording of the story using the child's own voice (with the Itbook classics), or the theatrical re-writing of the story using combinations of scenes, characters and elements (with the works of Tales Apart), as occurred in the private context. In the school the teachers also confirmed that the use of the iPad allows the children to increase some skills which are essential to this age group, such as fine motor skills.

It is worth mentioning, however, that the intervention of the adult in the reading event was essential in order to advance beyond compulsive touching of the screen and the mere playing of games, as evidenced by the independent reading of Itbook's *The Three Little Pigs* in the first session we observed (even after a year's familiarisation with the app, interactive confusion occurred, with conflicts included). Ludic uses also predominated in the classroom when the children were in charge of the device, although they were unable to access the Internet to watch their favourite television shows or to play online video games (options that were not available in the school). When the children were given free rein, the firm favourites were the options that offered tactile interaction and ludic elements both inside and outside the context of the stories. It was only the facilitation – which regulated the pace of the reading in order to focus the children's attention on specific elements by means of questions and observations similar to those that guide activities relating to printed books – that compensated this dynamic and placed the literary components in their rightful place in terms of reader training. Although it was also observed, concurrently, that facilitation could reach a point where it neutralised the fragmentary nature of digital reading (predominant in independent reading) if the linearity of analogue reading was unconsciously reproduced through the manner in which the text was accessed.

One of the significant distinguishing factors between independent and guided reading was provided in the observational sessions by a reading event with *Emma Eats*, one of the favourite apps. Without the intervention of the teacher the children laughed and had fun using their fingers to move the little bear's head and cover it with tomato sauce, etc. They simply enjoyed playing, and while they occasionally commented on what they saw, touching the screen and seeing what happened when they did so interested them above all else.

Indeed this app offers a ludic and fragmented proposal that is very suitable for users in their early childhood years. With teacher guidance, however, the reading experience is modified and enriched. As a result of the open questions, indications designed to focus the children's attention and the synthesis of the children's contributions, the children's enjoyment of the interactive literary game did not decrease; they also simultaneously commented on the essential features of each scene (the space, the protagonist and her actions), identified some of the elements (secondary characters and objects), comprehensively developed possibilities for intervention (such as placing an entire series of objects, rather than just one, when this was requested), detected and verbalised structural components of the work (humour) and, based on the facilitation, even reached the point of establishing cause-effect relationships (eat-grow), an aspect that is still complex for two- to three-year-old children. The children experienced the pleasure of digital reading while simultaneously developing reading skills and acquiring knowledge that would prove useful for accessing other literary texts and understanding them more fully. However, this was a linear reading that did not attend to the structural fragmented nature and hence equated digital reading with its analogue counterpart.

It is facilitation therefore that guarantees the optimum exploitation of digital works (as occurs in printed editions) in terms of literary education (Munita, and Manresa 2012). Further proof of this was provided in the guided reading event of *The Red Apple* during the second observational session. Although this app is not very interactive and had not aroused interest during the year, the simple fact that it was proposed by an adult, the beginning of the story (read in a small group and with the tablet visible to all) immediately caught the children's attention, put a stop to the unbridled tactile impulses of the principal interactors and soon attracted children that were involved in other activities. During the reading event the facilitator employed resources of shared meaning construction (e.g., the link between life and literature, with the resulting involvement of the children), fostered diverse strategies (forming hypotheses based on the paratexts, foreseeing the events in the story – with the implicit learning of the structural comprehension of the storyline, expressed in repeated sequences – or detecting intertextual links) and finished by explicitly stating what had been learned in a final summation. A whole different reading story, in other words.

Conclusions

From all the above the following conclusions can be reached:

1. Recent research indicates that apps allow the incorporation of multimodal and multilinear production that diversifies uses and reading experiences and requires new modes of experimentation, reading and thinking, with the corresponding benefits for the general development and literary training of young children.
2. Children between the ages of two and six show great interest in tactile devices and apps generate great expectation among them.
3. These devices allow them to develop autonomy in leisure activities as well as other abilities, such as fine motor skills, which are essential to their stage of development.

4. Children attain reading autonomy at an earlier age, which they find satisfying due to the user-friendliness of touch tablets; they master them very quickly and, due to the multimodal nature of digital literature, the audios replace the need for the adult intervention required with printed books.
5. The initial interest in apps progressively decreases when used independently by children. If they discover that the tablet allows them to watch television and play video games, reading soon becomes less important, although use of the device as a preferred leisure activity remains.
6. Children's interest in apps does not disappear with shared use accompanied by adequate guidance because interaction and playing enrich and enhance the reading experience through focalisation on the literary aspects.
7. In the absence of facilitation children's reading usage of digital literature becomes completely gamified. In the home environment playtime is associated with apps and the tablet, while reading is associated with books and adult intervention. In the classroom, facilitated reading counteracts the predominance of playing in children's independent reading events.
8. The inherently fragmentary nature of digital reading (facilitation has little effect without corresponding training) presents a clear evolution among children under six, from total ignorance and random selection to conscious selection of scenes with more emphasis on interaction and ludicity.
9. The favourite apps are, in the following order: fictional apps that display a high level of interaction and playing, the new gamified versions of popular classics, non-fictional apps that offer multi-sensorial experiences and works that offer the possibility of special identification or personalisation.
10. Digital literature promotes a more personal reading experience that is attractive to young children and expands their possibilities for autonomous learning and creation in literary and linguistic terms.

These conclusions point towards the logic of introducing children's digital literature from the earliest stages of education as a complement to printed books. Schools should democratise access to a body of work that encourages implication, offers very intense reading experiences and calls for the introduction of different modalities of participation, comprehension and interpretation in order to contribute to digital (literary) literacy without desisting in the regulation of certain specific uses that eventually relegate literary apps to the level of strict game playing, or obscurity, in favour of other leisure possibilities offered by touch-screen devices. It is recommendable to diversify the forms of presenting e-lit in the same manner that didactics suggests in the case of printed books (Fittipaldi 2013). Some formulas do not differ significantly from what is already practiced in the schools, although specific teacher training in e-lit for children is necessary. The decisive issue is to provide educational staff with the resources required to correctly cultivate this literature in pre-school classrooms. Without this it will be difficult to provide a response to one of the principal social challenges of the 21st century.

Works Cited

Primary Works Cited

Alice's Adventures in Wonderland. Valencia: Itbook, 2010. iPad edition.

Barefoot World Atlas. London: Touchpress Limited, 2014. iPad edition.

Bauer, Jutta, and Carlsen. *Emma Eats*. Hamburg: Carlsen, 2013. iPad edition.

Bizzy Bear Builds a House. London: Nosy Crow, 2012. iPad edition.

Bizzy Bear on the Farm. London: Nosy Crow, 2011. iPad edition.

Blasco Grau, Irene. *Rita the Lizard*. Valencia: Irene Blasco Grau, 2012. iPad edition.

Canyelles, Anna. *Saint George and the dragon*. Barcelona: SAU – La Galera, 2013. iPad edition.

Douzou, Olivier. *Fourmi*. Arles Cedex: Rouergue, 2012. iPad edition.

Dubuc, Marianne. *In front of My House*. London: WingedChariot, 2011. iPad edition.

Hat Monkey. Berlin: Fox&Sheep, 2014. iPad edition and Google Playstore.

La coccinelle. Ill. Silvaine Peyrols. Paris: Gallimard Jeunesse, 2011. iPad edition.

Little Red Riding Hood. Ill. Ed Bryan. London: Nosy Crow, 2013. iPad edition.

Main, Brian. *Lil'Red. An Interactive Story*. Brian Main, 2013. iPad edition.

Oral, Feridun. *The Red Apple*. London: WingedChariot, 2011. iPad edition.

Parker Penguin. London: Nosy Crow, 2013. iPad edition.

Puss in Boots. Valencia: Itbook, 2012. iPad edition.

Raud, Piret. *Emma Loves Pink*. London: WingedChariot, 2010. iPad edition.

Ruillier, Jérôme. *Four Little Corners*. Madrid: Dada Company, 2013. iPad edition and Google Playstore.

Sleeping Beauty Puppet Show. Barcelona: Tales Apart, 2012. iPad edition.

SnowWhite and the Seven Dwarfs. Barcelona: Tales Apart, 2012. iPad edition.

The Three Little Pigs. London: Nosy Crow, 2011. iPad edition.

The Three Little Pigs. Valencia: Itbook, 2012. iPad edition.

To the Farm! Premià de Dalt: Sanoen, 2012. iPad edition.

Wittlinger, Heidi, and Fox&Sheep. *Nighty Night*. Berlin: Fox&Sheep, 2013. iPad edition and Google Playstore.

Secondary Works Cited

Al-Yaqout, Ghada, and Maria Nikolajeva. "Re-conceptualising Picturebook Theory in the Digital Age." *Nordic Journal of ChildLit Aesthetics*, 6 (2015) Web. 22 Feb. 2015.

Aliagas, Cristina, and Ana María Margallo. "Children's Responses to the Interactivity of E-storybooks in Family Shared Reading Events Involving the iPad." *Literacy* (in press).

Bach, Jean François, *et al. L'enfant et les écrans. Un avis de l'Académie des sciences*. Paris: Éducation Le Pommier, 2013. Print.

"Bologna Ragazzi Digital Award." *Bologna Children's Book Fair. Bologna.* Bologna Children's Book Fair, n.d. Web. 26 Nov. 2014.

Borràs, Laura. "Había una vez una app… Literatura infantil y juvenil (en) digital." *Revista de Literatura*, 269 (2012): 21-26. Print.

Christakis, Dimitri. "The Effects of Infant Media Usage: What Do We Know and What Should We Learn?" *Acta Pediatrica*, 98 (2009): 8-16. Print.

CLAAB: Children's Literature Apps and Books Club. 2014. Web. 26 Nov. 2014.

Colomer, Teresa. *Introducción a la literatura infantil y juvenil.* Madrid: Síntesis, 2010. Print.

Common Sense Media. *Zero to Eight: Children's Media Use in America.* Common Sense, 2013. Web. 16 Jan. 2015.

Correro, Cristina, and Neus Real. "Panorámica de la literatura digital para la educación infantil." *Revista Textura (ULBRA)* 16.32 (2014a): 224-244. Web. 20 Jan. 2015.

—. "Aplicacions per a primeres edats." *International Symposium: Electronic Literature: Texts, Readers and Teaching Practices.* 3-4 Oct. 2014, Barcelona. Barcelona: Universitat Autònoma de Barcelona, 2014b. 37-43. Web. 20 Jan. 2015.

DigiLitEY: The digital literacy and multimodal practices of young children. 2015. Web. 19 Oct. 2015

Fittipaldi, Martina. "¿Qué han de saber los niños sobre literatura? Conocimientos literarios y tipos de actuaciones que permiten progresar en la competencia literaria." Diss. Universitat Autònoma de Barcelona, 2013. Print.

Gremi d'Editors de Catalunya. *Hàbits de Lectura i Compra de Llibres a Catalunya 2013*. Barcelona: Gremi d'Editors de Catalunya-Associació d'Editors en Llengua Catalana, 2014. Web. 10 Feb. 2015.

Hayles, N. Katherine. *Electronic Literature: New Horizons for the Literary*. Notre Dame: U of Notre Dame P, 2008. Print.

Horne, Lars Korsemann. "Apps: A Practical Approach to Trade and Co-Financed Book Apps." *Publishing Research Quarterly*, 28.1 (2012): 17-22. Print.

La Joie par les livres. Centre national de la littérature pour la jeunesse. Web. 26 Nov. 2014.

"Le Prix du livre numérique jeunesse." *Bibliothèques municipales de Grenoble*. Bibliothèques municipales de Grenoble, n.d. Web. 10 Mar. 2015.

Leveugle, Odile, and Valérie Leblanc. *Applimini*. 2012. Web. 26 Nov. 2014.

"LIJ Digital." *GRETEL: Grup de recerca en literatura infantil i juvenil i educació literària*. GRETEL, 2014. Web. 10 Mar. 2015.

Munita, Felipe, and Mireia Manresa. "La mediación en la discusión literaria." *La literatura que acoge: Inmigración y lectura de álbumes*. Eds. Teresa Colomer, and Martina Fittipaldi. Caracas/Barcelona: Banco del Libro-Gretel, 2012. 119-143. Print.

Ministerio de Industria, Energía y Turismo. Secretaría de Estado de Telecomunicaciones y para la Sociedad de la Información. *La sociedad en red 2013*. Madrid: Ministerio de Industria, 2014. Web. 10 Feb. 2015.

National Center for Infants, Toddlers, and Families. *Zero to Three*. 2014. Web. 10 Mar. 2015.

Quenqua, Douglas. "¿Qué han de leer los bebés? ¿Hora de leer cuentos o de mirar otra pantalla más?" *El País* 3 Oct. 2014: Suplemento – 1 y 5. Print.

"Recursos digitales." Fundación Germán Sánchez Ruipérez. Web. 26 Nov. 2014.

Ribes i Guàrdia, Francesc Xavier. "Las emisoras de radio del Estado español en Internet. Las *bitcasters*." Diss. Departamento de Comunicación Audiovisual y de Publicidad, Universitat Autònoma de Barcelona, 2014. Web. 10 Mar. 2015.

Roskos, Kathleen, Karen Burstein, and Byeong-Keun You. "A Typology for Observing Children's Engagement with eBooks at Preschool." *Journal of Interactive Online Reading*, 11.2 (2012): 47-66. Web. 10 Dec. 2014.

ScreenKids. "La Souris Grise." 2010. Web. 26 Nov. 2014.

Sheppard, Dale. "Reading with iPads – the difference makes a difference." *Education Today*, Term 3 (2011): 12-15. Web. 26 Nov. 2014.

Stichnothe, Haddassah. "Engineering Stories? A Narratological Approach to Children's Book Apps." *Nordic Journal of ChildLit Aesthetics*, 5 (2014). Web. 17 Apr. 2015.

Stiftung Lesen. "Digitale Lesewelten." Web. 26 Nov. 2014.

Strasburger, Victor C., and American Academy of Pediatrics. Council on Communications and Media. "Policy Statement-Media Education." *Pediatrics*, 126.5 (2010): 1012-1017. Print.

Strasburger, Victor C., Amy B. Jordan, and Ed Donnerstein, eds. "Health effects of media on children and adolescents." *Pediatrics*, 125.4 (2010): 756-767. Web. 26 Nov. 2014.

Turrión, Celia. *Literaturas exploratorias*. Web blog post. 2011. Web. 10 Mar. 2015.

—. "Multimedia Book Apps in a Contemporary Culture: Commerce and Innovation, Continuity and Rupture." *Nordic Journal of ChildLit Aesthetics*, 5 (2014a). Web. 20 Mar. 2015.

—. "Narrativa infantil y juvenil digital. ¿Qué ofrecen las nuevas formas al lector literario?" Diss. Universitat Autònoma de Barcelona, 2014b. Print.

Yokota, Junko. "From Print to Digital? Considering the Future of Picturebooks for Children." *Bologna: Fifty Years of Children's Books from around the World.* Ed. Giorgia Grilli. Bologna: Bononia University Press, 2013. Web. 10 Dec. 2014.

Yokota, Junko, and William H. Teale, "Picture Books and the Digital World: Educators Making Informed Choices." *The Reading Teacher*, 67.8 (2014): 577-585. Print.

Reading Literature on Screen in a Classroom Library

Teresa COLOMER
Universitat Autònoma de Barcelona

Karla FERNÁNDEZ DE GAMBOA VÁZQUEZ
Universitat Autònoma de Barcelona

Most schools in our environment use information and communication technology (ICT) at different levels and in various facets of their teaching. Teachers and students commonly use the computer to search for information or to perform activities in different knowledge areas (Jimoyannis, and Komis 2008) and digital reading education has already been incorporated into the school objectives to the point where they form part of international evaluations. However, when these teachers and students participate in activities for the promotion and creation of reading habits they use only printed works. The reading of digital fiction and the interpretive learning of multimodal works practically takes place outside the school.

We at the GRETEL research group asked ourselves what would happen if children had a corpus of fiction available in the classroom library that included both printed books and digital works. What effect would it have on their reading practices? What would their preferences be? How would they assess these works in shared conversation activities? Would this influence the conceptualisation of literary reading expressed by the children? The answers to these questions should give us clues to the didactic benefit of integrating this type of literature in current literary education.

Research description[1]

One of the actions carried out by our team was to conduct exploratory research on reading habits by introducing digital works of fiction into a primary school classroom library.

---

1 A first description of this research can be seen in Colomer, and Fernández de Gamboa 2014.

Choosing the school situation to be observed

The research was carried out in a primary school classroom located on the outskirts of a Catalonian city, with a sixth-year class of eighteen students aged between eleven and twelve.[2] We started by introducing into the classroom five iPads with sixteen fictional apps, freely mixing them with books for five months.[3] We then set about observing the independent reading of the students during that period.

It must be pointed out that the school is located in a low-level socioeconomic and cultural area and has an adult population with primary-level education. This implied a low level of familiarity with technology which was beneficial from the point of view of observing motivation and the ways in which the children approached digital fiction. Moreover, this group of students had read a large number of books and had developed a high level of reading skills over the previous three school years with the same teacher they had at the time of the research. This situation allowed us to access abundant information on the previous reading habits of the children in order to contextually interpret the behaviours we observed. In addition, as described by Reyes (2011), the group routinely carried out independent reading practice and literary conversations which facilitated the observation of their reading and the obtaining of the children's explicit and spontaneous reflections on the digital reading experience.

How the information was obtained

The observation was conducted two days a week from January to May 2013. Two activities of the group were observed which were habitual for them since the third year of primary school: half an hour daily of independent reading and one hour per week of conversation and recommendation from the children on the works read.

After analysing the existing digital production, the works were selected based on criteria of quality, scope and diversity of digital resources, their age-appropriateness and on the possibility of text in Catalan or Spanish. The selection of the corpus inevitably reflected the poor amount of digital literary production on the Spanish market at the time of the research (Borràs 2012) which distorted the comparison of the children's reading preferences with respect to the written corpus. As this was the real situation of the children's reading material on offer, it seemed relevant to explore the advantages and disadvantages of introducing it into the school environment under the current conditions. Analysis worksheets of

2 This is the Francesc Aldea i Pérez School in Terrassa, with Lara Reyes López as group tutor.

3 To see a list of some of the apps see Primary Works Cited.

the selected corpus were created following the Turrión (2014) model for subsequent contrast with the reading results obtained. Six digitised works were also selected, including some printed works already in the classroom library. The objective here was to examine the children's interest in works which merely added the novelty of the screen to the printed format. The children anonymously answered an initial individual questionnaire on their reading context, use of ICT, experience in specific reading of digital fiction and expectations for extending the classroom library with works of this type.

Observation guidelines were drawn up for the independent reading practice in order to collect data on the reading uses of digital literature. The guidelines were complemented by a researchers' observation diary which would also be used for the observation of the conversation sessions.

Five iPads were loaded with a first corpus of ten digital and six digitised works. Two months later, six more digital works were added to maintain the children's interest and continued reading possibilities. The tablets were placed in the classroom library and the rules of use were equivalent to those for reading books: they could read in pairs or groups, they could change reading material and reserve the device for the next session if they had not finished reading. Instructions on the basic operation of the device (turning it on, changing application, etc.) were given, but this was postponed to see how specific autonomous learning of the management of the apps developed, imitating the real context of coexistence of a printed and digital corpus.

Throughout the process eighteen independent reading practice sessions and four conversations were audiovisually recorded. In the first case, the static camera allowed us to capture the group reading activity and the use of the devices; it did not however allow us to see the interaction of each reader with the digital work they were reading, an aspect that has not been considered here. In the second case, the recordings of the sessions were transcribed for subsequent analysis of the students' discursive construction on digital reading.

The students' individual reading diaries were also available to the investigation: a record of all the works that the children had read over the previous three years, to which a separate section was added for digital works.

What information was obtained?

After the observation and data collection phase, we proceeded with the process and analysis stage. First, the data from the initial questionnaire, the observation guidelines and the comments made by the researchers in their diary on the independent reading practice (Table 1) were exported.

This yielded results on the starting point of the students, the expectations created by the experience, the learning of the use of the devices and the development of digital reading practices in a classroom library situation.

Second, the students' digital reading diaries were transcribed to a chronological and title-based table (Table 2), which showed how many times each work of the corpus had been read, the distribution over time and which specific students had read them. This information revealed the evolution of the students' involvement in the digital reading as well as the reading preferences from a quantitative point of view with respect to the printed works and a qualitative point of view regarding the digital titles.

Third, the reading rate obtained for each work was compared to its descriptive characteristics sheet. With this information we attempted to establish a correlation between both sets of data to reveal the incidence of the type of digital works on reading choices. In the same way we incorporated the results of the analysis of the transcriptions to see the evaluations expressed by the children for each specific title. This allowed us to obtain results on the evaluations according to the specific characteristics of the digital and digitised texts.

Fourth, we performed an in-depth analysis of the transcriptions of the conversation sessions on the works. For this we used the inferential content analysis method (López-Aranguren 2000), with thematic patterns and definition of emergent categories. The thematic results of the transcriptions were crosschecked with the researchers' diaries in order to achieve a clearer interpretation of the topics of interest for the research (Table 3). This allowed us to show the aspects highlighted by the children regarding the works and digital reading, and to characterise the discourse built upon the differences between printed and digital reading.

Explanation of some of the results

Here we will discuss some of the findings obtained in the reading practices, preferences between the print and digital corpus, preferences according to the characteristics of the digital works and the collective construction of the discourse regarding the interest in digital reading.

Reading practices using digital devices

The initial questionnaire was designed to describe the reading context of the sample along with their previous reading experience with digital devices and expectations for the experience. Some of the results describe the sample as a group of students with mothers who read daily (17%) or "sometimes" (72%), and 67% of fathers who "never" read. Despite this context of limited reading practice, their school education had achieved that 83% of the girls and boys rated themselves as "big readers" or that they "read quite a lot" and 94% of them read daily or almost daily. Also, despite the lack of family literacy, new technologies had made their way into the home: 67% of the children had the Internet at home and used it to write in the school blog or in social networks (94%), to play (72%), to watch films (28%) or to read (22%). However, no one said they had ever read fictional texts on a digital device.

Their expectations for the upcoming experience were positive, although 85% simply gave different variations of inexpert answers in the questionnaire saying they expected it to be "fun", and only in some cases did the reflection seem to respond to a more specific knowledge of digital fiction, giving clues to their consideration that this was something hybrid, close to the audiovisual, and even traces of suspicion from some students who seemed to especially enjoy books:

> I think it will be an innovative experience, because reading digitally is a really new thing. On the other hand I don't think I'll like reading with the iPad as much as reading on paper because we won't be able to physically have the story, and with the music and special effects some will have, it'll look like a film.[4]

Integration of reading with digital devices into the regular reading habits

Reading with digital devices was very quickly integrated into the regular reading habits of independent reading. The curiosity of the students for an unfamiliar reading format created a great demand for the devices during the first weeks. However, it soon became obvious, and even surprising, that digital reading became merely another option, to the extent that some devices were left on the shelf during some sessions.

Collaborative learning: operating the devices

Reading with digital devices did not promote more socialised reading situations to the expected extent. The results of the observation (Table 1) show that students chose to read digitally in pairs 43% of the time, especially in the beginning (Figure 1). They also did so more often compared to picturebook reading in pairs over the same period. But it is very remarkable that they opted for individual reading with digital devices in 57% of the occasions and that this behaviour prevailed after the exploratory period. Another sign of normalised integration regarding regular reading habits.

4 English translations of all quotations in other languages have been provided by Tim Mc Quaid.

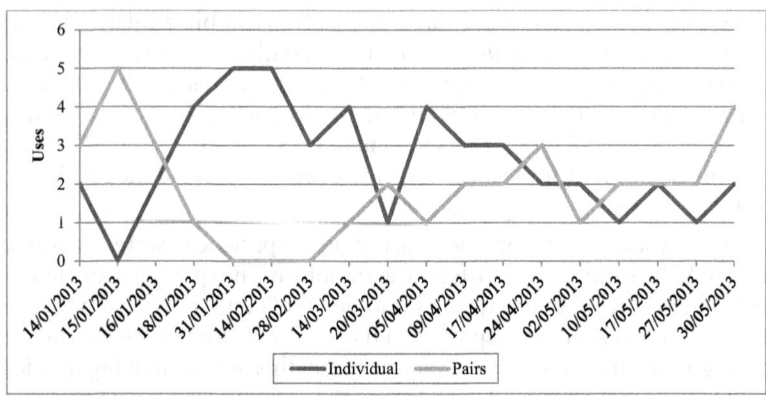

Figure 1. Distribution of the device

Moreover, the children not only opted mostly for individual reading, but they also only made comments among each other 60% of the time and did so above all to jointly learn how to operate the devices and apps.

Familiarisation with the use of the formats is certainly very important for the practice of digital reading, therefore the guidelines and the observation diary paid special attention to this aspect. At first the children treated the devices with a certain fear of damaging them; they chose to shut them down immediately when messages appeared that they did not understand (often a message in English) and it took them some time until they discovered different operational features, such as the advantage of using both hands, the ability to mark the page where the reading stopped, the need to move the device to be able to operate the application, the different ways to turn the page (click, drag, etc.), the use of the "hint" indication to activate effects, etc.

These discoveries were made informally through interaction among the children and occasional requests for help from the adults. Of the 60% of interactions that occurred while reading, 17% took place among reading pairs who were arguing over which application to choose, were finding out how to activate animations or audio, or happily commenting on how the reading was going. The other 42% occurred among students who were reading on different devices, alone or in pairs, and were calling upon other children to obtain or offer help on the use of the apps and devices.

Table 1. Results of the observation guidelines for the observed reading sessions[5]

Who do they read with?	Individual reading	46
	Reading in pairs	33
	Group reading	Not detected
How do they read?	Uninterrupted reading of a text	70 (14 titles)
	Fragmented reading of texts ("sampling")	67 (20 titles)
	Reading accompanied with audio	Almost always whenever possible
	Reading without audio	19 (mostly digitised works)
How do they read an app?	Reading focused on the text (interaction simultaneous to the reading or without interaction)	Reads the text and later enables effects and animations (27). Turns the page before animations end (2). Reads the text without enabling any animation (5). Enables animation while listening to the text (2).
	Reading unfocused on the text (interaction previous to reading or without text reading	Continuously touches the screen (3). Turns page without stopping to read the text (3). Reads the text but repeats animations continuously (4).
Behaviour of students reading digitally	Focused on their reading	19
	Discussion with their partner or group that are reading the same device	8
	Discussion with classmates around them	25
Behaviour of students reading in print	Focused on their reading	19
	Occasionally look at the devices around them	6
	Constantly look at the devices around them	Not detected

5 The numbers in this table indicate the amount of times that a particular attitude or usage was detected during the non-participative direct observation sessions. Some irrelevant items have been deleted, such as the way the devices were distributed and the choice of language. The titles of the works are not included for reasons of space.

The possibility of alternating the languages included in the application is a good example of the exploratory and collaborative forms of learning that the children followed in their use of the new technologies: some followed the stories despite the fact that they did not understand the language well, others abandoned them and others investigated until they found a way to change the language; this knowledge was quickly transmitted among them:

Álvaro: *Animalarium* was in English.

Andrés: But you could change it.

Teacher: Was yours in English?

David: We changed it to Spanish, which was the other language we had, it wasn't in Catalan.

[…]

Luis: I chose the same one and it was in English.

Tamara: I know, but I put it into Spanish. Where there's a globe of the world, you touch it there.

Orality, fragmentation and interactivity

Some of the more specific and notable new features of the multimodal formats are the incorporation of audio (Yokota, and Teale 2014), fragmented reading (Stichnothe 2014) and the interactivity proposal (Turrión 2014). The children's response revealed interesting aspects in relation to these three characteristics.

First, the addition of orality was an aspect very much appreciated by the readers. The children always read with headphones except in cases where the works lacked audio (as in the works that were simply digitised) and only after establishing conclusively that there was no such possibility. The audio was activated even when they read individually and even though the readers had decided to dispense with the animations to concentrate only on the text. Therefore, if one of the advantages of the new formats is the recovery of the oral narrative, it seems to find an immediate response in the preferences of the readers. This is corroborated by the fact that 15% of conversation session time was taken up with positive comments on the emotive nature of the reading situation created by the audio:

David: It's as if the text was being explained to you, as if it was talking to you, it's not like another story where it's a narrator who's explaining it, it's explaining it to you and, as you listen to it, I don't know, I felt very much inside the book.

Second, the students showed resistance to the reading fragmentation produced by digital exploration. The distinction between uninterrupted and fragmented reading of the works (regularly opening and closing apps) revealed a considerably balanced outcome for both types. However, many of the fragmented readings were not due to dispersed reading but rather happened during the process of selecting the application. Moreover, students chose mostly short works that could be read in one reading session (68%), closing the apps containing longer stories even though the possibility to reserve the device to continue reading during the next session was made clear, the same as with the printed works. These short pieces were also the most explicitly valued by the children, so the tendency towards uninterrupted reading of short works was the most prominent behaviour.

Thirdly, the usual behaviour of most students regarding interactivity was to read the text linearly and touch the screen only once to activate animations and effects, either at the moment they appeared or later (60%). This general behaviour alternated with other procedures: on the one hand, the initial or central exploration of the effects was the norm in the first sessions, but only a few students continued to do this – those who left the text in order to play and repeatedly activating the animations (17.78%). On the other hand, other children seemed to enjoy combining the textual and interactivity aspects, but stopped several times with the animations (8.89%); and finally, the tendency to focus almost exclusively on the text was also observed with readers who jumped to the next screen page without waiting for the effects to finish or those who only read the text without activating any animations (13.33%).

From the proportion and relation between this continuum of behaviours it seems that the children mostly projected their printed-text reading skills onto the digital reading devices and took the animations as anecdotal, as a post-reading extra, to explore superficially and focus on later, to pay it some attention but only until their impatience to follow the story got the better of them, or simply something they could completely do without in order to fully enjoy the work as an oral and written narrative.

Living in a technological world

Another facet of digital reading practices is their tendency to promote more extensive forms of information and socialisation through ICT. In spite of coming from a social context with so little experience with technology, we observed that the children soon adopted expert attitudes when using the devices. They commented on the features of the more or less modern tablets, their reduced weight, their screen resolution, ease of use, etc., for almost 20% of the time devoted to discussing their operation in the conversation sessions. They soon also resorted to the Internet to gather contextual information on the works or to provide information on commercial aspects of price and forms of purchase, so this extension of social practices (Cassany 2008) seems to be confirmed as behaviour immediately induced by digital practices:

> Diego: This Easter I read *Wormworld* on the Internet because it couldn't be downloaded here. I found out it's not finished yet, and more or less this month the author will publish the fifth one. I checked it out because I saw a blog and it said that the last one wouldn't be published for a long time.

Assessment of reading with digital devices

The total number of complete digital readings recorded in the children's reading diaries was two hundred and forty-seven; 93.52% of these were digital works and only 6.48% were digitised printed works. This gives an average of 13.72 digital readings per student during the five months of observation – a fact that can be contrasted with an average of 40.92 printed readings for the same students during this period. Undoubtedly we must not forget that there were only five digital devices available and the total number of printed narrative texts that students had available during the research period (around sixty picturebooks and fifty novels) far exceeds that of the digital works (sixteen apps and six digitised works) since the investigation was not designed to establish a balanced corpus for measuring preferences but to include this type of fiction in a natural reading situation in the classroom. Nevertheless, it must be observed that the majority trend was to continue reading printed works with occasional forays into the digital format.

The lack of attention paid to the simply digitised works also stands out in these results. The children's comments show their scant interest in reading works which did not provide any other added value to the printed books apart from simply reading on a screen and the technical disadvantage of their slow loading process. It becomes clear then, that technological innovation alone does not outweigh the attractiveness of the printed book, although the use of digitised works can be advantageous for other already very widespread school uses, such as group reading and discussions.

The evolution of digital reading through the experimentation period was significant (Figure 2). Abundant initial use is clearly visible in the first month followed by a sharp decline. It is a graphic depiction of how, when the novelty effect had worn off, the children returned to their usual habit of reading printed books. However, digital reading increased as the children progressed in their learning of how to best use the possibilities of digital works after the quality of the available corpus was improved and after the group's social evaluation of the quality of some titles increased in the discussion sessions. With the change of these three factors the prestige of the digital corpus increased in terms of literary reading and also became a worthy option for the children.

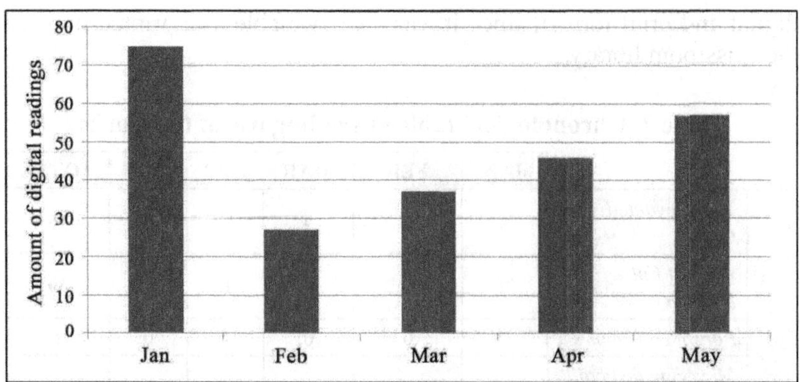

Figure 2. Evolution of digital reading during the experimentation period

The influence of the corpus of works

The importance of the corpus in the reading preferences inevitably leads to the analysis of the most read titles. Since the children explored virtually all the apps, we can now ask ourselves why certain titles remained as a reading choice over time.

The comparison between the analysis worksheets of the titles and their success in the classroom provides some clues to this question. Some works, such as *A Chest Full of Monsters* (with the highest number of readings) or *Doctor W.*, had a large initial attraction, but their reading later declined (Table 2). These are works with extensive use of animation, effects and audio; but these resources are not there to serve the story, in such a way that after the novelty factor wore off interest in them faded. The students identified them as more ludic proposals – 7.17% of the time dedicated to establishing this contrast in the conversation sessions –, as one student said, "they distracted you a lot" and she "wanted to read more".

In accordance with this assessment and following the success of *A Chest Full of Monsters*, the most read titles were the works with good fictional construction and an integrated use of digital resources – works with a consistent storyline, an effective use of intrigue or an important literary and aesthetic component such as *The Wormworld Saga* or the titles of *Moving Tales*; sometimes with formats similar to an audiovisual narrative, such as *Numberlys* or *The Fantastic Flying Books of Mr. Morris Lessmore*, and others with animations clearly integrated into the work, as in *El Libro Negro de los Colores* (The Black Book of Colours). Some titles such as *El Libro Negro de los Colores* or *Professor Revillod's Universal Animalarium* interested the students for their comparability between the digital and print format, since it was also available as a printed book in the classroom library.

Table 2. Chronological table of reading use of the works

		JAN	FEB	MAR	APR	MAY	TOTAL
Digital works	*The Unwanted Guest*	6	5	4	0	0	**15**
	A Chest Full of Monsters	26	3	4	0	6	**39**
	Forgotten Colours	0	0	0	1	0	**1**
	Mi vecino de abajo (My Downstairs Neighbour)	5	5	1	0	4	**15**
	Doctor W	7	2	0	0	1	**10**
	The Lost Houses	0	0	1	1	0	**2**
	Profesor Revillod's Universal Animalarium	10	4	1	0	0	**15**
	The Wormworld Saga	0	0	10	17	3	**30**
	El libro negro de los colores (The Black Book of Colours)	12	2	1	0	9	**24**
	The Numberlys	3	6	7	1	5	**22**
	The Heart in the Bottle	–	–	4	4	4	**12**
	The Fantastic Flying Books of Mr. Morris Lessmore	–	–	–	9	4	**13**
	iPoe Collection, Vol. 2	–	–	–	11	8	**19**
	This Too Shall Pass	–	–	–	2	4	**6**
	Underground Kingdom	–	–	–	0	7	**7**
	Children's Tales	–	–	–	0	1	**1**

		JAN	FEB	MAR	APR	MAY	TOTAL
Digitised works	*Matilda*	0	0	2	0	0	**2**
	Crictor	0	1	0	0	0	**1**
	The Witches	2	0	0	0	0	**2**
	Otto	2	2	0	0	1	**5**
	El autobús de Rosa (Rosa's Bus)	1	1	1	0	0	**3**
	Little Bird	1	1	1	0	0	**3**
TOTAL		**75**	**32**	**37**	**46**	**57**	**247**

Thus, the interest of the children in works that truly provide new reading possibilities can be seen by the total amount of readings obtained for each title and by their temporal evolution, while those that exploit the ludic and entertainment possibilities obtained only fleeting success.

The analysis of the conversation sessions, however, provided another factor for the success of specific titles: the impact of social recommendation of the works at the peak of their popularity. Spontaneous comments on digital works took a long time to emerge and, as we shall see, they happened to a limited extent. When they talked about the books they had read, the children seemed to forget the time they spent on digital reading and revealed their opinion that these works were not worth their analytical attention or their endorsement. From their remarks we can conclude that the printed corpus was deserving of their trust because it had been selected by the school, while the apps seemed to come from a world foreign to the school and to truly consistent fiction.

It seems plausible that this consideration is reinforced by two factors: the absence of presentation and "endorsement" by the facilitators and the poor quality of the digital corpus. The presentation and teaching guidance of the works as a school activity proved to be an important factor that gave the children confidence and attracted them to reading, while the artistic weakness of most of the digital corpus was a reality which was immediately detected by the children. Therefore, the first recommendations to appear in the discussion were those referring to the digitised picturebooks, works that the children could evaluate on the same level as the printed works they already knew from their literary experience. Later, when the corpus was improved with the introduction of new works such as *The Heart in the Bottle*, *The Fantastic Flying Books of Mr. Morris Lessmore* or *This Too Shall Pass*,[6] and when the children's

6 Two months later, six more digital works were added to the initial corpus of ten digital and six digitised works.

conception of the significance of reading digital fiction was gradually restructured, there was a marked change in their initial opinion on the apps as an added reading space unworthy of their analytical attention. Only then did some recommendations of digital works begin to emerge – and the titles mentioned correlate closely with the increase in reading as shown on the chronological table of reading use of the works (Table 2).

Construction of the children's discourse on digital literature

As we have seen, the expectation regarding the arrival of the digital devices gave way to collaborative learning and the enjoyable exploration of the apps, but the topic of digital reading took some time to emerge in the weekly conversations and recommendations. The teacher's questions were then addressed to elicit the clarification of their opinions using the didactic resource of comparing print and digital reading. This comparative resource allowed us to focus on the effects and reception of the digitalisation and stimulated an expert reader perspective, providing a distance from both types of reading and thus enhancing the analysis and conceptualisation of the experience. Despite this, the time spent on digital reading was only 7.85% of the four hours of literary conversation recorded. The analysis of the time spent on digital reading shows the main topics that arose and how much time was spent on them:

Table 3. Topics that arose in the analysis of the transcribed conversations

Topics	N° of interventions	Time spent
Technical issues/device operation	47	19.83%
Narrative construction (fictional aspects, artistic resources)	38	16.03%
Description of features and affordances of the digital corpus	32	13.50%
Future of reading and literature	32	13.50%
Opinion/evaluation of audio (music and sound)	23	9.70%
Opinion/evaluation of animations and effects	19	8.02%
Fictional reading vs. gaming	17	7.17%
Printed literature vs. digital literature	16	6.75%
Opinion/evaluation about the orality incorporated into the works	11	4.64%
Expectations	2	0.84%

In terms of their impressions over time, the first were of surprise and fun regarding the apps and resulted in descriptive reports on the interactive possibilities (13.50% of the recorded time). Soon however, the distinction between game-playing and reading came to the fore; "it was a game, not a story" as Roberto said – or as Mireia said with the support of Tamara:

> Mireia: You can laugh, but that's it, it's not… And now I just realised there are two types, this one *A Chest Full of Monsters* which is more like with effects and so on, and then the other one, like the one Tamara mentioned [*The Unwanted Guest*], which is a story but it's more… enjoyable.
>
> Tamara: I agree with Mireia because we were reading *The Zombie* [refers to *A Chest Full of Monsters*] and you didn't even know who the main character was. People popped up and I kept pressing. But now I'm reading a book which doesn't have many sounds or anything. And I'm enjoying the story more. I've found the difference that there're less sounds that distract you a lot, and that's very good, it's fantastic that one…, what's it called? The poverty one [*The Unwanted Guest*].

As mentioned, the digitised works were the first to be recommended because the children felt safe with their assessment criteria and their consideration of them as "stories" was evident. When assessments of digital works began to emerge they were made with judgments based on the feelings they had and on the description of the emotions that they experienced during the reading. In contrast, in their assessments of the coexisting printed works, the children used a more conceptual and analytical language centred on the works themselves. This therefore shows that the children adopted a certain "relapse" to a more casual and less academic language when speaking about the digital works, a more "naive" reader position, which seems to reveal that literary learning did not initially transfer to the new forms of fiction.

This response leads us to analyse to what extent received learning is transferred between forms and artistic codes and to consider the need to include the reading of digital fiction in the reading training of current generations. In this way, the continuity of the experience and the teaching guidance began to promote more elaborate analyses on the fictional aspects and artistic resources of the digital works; these analyses increased to the point of 16.03% of the conversation time.

> Andrés: I think *Wormworld* is the kind that has a plot that builds up.
>
> Diego: But in the first part it doesn't build up much, only at the end when it says, 'but he did not know the adventures he was going to go through'. And you go, what? Now that the story was just starting!
>
> Christian: You might say it's great, but humorous? I don't think so.
>
> Carolina: It's true, because I don't think flying books are funny.

Álvaro: It's pretty sentimental, because Morris always has his book, he's writing everything that happens and that's when the whole book gets deleted at the beginning, but then he rewrites it when he's leaving, because he's the new one who flies, his book returns.

Verónica: When I read it I saw there was a flash back, right? First he's old and then he's flying.

Teacher: So, do you think that the black and white [*The Unwanted Guest*] is to show that it's old?

Natalia: It's because of the sadness.

Judgments of this type may have occurred due to the good reading level of the group under analysis which shows that good readers have a high level of expectation, competent criteria and the ability for critical distance that allows them to judge whether digital features add meaning to the story. But it also demonstrated the difficulty to adjust the learning from print reading to new formats. The students had learned to maintain a certain distance from the storyline and the intrigue of the works in order to observe their artistic creation, and their comments on the printed works showed this; but they had not been educated as digital readers and when faced with the new formats they felt discomfort at abandoning the plot and straying towards the digital attractions to linger on the evaluation of unusual aspects. If works build their readers, then undoubtedly digital works also build theirs. If they are not addressed to a player but to a reader of artistic fiction, they require a reading that allows the observation of the design and creation of works of this type and their effectiveness at achieving the effects. As with the printed forms, school education and the quality of the corpus prove to be essential instruments in the training of more flexible readers.

Finally, we would like to underline the recurrence of the social debate on the future of reading (which occupied up to 13.50% of the time) in the children's discussions who, as book lovers – or susceptible to social clichés – discussed the future of exclusively digital reading:

Roberto: It's like it was the book of the future.

[…]

Ana: I'll definitely keep reading on paper.

Mireia: I may agree a bit with Roberto because maybe one day we'd stop cutting down trees. And if someone wants money, perhaps this way with iPads, people would pay and they could make money.

Álvaro: But Mireia, printing houses and bookshops would close down. […]

Natalia: No, they'd use iPads.

Verónica: Instead of a library with books it would be a library with iPads.

Mireia: It would stop being so expensive.

They delved into their own experience of reading learning to defend the impossibility of reproducing it through digital reading:

> Verónica: Children won't be able to read on iPads. […] Because reading picturebooks is easy, they don't know how to handle the iPad.
>
> Andrés: […] [B]ut if the first book you read is an iPad, it's not complicated, it's just like moving your fingers like this to turn the page.
>
> Álvaro: Maybe they wouldn't be able to analyse picturebooks so well and all that, because the children would get distracted by the sounds and it would be a big mistake not to use paper books.

And they expressed their fears that stories would be converted into mere fragmented games:

> Mireia: […] [S]tories will stop being so good because maybe they'll focus more on making more of those funnier special effects that make children laugh, and then the story will be nonsense, just to keep the effects and make them relate.

Conclusions

The results of this exploration provide diverse indications on the digital reading practices of students between eleven and twelve years old using digital devices integrated into the classroom library. From the point of view of their didactic interest they can be summarised in the following conclusions.

Firstly, we can confirm that fictional reading in different formats can coexist without undermining the interest in the reading of printed works in a group of students with a good pre-existing reading level and with the added benefits that the new format provides regarding technological learning.

Secondly, we see a majority tendency to transfer print-reading habits to reading on digital devices with a certain preference for individual reading, short, uninterrupted and dependent on the text, but with the immediate incorporation of audio and a gradual acceptance of interactivity if this forms a real and significant part of the resources of the story.

Thirdly, the quality of the fictional experience of the corpus is a decisive factor in the reading preferences and practices in the school context, with the readers making a clear distinction between playing and reading. The majority preferred narratively consistent stories, an outcome which digital production must take into account if it wants to enter the field of school education.

Finally, the socialisation elements in the classroom community are also essential. If students are to pay attention to digital fiction in the school, it would appear that a teaching guidance process is necessary, as well as one of conceptualisation and agreed assessment of the group on reading in new formats. Similarly, the resistance and slowness in the transfer of children's analysis and literary assessment abilities to digital fiction demonstrates the need for specific learning on the artistic functioning of the multimodal resources of the works.

In conclusion, the exploration carried out shows the real possibilities for the integration of children's digital literature in the classroom library, it outlines the existing limits in the current corpus in order to achieve this, it suggests the desirability of creating spaces for conceptual development to extend the students' understanding of reading and reveals the need for teaching guidance, both in the introduction of the works and in the inclusion in literary education of the analysis and specific assessment of multimodal resources.

Works Cited

Primary Works Cited

Cottin, Menena, and Rosana Faría. *El libro negro de los colores*. México D. F.: Ediciones Tecolote, 2012. iPad edition.

Joyce, William. *The Fantastic Flying Books of Mr. Morris Lessmore*. Shreveport: Moonbot Studios, 2011. iPad edition.

—. *The Numberlys*. Shreveport: Moonbot Studios, 2012. iPad edition.

Lieske, Daniel. *The Wormworld Saga*. Barcelona: Robot Media, 2011. iPad edition.

Lluch, Enric. *A Chest Full of Monsters*. Valencia: Itbook, 2013. iPad edition.

Neira, Muyi, Martín Guido, and Karina Letelier Oteiza. *Doctor W.* Barcelona: PipilApps, 2014. iPad edition.

Nesquens, Daniel. *Mi vecino de abajo*. Mobile Republic, 2011. iPad edition.

O'Rogers, Jacqueline *The Unwanted Guest*. Gibsons: Moving Tales, 2012. iPad edition.

Sáez Castán, Javier, and Miguel Murugarren. *Profesor Revillod's Universal Animalarium*. Barcelona: Fondo de Cultura Económica. iPad edition.

Secondary Works Cited

Borràs, Laura. "Había una vez una app… Literatura infantil y juvenil (en) digital." *Revista de Literatura*, 269 (2012): 21-26. Print.

Cassany, Daniel. *Practicas letradas contemporáneas*. México: Ríos de Tinta, 2008. Print.

Colomer, Teresa, and Karla Fernández de Gamboa Vázquez. "La incorporación de literatura infantil digital a la biblioteca de aula." *Anuario de investigación en literatura infantil y juvenil*, 12 (2014): 19-36. Print.

Jimoyiannis, Athanassios, and Vassilis Komis. "Examining Teachers' Beliefs about ICT in Education: Implications of a Teacher Preparation Programme." *Teacher Development*, 11.2 (2008): 149-173. Print.

López-Aranguren, Eduardo. "El análisis de contenido." Comps. *El análisis de la realidad social: métodos y técnicas de investigación*. Manuel García, Jesús Ibáñez, and Francisco Alvira. Madrid: Alianza, 2000. 383-414. Print.

Reyes, Lara. "Fer lectors en un context advers." *Articles de Didàctica de la Llengua i la Literatura*, 53 (2011): 58-67. Print.

Stichnothe, Haddassah. "Engineering Stories? A Narratological Approach to Children's Book Apps." *Nordic Journal of ChildLit Aesthetics*, 5 (2014). Web. 20 Mar. 2015.

Turrión, Celia. "Multimedia Book Apps in a Contemporary Culture: Commerce and Innovation, Continuity and Rupture." *Nordic Journal of ChildLit Aesthetics*, 5 (2014). Web. 20 Mar. 2015.

Yokota, Junko, and William H. Teale, "Picture Books and the Digital World: Educators Making Informed Choices." *The Reading Teacher*, 67.8 (2014): 577-585. Print.

Part V

Creating Digital Texts: Two Reflections

Inanimate Alice – How We Accidentally Created a Digital Story for Schools

Kate PULLINGER

Bath Spa University

From viral marketing tool to pedagogical blockbuster, *Inanimate Alice* (The Bradfield Company 2005-2015) has had a slow, steady and largely unexpected rise to international prominence. In 2005 the Bradfield Company commissioned Chris Joseph and I to create a series of interactive stories for a marketing campaign for a feature film that has yet to be made. From that inauspicious beginning, *Inanimate Alice* has gone on to become one of the most popular digital stories in classrooms around the world. In this paper I discuss how and why this happened.

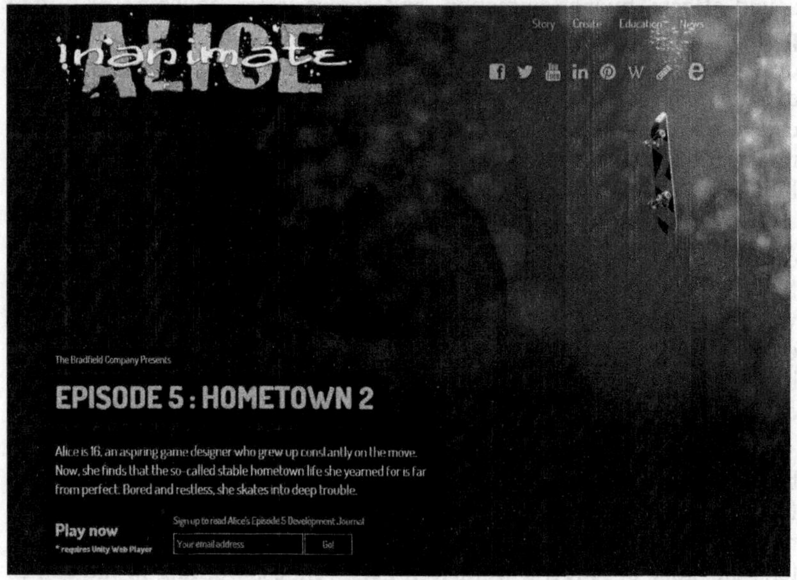

Image 1. *Inanimate Alice.* Episode 5: Hometown 2. Initial screen

The story of *Inanimate Alice* is a story of mistakes, dead-ends, lucky accidents, good decision-making, and spectacular success.

In fact, there are two stories to tell here: one, the story of Alice herself, and two, the story of the project overall and how, despite all odds, *Inanimate Alice* continues to thrive as a digital fiction for the 21st century.

The first story, the real story, is this: Alice is a young girl growing up surrounded by technology. Her father, John, works in the oil and gas industries, and Alice and her mother, Ming, travel the world with him, often living in remote locations. Alice is home-schooled by Ming, who is a painter, and John, who is an engineer. In each episode of the digital story, Alice is a little older – in episode one she is eight years old and by episode six, which is in production at the time of writing (March 2015), she is nineteen. Alice is curious and intrepid; she loves gadgets and computers and wants to be a games designer when she grows up, and she has an imaginary friend called Brad. Ten episodes are planned. Episode five was launched in December 2014.

The second story, and the one I'll focus on here, is the story of the project overall, how it was made, and how it was nearly un-made in the process.

First, a definition: *Digital Fiction*, which is the term I use most often to describe *Inanimate Alice*: works that combine text with images, video, sound effects, music, animation, and games: often collaborative, often participatory, usually transmedia. This definition is not from a dictionary or a work of critical theory; I made it up myself. *Inanimate Alice* is an exemplar of a field that is so new that consensus on terminologies and categories is also still emerging; elsewhere, digital fiction is sometimes referred to as interactive narrative, multimodal online fiction, or electronic literature.

For me, as the writer of the stories, the key media, the key narrative-delivery mechanism, is the use of text; it is the use of text and the primary focus on text that makes *Inanimate Alice* literature as opposed to film, video, or other screen-based visual forms. I have a background and an on-going creative practice as a novelist; my interest in digital fiction has always been in the potential for new forms of literature, new forms enabled by digital platforms, software, devices and technologies.

As I have mentioned above, *Inanimate Alice* had rather inauspicious beginnings. The project began life as a viral marketing campaign for a film, *E-Mission*, for which the project producer, Ian Harper, hoped to raise financing. The film script, written by Harper, is an eco-thriller that tells the story of Alice, a women in her twenties, working in the games industry in the United States. Harper had the idea that telling the back-story of Alice through a series of online digital stories might be a way of generating interest in the film, so in 2005 he commissioned me to create these stories, and I brought Chris Joseph on board as web developer, designer, and sound and music artist.

As mentioned above, we knew from the start that we were creating a hybrid storytelling form so new we had no idea what to call it; bearing in mind that YouTube was less than a year old and tablets, smartphones and e-readers had yet to reach the mainstream, we referred to episode one as a *webvid*, a term that, happily, did not catch on. Our budgets were very small and our creative team consisted of myself in London and Chris Joseph, who was living in Montreal. We had no idea who our audience might be – if an audience even existed. Between 2005 and 2008 we created four episodes of the story. They were built using Flash, a web technology that has since become rather outmoded. They are available online, via the *Inanimate Alice* website, for free.

From the project's inception, Ian Harper, the project producer, embarked on attempting to create a business model for the work, meeting with potential investors from film, television and publishing, in the United Kingdom, Europe and the United States. But the business models weren't there yet; the first mainstream tablet wouldn't arrive until 2010. At the time it was still common for the producers of culture to say that people didn't want to read text on a screen.

So production on *Inanimate Alice* stalled: we ran out of money. Six years passed.

In the world of content production six years between episodes – episodes of anything from television series to book series, let alone emerging forms of digital fiction – is a very long time.

However, as is often the case with creative work, these somewhat difficult and restrictive circumstances resulted in a series of lucky accidents.

The film script, and the idea of developing an episodic backstory for the film of Alice's life beginning aged eight, gave us a sturdy narrative framework for the project that we have been able to rely on across many years and with a creative team that has grown and changed.

The founding format of the episodes – Alice and her family on the move across the world, in new places, dealing with new challenges with every episode – has allowed us to range freely across international borders and storylines, giving the story a global appeal. The near-future setting and the future-retro design aesthetic of the episodes means that it hasn't yet begun to look dated.

As well as that, Alice is popular – readers like this character, and they like her imaginary friend Brad.

Getting in at the beginning of an emerging art form – hybrid, multimodal, digital storytelling – meant that for several years *Inanimate Alice* was able to show herself off in an uncrowded field.

Tight budgets meant that when we were first working on the visual look of episode one, we considered paying to use still photographs of actors and later we considered animating the characters but decided against both these things. This was one of our first lucky accidents: it has become clear to us that an important aesthetic feature of *Inanimate Alice* is that Alice herself is never represented visually on screen. The fact that she remains off-screen throughout renders this hybrid form of storytelling closer to that of reading a book, where it falls upon the reader to imagine the main character's appearance throughout the text, unlike watching a film. This aspect, combined with the first person narrative voice, draws the reader into Alice's world, allowing readers to identify with Alice, to place themselves in the story as they do when reading a book.

The creative corollary of the dearth of business models meant we had no idea who our audience might be; in fact it is probably safe to say that the audience didn't exist yet. Chris Joseph and I did not initially consider the fact that a work about a child might appeal to children, a factor that seems obvious with hindsight. However, children's writers often maintain that they write for a general audience, and for us it has been important that the work appeals to an adult audience as well as younger readers.

Another lucky accident was the fact that Alice wants to be a games designer when she grows up. It is this aspiration that allows us to embed games into the digital stories in a way that makes narrative sense; in each episode the games included are representative of what a child Alice's age might be able to create – there's a narrative reason for the interactivity. Accordingly, the level of interaction and gaming skill required by the reader increases with each episode as Alice reaches age eight, ten, etc. By episode six, Alice, now nineteen years old, is at art school, studying game design; the episode includes a much more sophisticated game interface than seen in the episodes to date.

This gradual increase in interactivity through the episodes has meant that the work has a secondary function as a primer or introduction to digital fiction and interactivity for readers new to its potentials. Early anecdotal reader responses showed us that our audience is split evenly between readers who enjoy playing the games embedded in the stories and readers who do not, so we took a decision to accommodate both types of readers. Episodes three and four have two versions: "read-only" and "full version". In the full version readers need to complete games before they can move on in the story; in the read-only version the games are by-passed. We'll maintain this dual approach throughout the series, accommodating, wherever possible, both types of reader.

Early responses to the episodes also brought to our attention the fact that teachers were responding positively to the stories. In 2007 I met a PhD student, Jessica Laccetti, who was researching multimodal fiction, including *Inanimate Alice.* Laccetti was very interested in digital pedagogy – using multimodal fiction in classrooms – so the project producer commissioned her to write a set of teacher's notes, an Education Pack, and from that date onward we began to cultivate and communicate with a number of educators around the world. The dual approach to episodes three and four – "read-only" vs "full version" – has also meant that the teachers can approach the work in two ways: driven by story alone, or through foregrounding interactivity and this has proven to be a useful pedagogical tool.

In another happy coincidence Laccetti, a Canadian with Italian parents, translated the text of the stories into Italian, and then other translations were commissioned in German, French and Spanish. This multi-lingual approach expanded the reach of the project exponentially and enabled its use as a resource for teaching English as a second language. Autumn 2014 saw the launch of translations of all the episodes into Japanese and Indonesian, commissioned by Education Services Australia.

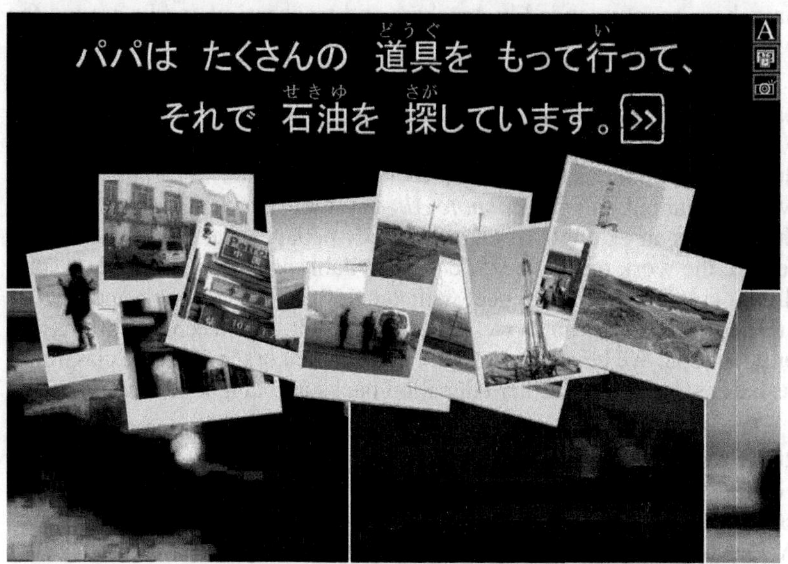

Image 2. *Inanimate Alice*. Translations into Japanese and Indonesian

But despite all this, one disappointing fact remains true: *Inanimate Alice* had no new episodes for six years, practically a lifetime in our rapidly evolving digital landscape. How did the project remain current, visible and relevant across all these intervening years?

One major factor is that the work has won many awards and accolades. In 2006 *Inanimate Alice* won Italy's Premio per l'arte digitale, a digital media prize sponsored by the Italian ministry of culture. This prize sparked a cavalcade of prizes and honours, including being chosen as a finalist in 2006 at NICOGRAPH International (Seoul, Korea), a finalist in the Digital Media Awards (Dublin, Ireland) in the Hall of Fame category, and winner of the IBM New Media Prize at the twentieth Stuttgarter Filmwinter (Stuttgart, Germany) in 2007. In 2008 *Inanimate Alice* was a finalist at CULTURAS Intercultural Dialogue Awards (Madrid, Spain). The episodes have featured in the Electronic Literature Collection, Volume I (Hayles *et al.* eds. 2006) and Volume II (Borràs *et al.* eds. 2011) in the United States; we've partnered with the United Kingdom's *The Guardian* newspaper as well as the BBC's The Space; and bespoke Alice stories have been commissioned by Education Services Australia. In 2012 *Inanimate Alice* was named one of the American Association of School Librarians' Best Websites ("Best Websites for Teaching and Learning" 2012), and in 2013 was cited as "a masterpiece of transmedia storytelling" in EdTech Digest (Hovious). Perhaps most crucially we have been recommended by teachers and teachers' networks around the world (Facebook Group).

Another factor has been the rise of transmedia and transmedia pedagogy, a newly developing field that *Inanimate Alice* fits into very well. But as well as that, and more importantly, I put our continuing growth down to the countless educators, teachers and teacher-librarian advocates who blog about using *Inanimate Alice* in their classrooms, who present the story as an example of digital literacy pedagogy at conferences, who feature the work on university course syllabi, using it as a tool to inspire digital creativity, who connect with each other via Facebook and Twitter and other social media as well as through their own teaching forums and publications. We have worked with these educators to produce classroom resources, including further education packs and language resources.

For me, a pivotal moment in the history of this project came in March 2009 when my Google Alerts first brought to my attention multiple versions of *Inanimate Alice: Episode 5.* Chris Joseph and I had not yet created a fifth episode. Through following the links I discovered that an American high school English teacher, Diane Aronow, had been using *Inanimate Alice* with a group of teenagers that her school system had deemed 'hard to reach' and she had encouraged them to create their own versions of episode five. Aronow then published these episodes on her class blog.

Discovering these episodes gave new meaning to me for the potential of "interactivity", a term often heralded as a new paradigm for reading and writing. When Chris Joseph and I began working on *Inanimate Alice*, we thought that interactivity meant games, finding a way to introduce gameplay into digital narrative which, as stated, is key to our project. But discovering these student-created and published new episodes reshaped and refocused my ideas about the potential for interactivity, and since then this has been an aspect of pedagogical engagement that the team behind *Inanimate Alice* has been very keen to encourage and embrace. It was flattering to discover our text disseminated and reconstructed in this manner, of course, but more importantly, these new episodes are a true indicator of the potential for digital fiction in the classroom. New episodes have continued to appear online regularly since then and as part of the launch of episode five the *Inanimate Alice* website was redesigned by our new Creative Director, Andy Campbell, to include a gallery of reader-created episodes, showcasing episodes from around the world.

While *Inanimate Alice* itself is a work of disintermediation – self-published, created outside the frameworks of educational publishing and digital publishing – it has gained from further disintermediation, as episodes are created and published across the web. It is a work of spreadable media, as so usefully defined by media theorist Henry Jenkins (Jenkins, Ford, and Green 2013). It is a work that has continued to iterate, adapt and change. And, most importantly, it is a work that relies on participation and engagement to survive.

It has been a fascinating process to observe how *Inanimate Alice*, which was not originally intended as an educational title, is adopted, adapted, and augmented by educators. Because of the serial nature of publication, we have been able to capitalise on that interest by creating pedagogical tools and spaces for discussion specific to *Inanimate Alice*, while continuing to create episodes that stay true to the underlying principles of the project. The sizable audience of children for the work has redefined the work as children's literature, while its popularity with educators has repositioned it as a classroom resource. Here's hoping that we find a way to continue to iterate and respond well beyond episodes five and six, and into the future.

Works Cited

Primary Works Cited

Pullinger, Kate. *Inanimate Alice*. London: The Bradfield Company, 2005ff. Web. 23 Feb. 2015.

Secondary Works Cited

Aronow, Diane. *Aronow's English 10*. 2010. Web. 17 Mar. 2015.

"Best Websites for Teaching and Learning." *American Association of School Librarians (AASL)*. American Association of School Librarians, 2012. Web. 17 Mar. 2015.

Borràs, Laura, *et al.*, eds. *Electronic Literature Collection*, Vol. 2. Maryland: Electronic Literature Organization, 2011. Web. 17 Mar. 2015.

Facebook Group. iTeach with Inanimate Alice. Web. 15 Jan. 2015, 17 Mar. 2015.

Fleming, Laura. *Inanimate Alice on Facebook*, 2010. Web. 1 May 2011.

Hayles, N. Katherine, *et al.*, eds. *Electronic Literature Collection*, Vol. 1. Maryland: Electronic Literature Organization, 2006. Web. 17 Mar. 2015.

Hovious, Amanda. "Exploring Inanimate Alice." *EdTech Digest*. EdTech Digest, 11 Oct. 2013. Web. 17 Mar. 2015.

Jenkins, Henry, Sam Ford, and Joshua Green. *Spreadable Media*. New York: New York University Press, 2013. Print.

Change of Direction

Arnal BALLESTER

Escola Massana. Centre d'Art i Disseny

Over the last decade studies on children's literature have undergone an extraordinary development, but only very recently have they begun to look at the world of electronic devices.

Computers, e-readers, tablets, mobile phones, all form part of our everyday environment, although some have been around for several decades it was the relatively recent appearance of tablets (in 2010) that really caught the interest of the wider public in apps, or applications designed for digital handheld devices.[1]

The idea of many of these applications is to immerse us in a defined storyline which in certain instances is combined with an interactive game, and in others is based upon it. These are what we call book apps. Some of these are derived from analogue editions while others are native, in other words, created from the specific possibilities offered by digital technology. These are different productions from those destined for e-readers because they do not follow the reading logic of the book codex.

The effect of this new reality on the future of books has been interpreted in many different ways, some of them hostile, some very enthusiastic, and most of them sceptical. Beyond the emotional responses however, their very existence poses important questions starting with the definition of the concepts of *book* and *reading*. We will not expound on this aspect as we are more interested in its place in our cultural development than explaining its identity in etymological terms – can something without pages be considered a book?; can following a multi-language itinerary on an app be considered reading? It is important to understand what place this issue has in our cultural development. Moreover, specific to their very nature is the virtuality of texts and images that only exist as a group of electronic impulses which gives them a permanent malleability – a quality completely alien to analogue creations.

1 From *application* in English, used to describe any computer application, but has acquired a more restricted meaning in colloquial use.

In truth this reflection had a timely beginning; at the turn of the century one of the great contemporary scholars of books and reading, Roger Chartier (2000), gave us a keen analysis of the nature of reading on personal computers and the Internet, which at that time were no longer such new devices, and summarised a large part of his conclusions affirming that these new media made the reader freer. According to him this freedom was linked to the dematerialisation of the reading surface, a factor that emancipated us from the restrictions of the book codex structure as it allowed to mould the flow of information, alter the predetermined order of reading, and link it to other textual flows (17).

The successes and limits of an analysis

Chartier (2000) proposed another key idea in which the digital medium could make one of the fundamental ideals of the Enlightenment come true – the real, simultaneous universalisation of both authorship and knowledge:

> [...] the electronic book requires collaboration from the readers who can henceforth write in the book themselves and in the wall-less library of electronic works [...]. As with the Enlightenment project, electronic text creates an ideal public space in which, as Kant imagined, the public use of reason can and should be freely used without restrictions or exclusions. (110)[2]

Despite its perceptiveness, this approach to the subject did not, however, exhaust everything offered by the new environment, neither could it do so at that time because the analysis prudently circumscribed the question of exposure of the written text to digital technologies without examining in detail aspects such as the effects of the articulation of different types of languages (written text, sounds and images) or the possibilities of influencing the integrity of external text through the manipulation of its structure and content.

However, if the new digital medium represents a new paradigm of exchange and dissemination, this is not only due to the speed of propagation of the contents (a purely quantitative aspect) or to the possibility to link texts from different sources (one of its qualitative aspects), or even to the capacity to combine diverse languages, but to the potential it has to take and directly alter any input circulating on the web. In reality the turning point of a new reader model is based on this plasticity of the digital medium which allows the dissolution or at least the relativisation of the concept of uniqueness of a specific work, and for the same reason, of the concept of individual authorship.

---

2 English translations of all quotations in other languages have been provided by Tim Mc Quaid.

A stranger in the debate: the video game

To appreciate the true nature of this change perhaps we should move our focus away from the realm of books and the written word and examine the world of video games. Since the 1970s of the last century this has foreshadowed the most radical aspects of the mutation, and due to its mass culture and the global nature of its activity it has extended new ways of relating the public to textual, iconic and audiovisual contents.

The video game was ignored if not scorned for a long time as a cultural sub-product by the majority of critics and until recently occupied a very marginal place in academic studies.[3] To a certain degree, history has repeated itself just as happened in its day to films, comics… or the printed book itself which were initially forms of popular entertainment and were full of topics outside of those accepted by a cultured and sophisticated public. However, this fact has clouded the analysis of two important questions: on one side the progressive, now mass, appearance of very varied proposals with increasingly more complex discourses; on the other, the consolidation of a very wide public which, unlike the analogue reader, is not content with simply receiving the proposals and mentally re-working them, but instead redirects and reconstructs them through a tangible action and in connection with the actions of others.

As Professor Óliver Pérez Latorre (2012) explained in his essay *El lenguaje videolúdico. Análisis de la significación del videojuego* (The Video Game Language. Analysis of the Meaning of the Video Game):

> The video game genuinely does not "only" deal with "stories" or "storylines"… but with a group of stories which on a profound level make up the image of a "world" and form an underlying discourse on the Subject/Environment relationships which occur in that world. Ultimately it appears that where the traditional narrative has always given us discourses about our relationship with our objectives (desires, necessities, dreams…), video games also give us (and some in particular) discourses about our relationship with worlds, which is to say, with certain environments (natural, social, cultural…). (51)

This relationship is not one of a solitary spectator because the video game has expanded as a possibility to collectively share an experience through an action which modifies it in real time. This, commonly called interactivity, has consequences which go farther than the individual, deferred and one-directional relationship with the narrative; it is a characteristic of the print culture with which we were educated and has

3 Academic interest in the language of video games has been expressed in the consolidation of journals specifically dedicated to the study of gaming such as *Games and Culture* (web: gac.sagepub.com) and *Games Studies* (web: gamestudies.org/1402).

also impregnated and even dominated our experience of the visual and the theatrical.

Images, words and the digital world

In short, it is a matter of recognising the impact it will have on global cultural practices, the fact that various generations now see the video game as a completely normal activity, in the same way that cinematographic culture modified our way of reading images over the last century.

In relation to this latter point it should be pointed out that the analysis of the role of illustrations in books has not always sufficiently explored this relationship between cinematography and narrative forms through, or with, image. Comparative studies are still needed on the languages employed in cinema and book illustration and the way this is received by the reader. However, there are many studies that look at this question from a viewpoint that could be qualified as autocratic because there is more interest in pointing out, sometimes in an artificial way, the specificity of the reading context of the image (the book) than in establishing the necessary connections with other practices that characterise the cultural life of the reader. This is a somewhat urgent issue and in this case should now be related to the evolution of the languages driven forward by the new digital reality.

We must play down the importance of the fact that in the last decade there has been an enormous increase in the production of illustrated books and, at the same time, the advance of electronic proposals from the publishing world has occurred much more slowly than one would expect given the technological possibilities. Both phenomena have a lot to do with short-term economic realities. The avalanche of titles, which many have seen as an explosion of creativity, has camouflaged the absence of evolution in graphic languages and narrative structures with the repetition of known formulas, the reuse of past experiments and above all the *spectacularisation* of graphic forms and editing formats at the expense of narrative content robustness.

Despite this it is significant that the same areas that celebrated the boom of the picturebook also recognise that this expansion has in some way been a response to the advance of the digital world, also criticised for its lack of great works. It is also true that it is at an initial stage which could be qualified as hybridisation, common to the first steps of all the artistic manifestations we know. At the start of this process mechanical transposition formulas were explored based on the logic of the codex with certain added touches of interactivity. This, however, came to a dead end and soon gave rise to proposals which converted the relative liberty of itineraries and the combination of different media – written, iconic, cinematographic and sound – into steps of progress for the narrated story.

The adaptations of some books by Oliver Jeffers, or the more recent *Lil' Red*, a native production, are some examples among many of this type. There have also been some authentically refreshing proposals based on the knowledge plane specially aimed at children readers such as *Metamorphabet*, one of the most recent creations from Vectorpark. In this case the combination of voice and image is transformed in a surprising way by the actions of the reader. It lays down knowledge and at the same time stimulates a poetic experience in a way which the best illustrated alphabet books never managed to achieve.

It is equally true that all production has remained within the limits of the short piece. The native equivalents of the great sagas in the style of the Harry Potter Series, or series like Jim Knopf by Michael Ende, are not to be found. It will take some time before these appear, but once again it would be worth looking back at the video game to glimpse the future possibilities the medium has regarding the production of long-haul narratives. We would then see that the current limits are not in the areas of creativity or of language, but instead in the economic resources to produce them or, in any event, in the access to the necessary technological tools within reach of the creators.

Another way of thinking

Without a doubt we are at the beginnings of a process whose most elaborate forms we are still far from being able to predict, but we can already highlight base tendencies which we should pay attention to. Perhaps the most important of these is the establishment of the figure of a reader-public that is also an active element in the building of a work both unitary and dynamic. This obliges us to rethink the function of the creators, writers and illustrators of the books of the future.

If there is an insistence on the production of works based on the specific resources of the medium, narration structures will start to emerge that no longer conceive the storyline as a one-directional track with more or less secondary offshoots, as still occurs nowadays, but as a launch-pad towards multiple variables of a general story whose authorship is shared with the reader. The writing of storylines will no longer be seen as a line drawn between two points with intermediate asides, but as the definition of an equation whose outcome depends on the specific magnitudes of the terms and will be provided by the readers themselves.

As far as illustration in the digital medium is concerned, it is clear that the tempo of the images will be linked in one way or another to their movement. Equally, all the acoustic sensations evoked in visual language through synaesthesia can now materialise in real sounds. The atmosphere transmitted by images in books through exclusively graphic-visual channels is now achieved by a combination of physical sensorial stimuli. Lastly, in the same way as the writer, the illustrator has to move according to a logic to which he has not been accustomed: designing characters, settings and situations as a deployment of alternative forms where each image is conceived as a set of development potentials.

The visual formalisation of digital narrative productions will therefore require other skills. The question is not to recognise the indisputable collaborative character of the work of creation in this field, but to stop seeing it as the simple sum of the competences of its current actors (writing, graphics, animation and programming). It concerns changing the mind-set of the graphic artist, who will have to think about integrating at source the factors of movement and sound into the image. In order to do this they will have to incorporate skills into their day-to-day tasks that to date have been attributed to artists of other disciplines, regardless of whether they apply them individually or in collaboration with other actors.

Losses and gains

We are told that whatever the specific evolution is, none of the previous forms of reading will necessarily disappear with the arrival of the new ones. This is both a truth and a generalisation. No doubt we will continue to need to experience the sensation of "storytelling", but very possibly the codex form or the film form will be offered to us in other types of materials and on other types of devices, as is in fact already the case. It is also very possible that the linear story will no longer be the patrimony of those old and efficient formats because it will become another piece of more complex structures; this is already happening in apps and video games. We will have to wait and see to what extent the new media will integrate them or if they will place them in another position in our hierarchy of cultural habits.

In short, perhaps the time has come to put aside the considerations of technology and its contributions to focus instead on the evolution of our own impulses, needs and aspirations as social individuals, and realise that the tools do not change but rather the ways of telling the story – and if this is true it is because our relationship with the social and cultural medium also changes. With all the contradictions and reflexes inherited over centuries, we are headed towards more communal and participative ways of relating to knowledge and creation. The ideal of the Enlightened which Chartier referred to in his day is within our reach not only thanks to this new technological wealth, but also to the extension of literacy, of culture, and of the possibilities and the desire for learning of wide sectors of our societies.

Finally, we should also reflect on why the new narrative forms take on the logic of games, an activity essential in infancy but demoted to another plane of cultural values in adults. Playing is a fundamental element of our training, but through it we also learn to construct shared fictions and these are understood as symbolic and alternative projections of the world around us. In the new narratives gaming evolves into structure and connects the complex world of childhood with experiences from later stages. Playing makes us active and in this sense constitutes an immense and efficient school of expression and creation.

This road also leads us to recuperate forms of relating to the symbolic narrative which are set in the origins of our culture. The book born of the printing press extended the spread of words and images to limits that were unknown at the time and audiovisual media have made them universal. However, to date they have circulated in all these media as one-person messages. The hegemony of written culture represented, if not the disappearance of public participation, at least its relegation to a marginal place in the collective creation of stories that is so characteristic of oral culture. This is the skill that the new technologies allow us to recuperate, but on a larger scale, and in a different context where participation is not only a possibility but a necessity.

Works Cited

Primary Works Cited

Jeffers, Oliver. *The Heart and the Bottle*. New York: Penguin Group, 2011. iPad edition.

Main, Brian. *Lil'Red. An Interactive Story*. Brian Main, 2013. iPad edition.

Metamorphabet. Vectorpark, 2015. iPad edition.

Secondary Works Cited

Chartier, Roger. *Las revoluciones de la cultura escrita. Diálogos e intervenciones*. Barcelona: Gedisa, 2000. Print.

Pérez Latorre, Óliver. *El lenguaje videolúdico. Análisis de la significación del videojuego*. Barcelona: Laertes, 2012. Print.

About the Authors

Cristina Aliagas holds a BA and a PhD in Humanities from the Universitat Pompeu Fabra (UPF, Pompeu Fabra University, Barcelona, Spain). She is a Postdoctoral Researcher at The University of Sheffield and a member of the GRETEL research group. She researches literacy in the life of Catalan/Spanish children and teenagers. Her research covers a variety of topics: ethnography and literacy, social networks (e.g., Facebook and Twitter), literacy identities in adolescent subcultures (manga readers, rap singers, fanfiction members), family literacy practices and the complex interface between vernacular, digital literacies and the curriculum in secondary education.

Arnal Ballester is a graphic illustrator and professor of Visual Storytelling in the Escola Massana – Centre d'Art i Disseny (Massana School – Art and Design Centre, Barcelona, Spain) – affiliated to the Universitat Autònoma de Barcelona (UAB, Autonomous University of Barcelona, Spain). His artistic work has mainly been involved with the field of editorial illustration and animation.

Laura Borràs holds a BA in Catalan Philology and a PhD in Romance Philology from the Universitat de Barcelona (UB, University of Barcelona) where she is a professor, combining her teaching with e-learning and blended learning in literature. She has been Director of the HERMENEIA research group since 2000. Since 2007 she has been the Academic Director of the Master in Literature in the Digital Era of the UB. President of E-poetry 2009 and guest editor of Volume II of the Electronic Literature Collection, she is also a member of the International Literary Advisory Board of the Electronic Literature Organization (ELO), of Cultural Studies in Literary Interzones, Erasmus Mundus Joint Doctorate (Universitá degli studi di Bergamo [University of Bergamo], Italy) and of the Erasmus Intensive Program on European Digital Literatures (Université Paris 8 [University Paris 8], France). From 2010 to 2012 she was Visiting Professor at Kingston University (London, United Kingdom). In 2003 she was appointed Director of the Institució de les Lletres Catalanes (ILC, Institution of Catalan Letters) where she has promoted the lletrescatalanes.cat portal (also in Spanish and English).

Teresa Colomer is a Professor in the Department of Language, Literature and Social Sciences Education at the Universitat Autònoma de Barcelona (UAB, Autonomous University of Barcelona, Spain). She holds a BA in Hispanic Philology and Catalan Philology and a PhD in

Educational Sciences. She has published over two hundred and fifty articles and books on children's literature and on the teaching of reading and literature, and has received several awards for her research in Spain, Brazil and the United States. Currently, she is the Director of the GRETEL research group at the UAB. She is also head of the MEd. on Books and Literature for Children and Adolescents and of the MA on School Library and Reading Promotion. Her main fields of research are didactics of literature and literacy and social aspects of children's literature.

Cristina Correro holds a BSc in International Finance and Law from the F.H. Frankfurt a.M, (Germany), a BA in Catalan Philology from the Universitat de Barcelona (UB, University of Barcelona) and an MA in Research in Language and Literature Education from the Universitat Autònoma de Barcelona (UAB, Autonomous University of Barcelona, Spain). She is currently pursuing a doctorate in literature in early childhood education (PhD). She is a part-time lecturer and support technician with the GRETEL research group at the UAB's Department of Language, Literature and Social Sciences Education. Her areas of research include children's literature (zero-eight) and digital literature.

Karla Fernández de Gamboa Vázquez is a graduate in Pre-school and Primary Education from the Universidad del País Vasco / Euskal Herriko Unibertsitatea (University of The Basque Country, Spain). She also holds a Master's Degree in Research in Language and Literature Education, in School Library and Reading Promotion and in Books and Literature for Children and Adolescents from the Universitat Autònoma de Barcelona (UAB, Autonomous University of Barcelona, Spain). She is currently pursuing a doctorate in education as researcher in training (Personal Investigador en Formación, PIF [Research Staff in Training]) with the GRETEL research group at the UAB and working on a thesis on the characterisation of contemporary children's literature (eight-twelve).

Martina Fittipaldi holds a BA in Literature from the Universidad Nacional de Salta (National University of Salta, Argentina), and an MA in Research in Language and Literature Education, an MEd in Books and Literature for Children and Adolescents and a PhD in Language and Literature Education from the Universitat Autònoma de Barcelona (UAB, Autonomous University of Barcelona, Spain). She is a member of the GRETEL research group at the UAB. She works as a lecturer in the Universitat de Barcelona (UB, University of Barcelona) and in the MEd. on Books and Literature for Children and Adolescents (UAB) and her research work is on curricular analysis, reading responses and literary learning.

Anna Juan Cantavella holds a BA in Social and Cultural Anthropology and a PhD in Urban Anthropology from the Universitat de Barcelona (UB, University of Barcelona) and the Université Pierre-Mendès-France (University Pierre-Mendès-France, Grenoble, France). She works as a visiting lecturer in the Department of Language, Literature and Social Sciences Education at the Universitat Autònoma de Barcelona (UAB, Autonomous University of Barcelona, Spain) since 2013 and is a member of the research GRETEL group. Her current research is on spatial representation in picturebooks.

Bettina Kümmerling-Meibauer is Professor in the German Department at the Universität Tübingen (University of Tübingen, Germany). She has published fifteen books, including *Emergent Literacy. Children's Books from 0 to 3* (Benjamins, 2011), *Manga's Cultural Crossroads* (Routledge, 2013) and *Picturebooks: Representation and Narration* (Routledge, 2014). She is a co-editor of the book series Children's Literature, Culture and Cognition (Benjamins) and a member of the Management Committee of the EU-funded COST-action "The Digital Literacy and Multimodal Practices of Young Children".

Mireia Manresa holds a BA in Catalan Philology from the Universitat de Lleida (UDL, University of Lleida, Spain) and a PhD in Language and Literature Education from the Universitat Autònoma de Barcelona (UAB, Autonomous University of Barcelona, Spain). She is a member of the GRETEL research group, a secondary school teacher, an e-learning specialist (Institut Obert de Catalunya, IOC [Catalonia Open Institute]) and a part-time lecturer at the UAB. Her lines of research are based on the building of reading habits related to the training of literary readers in compulsory education. She is currently researching children's digital reading habits in and out of school and the reading response to electronic literature.

Ana Maria Margallo holds a BA in Hispanic Philology and a PhD in Language and Literature Education from the Universitat Autònoma de Barcelona (UAB, Autonomous University of Barcelona, Spain). She is a full-time lecturer at the same university and a member of the GRETEL research group. Her research focuses on the pedagogical affordances of Project-Based Learning as a tool to foster literary skills and literature, the usage of literature with newcomers in secondary schools and how to select literary texts according to pedagogical criteria. She is currently researching children's digital reading habits in and out of school.

Kate Pullinger writes fiction for digital, print, and hybrid forms. Her most recent novel, *Landing Gear* (2014), grew out of a participatory multimedia project, *Flight Paths: A Networked Novel* (2009). *Letter to an Unknown Soldier* (2014) is a digital war memorial created by letters written by 22,000 people in response to the centenary of outbreak of

World War One. She is Professor of Creative Writing and Digital Media at Bath Spa University (United Kingdom); she lives in London, England.

Lucas Ramada Prieto holds a BA in Hispanic Studies from the Universidad de Oviedo (University of Oviedo, Spain) and an MA in Research in Language and Literature Education from the Universitat Autònoma de Barcelona (UAB, Autonomous University of Barcelona, Spain). He is currently working on his doctoral thesis on children and adolescent electronic literature and literary education as a member of the GRETEL research group at the UAB.

Neus Real holds a BA from the Universitat Autònoma de Barcelona (UAB, Autonomous University of Barcelona, Spain), an MPhil (Arts) from The University of Birmingham (United Kingdom) and a PhD in Catalan Philology from the UAB. She is a specialist in women's fiction and is the author of numerous studies on contemporary Catalan literature. Since 2008 she has been a full-time lecturer in the Department of Language, Literature and Social Sciences Education at the UAB and a member of the GRETEL research group. She also works as a lecturer in the MEd. on Books and Literature for Children and Adolescents (UAB). Her current research is on early childhood, literary education and digital literature.

Lara Reyes López is a Primary Education graduate and holds a Master's Degree in School Library and Reading Promotion, in Books and Literature for Children and Adolescents and in Research in Language and Literature Education and a PhD from the Universitat Autònoma de Barcelona (UAB, Autonomous University of Barcelona, Spain). She wrote her doctoral thesis on literary education in Primary Education related to reading responses. She is a member of the GRETEL research group.

Celia Turrión Penelas holds a PhD in Language and Literature Education from the Universitat Autònoma de Barcelona (UAB, Autonomous University of Barcelona, Spain). She is a member of the GRETEL research group at the UAB. She studied contemporary picturebooks before writing her doctoral thesis on digital narrative for children. She has taught in the MEd. on Books and Literature for Children and Adolescents (UAB) and collaborated with various organisations in several training projects. She combines her work as a researcher with her job as an editor of children's literature.

Junko Yokota is Professor Emeritus at the National College of Education, National Louis University (Chicago, United States of America) and Director of the Centre for Teaching through Children's Books. She was a classroom teacher and school librarian for the first ten years of her career. Her research focuses on visual narratives in picturebooks, multicultural and international literature, digital literature for children and literacy instruction through quality literature. Her publications include five editions of a co-authored college textbook, *Children's Books in Children's Hands*, children's literature review columns, journal articles and chapters in edited books. She is currently a Fulbright Scholar at the Uniwersytet Wrocławski (University of Wrocław, Poland).

« Recherches comparatives sur les livres et le multimédia d'enfance »

Cette collection, destinée à créer un espace d'analyse sur les littératures et les productions culturelles dédiées à l'enfance et à la jeunesse, et ce quel qu'en soit le support – littérature orale, livre, multimédia, audiovisuel – se veut être un terrain d'échanges et un chantier ouvert à des questionnements éclairés.

Dans cette perspective, elle s'attache à insérer la réflexion dans le vaste champ des approches critiques liées à la littérature en général et aux sciences humaines, tout en ayant le souci de présenter des études compara-tives émanant d'horizons multiples et de pays divers. À ce titre, la collection, principalement orientée vers le monde francophone, pourra donner lieu à la publication d'ouvrages critiques en d'autres langues.

Collection dirigée par Rose-May Pham Dinh,
Présidente de l'Institut International Charles-Perrault
Institut international Charles-Perrault, Hôtel de Mézières
14, av. de l'Europe BP 61, 95 604 Eaubonne cedex 4, France
Tél : 01.34.16.36.88 / Fax : 01.34.27.69.60
communication.iicp@club-internet.fr

Comité scientifique

Institut International Charles-Perrault

L'Institut International Charles-Perrault a été fondé en 1994 en relation avec les universités et des professionnels des métiers du livre, il assure dans le domaine des littératures d'enfance et de jeunesse des fonctions de recherche, de formation et d'animation, sur le plan national et international.